Institutions in American Society

Institutions in American Society

Essays in Market, Political, and Social Organizations

John E. Jackson, Editor

Ann Arbor
THE UNIVERSITY OF MICHIGAN PRESS

Library of Congress Cataloging-in-Publication Data

Institutions in American society : essays in market, political, and
social organizations / John E. Jackson, editor.
    p.   cm.
    Includes bibliographical references.
    ISBN 0-472-10136-6 :
    1. Social institutions — United States.   I. Jackson, John Edgar.
HM131.I529   1989
306'.0973 — dc20   89-20359
                                        CIP

This book is dedicated to the memory of Dean William Haber. He was a valuable friend and inspiration to the Program, to the College, and to the University.

Acknowledgments

The contributors to this volume want to express their deep appreciation to Mr. A. Alfred Taubman whose initial question about what students know about the origins, functions, and operations of our society and whose generous gift to the University of Michigan initiated the program that led to the work included in this volume. His challenge and generosity are directly responsible for the development of this scholarship and it would not have occurred without his support. We want to thank Dean Peter O. Steiner for the encouragement and freedom he gave us as we explored the answer to Mr. Taubman's question and as we created a program that offered undergraduate students a unique educational experience. The actions of these two individuals provided a special opportunity for a diverse group of scholars and students to explore new ideas and curricular material. For this we are very grateful. We include the usual disclaimer that the contents of these essays reflect our own individual views and are not those of Mr. Taubman, Dean Steiner, or the University of Michigan.

We also want to thank Kathleen Dorando whose enthusiastic personality and untiring workstyle were critical to the program's success and to the completion of this book. The contributions of loyal, creative, and hard-working staff are necessary for all academic projects, and we were blessed with the best on all accounts.

Contents

Introduction

John E. Jackson

The Taubman Program in American Institutions at the University of Michigan began as an answer to the question, "What do students know about the origins, functions, and operations of the political, economic, and social institutions that give character and direction to our society?" This is the story of how the effort to implement the answer to that question generated faculty research directly from an undergraduate teaching program. Participants began with the task of designing an undergraduate curriculum and developing specific courses within that curriculum. What emerged from these courses and accompanying seminars was new scholarship examining our nation's institutions and pointing to directions for additional research on institutions. This volume presents that scholarship.

The first discovery in developing new courses was that we could not answer the prior question, "How do we as economists, historians, political scientists, and sociologists define and analyze 'institutions'?" There were two things we did know in searching for an answer: each course had to be interdisciplinary, as no one field can claim to describe fully any institution or social situation, and the courses had to present an analytical, problem-solving approach. We wanted students to confront, and ultimately attempt to answer, "Why?" and "What if?" questions about our society and its development. Each course had to be more than a description of an institution, its history, its functions, and its behavior. With these "guidelines" and the question to which we had no answer, we began in the fall of 1981 to develop a program on American institutions.

As the program progressed, a clearer image of how we were defining and analyzing institutions emerged. The vehicle for these discussions was a regular seminar attended by the teaching faculty. Initially, the topics of this seminar were the themes of the individual courses, which served to reinforce their interdisciplinary content. The seminars evolved into a discussion of the term *institution*, its meaning in the context of this program, and eventually into the preparation of the essays presented in this volume. The seminars also encouraged faculty to expand the original conception of their course and to explore new ways of studying and teaching about institutions and their role in our society. Just as our nation's institutions are evolutionary entities, so was our concept, use, and illustration of the term *institution*. This volume puts together a set of essays from program participants that exemplifies this process, documents the evolution of participants' thinking, and marks the current state of their research.

What Is an "Institution"?

The central theme in the beginning was that institutions are the connection between individual actions and collective outcomes. Society as a whole may be the sum of its individual elements, but this summation process is neither simple nor unique. Quite obviously, whatever the institutional structure, some individuals carry greater weight than others. More importantly, however, people interact to make the outcome far more than the simple sum or average of individual characteristics. Further, there are many ways to aggregate the same set of individual behaviors with each giving different collective outcomes. In many instances, the same method of aggregation will not even give identical results for the same individuals. The majority voting paradox identified by early theorists such as Dodson and Condorcet and formally proved by Arrow exemplifies this problem (see Chamberlin's essay in this volume for a presentation of this paradox). Our initial concern was to understand how different social structures (i.e., institutions) lead to different outcomes given similar individuals. Institutions initially became our term for the structures that accomplish this aggregation and yield collective outcomes. As evidenced in the following essays, our definition and analysis grew well beyond this use.

This initial concern with the process of aggregation is distinct from an interest solely with the aggregate outcomes themselves. Considerable work in the social sciences focuses strictly on aggregate outcomes and likely relationships among aggregate measures. The field of macroeconomics is the clearest example of these concerns, though there are analogs in political science and sociology as well. Our interest is in the connections between individual and collective actions. Our belief is that in the long run, the understanding of collective outcomes must rely on some knowledge of the aggregation process.

A second focus of the program and of the individual efforts was on the explicit design of institutions. In this regard, we were trying to understand, evaluate, and teach about the choices that created our institutions and that we continually make in reforming them. We wanted students to question the nature and performance of our social organizations and rules, to understand that these organizations and rules are subjects for debate and change, and to be prepared to recommend and implement changes where needed. The emphasis on the importance of history in the program served many purposes, but a central one was to underscore the fact that institutions can and do change, that change is often a consequence of choice, and that the perceived choices were derived from people's theory of institutions at the time.

This volume presents in a single place a summary of the thinking, learning, and teaching that evolved from the core courses in the Taubman Program in American Institutions at Michigan. The individual essays constitute new scholarship on their respective topics. More importantly, the collection of essays taken as a single entity contributes to the important and increasing amount of thinking and writing on institutions in the social sciences. Further, the interdisciplinary structure of the program, and of the individual courses, is evident in the separate essays and underscores the interdisciplinary nature of the effort to understand and study institutions. These studies are far from the final word on any of the topics, in fact most are important for the questions they raise and the future directions they chart. Collectively, they do further our exploration and understanding of the structures that connect individuals and society.

Organization of the Book

The initial essay summarizes the themes, content, and lessons of the program and the content of the seminar discussions, outlining the evolving use of the concept of an institution, the important role of institutions in our society, the many examples of institutions, and areas where additional scholarship is needed. This essay synthesizes what was learned during the program and evolved after the content of the other essays (and the associated courses) was established. It is not a framework around which the program and courses were organized, although some of the essays were revised on the basis of ideas reproduced in the overview. The similarities and differences from other approaches to studying institutions are outlined in this essay.

The essays by Corcoran and Courant and by Vinovskis illustrate several important themes. Because they deal with social norms in quite different contexts and time periods, particularly those related to gender and family, these essays powerfully complement each other. Corcoran and Courant present empirical evidence for the importance of norms in defining institutions and how they perform. In their case, the norm is the consequence of how women and men are socialized into different occupations and how that socialization affects lifetime earnings. Their essay explains some of the persistent female-male wage differences, but its real significance is in showing how the institution we call a labor market socializes its participants — both employees and employers — and it in turn is altered by this socialization pattern.

Vinovskis examines the organization of the family beginning in colonial times, how the roles of family members have changed, and the coincident changes in central social institutions such as schools and churches. His essay is an excellent example of the need to know the history of an institution in order to understand its current structure, as this structure is the accumulation of earlier experiences. For example, he traces how ability- and age-stratified schools responded to changes in social and family structure and in education theories. His description of the colonial family and its subsequent changes suggests an answer to one of Corcoran and Courant's questions. They claim to be unable to account for the origins of the concept of female and male occupations, but Vinovskis shows when these definitions evolved and how they differed previously. These two essays provide considerable evidence for the reciprocal relations between institutions, individual beliefs, and social outcomes and for the importance of historical analyses to help understand these relations.

The essays by Stafford and Robinson and by Zald present evidence about the importance of organizational structure in defining and differentiating institutions and their performance. Stafford and Robinson call for an institutional approach to the study of economic performance and for the significance of organizational design and incentives in developing an industrial policy for the United States. They argue that institutional variables are of equal or greater importance than natural endowments in contributing to a nation's competitive advantage in the international economy. Their essay is also a plea for us to reexamine some of the institutional arrangements that characterize our market structures if we are to remain competitive.

Zald, in his essay on the necessity to blend history and organization theory, points out several of the program's central themes. One is the necessity to understand the historical context of any organization. In this sense, he makes the same point as Vinovskis, only in the context of the development of the modern corporation in the United States. Zald also makes clear that organizational forms reflect choices made by individual entrepreneurs and managers in response to the economic, legal, and cultural circumstances that existed at a given time. Thus, we see both the evolution of our institutions and that this evolution is a matter of organizational design. Quite evident in this essay is the point that changes in legal rules and political structures as well as in economic circumstances will alter the nature of corporate organizations. Our current corporate entities are not the result of some set of invisible autonomous forces that dictate the "optimal" organizational structure.

The next three essays, by Walker, Aberbach, and Chamberlin, deal with political organizations and how they manage the conflicts inherent in people's different views of collective issues. Walker deals specifically with how different concerns get represented—which interests are easier to organize and how different organizations follow different political strategies. His study is important in two regards. First, differences in organizational ability and in strategy affect what influence different groups and types of issues have on the eventual outcome; variations in influence are critical to the analysis and evaluation of institutions as a means to aggregate individual preferences. Second, Walker demonstrates a strong relationship between the structure and actions of interest groups and the behavior of government agencies. For some interest groups, government support is critical to their ability to organize and be politically influential. At the same time, government agencies have a direct interest in maintaining these groups, as they become potent lobbyists for the programs that justify the agency's funding. In this context, government organizations, as political institutions, become far more than a neutral means to aggregate individual preferences. They become one of the set of interested organizations trying to affect the allocation of resources.

Aberbach presents a detailed account of how the formal and informal relations between institutions can be structured so as to control the actions and influence of each. A classic institutional problem is how to control the influence on outcomes possessed by those who manage the institution. A frequent control method used in the United States, and in varying degrees in other democratic societies, is one of competition and overlapping organizational interests. This control method is evident in elections in most jurisdictions, with competing parties, and in the economy, with competing firms. The U.S. federal and state governments were designed with different and overlapping branches to control and balance each other. Aberbach points out the effectiveness of this arrangement in controlling the bureaucratic institutions in the federal government through legislative oversight.

Chamberlin's essay elaborates very explicitly how rules governing decisions function to define institutions and affect their performance. He presents a number of different criteria by which to evaluate the performance of different rules governing decisions. These criteria do not seem very demanding and taken together would appear quite reasonable. But these criteria turn out to be mutually incompatible, meaning that no set of decision rules will produce outcomes that meet all the criteria, leaving us with a dilemma in which no one institution dominates others and so the choice of institutions is specific to the particular types of decisions being considered and the evaluation criteria one wishes to apply. This makes the empirical study of institutions and their performance all the more important, as the debate over likely outcomes and the importance attached to various criteria is central to institutional choice. Furthermore, as circumstances and the relative importance of criteria change, we should observe changes in the choices of institutions being adopted.

The concluding essay by McDonald offers explanations for the evolution and transformation of the state in this country and for the decline and return of an interest in institutions among social scientists. In the first explanation, McDonald takes issue with some institutionally oriented political scientists and sociologists who chart and analyze the rise of governmental institutions in the United States by the growth in the federal government, most of which occurred during and after the very late 1800s. McDonald points out that governments were very active and the subject of considerable debate in this country throughout the nineteenth century, but that the important institutions were those at the state, and particularly the local, level. In the account of how and when governments grew, McDonald traces important sources of growth to the interplay between individuals within the government and the mobilization of external interest groups. This analysis mirrors Walker's discussion of these relationships in their contemporary setting. McDonald's historical study strongly reinforces the earlier point that government institutions are far more than neutral and simple arenas for aggregating individual preferences into collective outcomes. Governmental organizations are active, and at times aggressive, participants in this process, with considerable ability to influence outcomes.

The fluctuating attention scholars have given to institutions, according to McDonald, is tied to the debate about the relative efficacy of culture, individual values, and institutions in shaping the character, content, and direction of society. The declining interest in institutions reflected increased attention to the role of individual interests and to the influence of citizens' needs and social and economic forces in determining the size and role of governments. McDonald ends by claiming that the study of institutions remains a central theme for social scientists and predicts a "(Re)Turn to Institutions."

These essays are to be read as accounts of the current state of this faculty group's continuing search for ways to study and teach about institutions in society. They are far from a complete statement of what we know and what interests us about institutions. Rather, they reflect our initial inquiries on the subject. The essays raise as many questions for further research as they answer. If nothing else, however, they should encourage a wide range of scholars to become interested in studying institutions and emphasize that this scholarship needs to be interdisciplinary in character. Institutions are not simply means by which to aggregate individual behavior, though this is a fundamentally important function. Nor are they primarily the means by which we structure, shape, and control individual values and experience, though institutions exert powerful forces on individuals. Institutions must be recognized as the structures that shape our society at the individual and collective levels and that reciprocally connect individuals and society.

CHAPTER 1

Institutions in American Society: An Overview

John E. Jackson

A major concern of social science is the collective performance of social processes, as distinct from individual behavior. Institutions are central determinants of these collective outcomes. Individuals are not isolated gas molecules moving about randomly, subject only to occasional collisions, where the collective properties can be described simply by these many individual movements and collisions. People exist within a social structure consisting of rules, behavior patterns, and organizations that aggregate their individual actions to produce collective outcomes. Institutions give identity and direction to these individual actions and insure that the whole is not merely the sum of the parts. These rules, behavioral expectations, and organizations in turn may be major influences on the values, beliefs, and actions that people exhibit in given situations. This essay summarizes what the contributors to this volume have learned about institutions and how to study them.

Institutions serve many purposes. As Zald points out, these functions range from providing "products and services," to "changing society," to discovering "human's relations to the ultimate grounds of being." The roles and behavior expected of institutions vary substantially. The variations in function and behavior affect how institutions perform and how well different institutions serve their purpose. For example, institutions such as private markets that perform well at providing certain goods and services may do a poor job of promoting social change. And institutions such as governments that can redistribute income generally do poorly at discovering and promoting religious values. No single institution will be optimal in every, or possibly any, situation. One purpose of the program was to better understand the nature and behavior of institu-

An early version of this essay was presented to the Annual Meeting of the American Political Science Association, New Orleans, Louisiana, September 1985. I want to thank Robert P. Inman and the participants in the American Institutions Program for their very helpful comments on early drafts, but absolve them from any responsibility for the content of this essay.

tions, to assess how institutional variations alter collective outcomes, and to evaluate how different institutions perform a wide variety of functions.

Collective outcomes clearly depend on individuals' characteristics, such as their values, beliefs, situations, and behavior. They also depend on the institutional framework within which people develop values and beliefs and behave. Given identical individual characteristics, variations in rules and organizations will yield different collective results. Institutions and outcomes also significantly contribute to the development of individual beliefs, preferences, and behaviors. Although not part of the traditional model of preference aggregation, these effects can be quite important. Institutions should also be evaluated on how well they contribute to the creation and articulation of preferences and to the development of certain norms and behaviors, particularly in domains where preferences are poorly formed and where a sense of community is important but lacking. These essays are a summary of what we have learned so far about the relations between individual characteristics, variations in institutional structures, and social outcomes.

Defining Institutions

An institutional analysis requires a description of how we conceive the term *institution*. This is a much used word. Many political scientists adopt an "institutional" approach while economists traditionally have striven to be "noninstitutional." There are continual references to political institutions, economic institutions, and social institutions. Even various individuals, behavior patterns, cultural norms, and formal organizations have been called institutions. In arguing for an institutional approach to the study of American society, we must first specify the elements that form and differentiate institutions.

A focus of the program was on the explicit design and alteration of institutions. The design and choice of institutions are a central part of public and social policy. We wanted to understand the choices that created our institutions and improve the decisions we continually make in reforming them. Of the many contributions historians made to this volume, a central one was to underscore the fact that institutions can and do change, that change is often a consequence of choice, and that the perceived choices are often derived from people's theory of institutions. A consequence of this focus was a desire to define institutions in terms of properties that are subject to explicit debate and change.

Organizational structure, formal rules, and norms constitute the three elements we use to define an institution. Variation in any aspect of these terms creates a different institution and is predicted to yield different individual and collective outcomes. By this definition single organizations — such as the University of Michigan, the National Organization for Women, General Motors, the Ann Arbor City Council — are not institutions, but examples of specific institutions called universities, social interest groups, firms, and legislatures. A single organization is an institution only to the extent that its structure, rules, or dominant norms are not replicated elsewhere. Thus, the United States Supreme Court and the United Nations are examples of institutions called courts and legislatures, respectively, and possibly are institutions in their own right, given their unique rules and structure.

Alternative Definitions of an Institution

Our way of defining institutions creates a meaning for the term institution that has both similarities and differences compared to the meaning currently used in sociology and political science. This definition evolves from both our interests in the design of institutions as a matter of public policy and in the choices that created our institutions and also our concern for their simultaneous aggregating and socializing roles.

The concept of institutions as the means by which individual actions or preferences are aggregated to collective outcomes is very similar to Riker's use of the term (Riker 1980). Riker is specifically talking about the voting rules that groups such as legislatures use to avoid the indeterminancy and cycles present in unrestricted majority voting. "The people whose values and tastes are influential live in a world of conventions about both language and values themselves. These conventions are in turn condensed into institutions, which are simply rules about behavior, especially about making decisions" (Riker 1980, 432). He quite clearly sees these rules as determining how individual tastes are summed to get a collective outcome. "Outcomes are, of course, partially based on tastes because some person's (not necessarily a majority of people's) tastes are embodied in outcomes. But the ways the tastes and values are brought forward for consideration, eliminated, and finally selected are controlled by institutions" (Riker 1980, 443). Our emerging view of institutions shares much with Riker, though we see institutions as embodying more than just formal decision rules.

A broader definition of institution, and a radically different role, is presented by March and Olsen (1984, 1987). They do not formally define a political institution, but state that "historically, political science has emphasized the ways in which political behavior was embedded in an institutional structure of rules, norms, expectations, and traditions that severely limited the free play of individual will and calculation" (March and Olsen 1984, 736). Unfortunately, they are not specific in how these, or other, attributes combine to form an institution, or how their variation creates different institutions. The examples they use, such as "the legislature, the legal system, and the state, as well as traditional economic institutions, such as the firm . . . " (March and Olsen 1984, 734), are quite broad and do not provide insights into how to compare institutions and their effects.

March and Olsen's major interest is not in the structure of institutions but in how institutions influence individual behaviors and beliefs. They explicitly distinguish between the view of institutions as a means of aggregating individual actions to reach collective outcomes and the view of institutions as a means of creating individual beliefs and guiding behavior.

> Parts of the new institutionalism are challenges to this primacy of outcomes. These challenges echo another ancient theme of political thought, the idea that politics creates and confirms interpretations of life. Through politics, individuals develop themselves, their communities, and the public good . . . . Politics is regarded as education, as a place for discovering, elaborating, and expressing meanings, establishing shared (or opposing) conceptions of experience, values, and the nature of existence. (March and Olsen 1984, 741)

This quotation may give too central a place to formal political institutions, but clearly it indicates their interest in institutions as determinants of individual attributes.

The view emerging from our discussions and empirical observations and expressed in these essays is that it is necessary to study institutions in their aggregating and socializing roles simultaneously. One gets only a partial, and possibly an incorrect, view of an institution if it is examined in only one context or as performing only one of these two tasks. Unfortunately, expanding the examination of institutions to include both functions greatly complicates the research task. Scholars studying the effects of institutional variations on the aggregation process have traditionally found it necessary to assume that individual attributes are determined independently of the institutional setting. Similarly, many people who examine how individual behavior differs among institutional settings frequently ignore the likelihood that institutional variations arise in response to individual behaviors. For example, political scientists routinely point out that party affiliation among U.S. voters is an important predictor of political attitudes. However, the behavior of parties in

choosing positions and strategies is much influenced by the structure of
and changes in these mass attitudes. The future research agenda is to
bring institutional choice and behavior into the model of individuals and,
for those studying institutions as methods of aggregation, to make individual preferences and behavior endogenous.

The considerable amount of writing on institutions in sociology has
a somewhat different focus than either of the above (see, for example,
Powell and DiMaggio 1989). As expressed by Jepperson (1989), an institution is seen as a regular, stable pattern of actions or behaviors, rather
than as a structure for aggregating or guiding behavior. In his terms,

> "Institution" represents a social order or pattern that has attained a
> certain property; "institutionalization" denotes the process of such
> attainment. By order or pattern, I refer, as is conventional, to stan-
> dardized interaction sequences. An institution is then a social pat-
> tern that reveals a particular kind of stability: "meta-stability" . . . .
> Put another way, institutions refer to those social patterns that will
> be reproduced, without requiring recurrent mobilization to secure
> such reproduction (i.e., "action"), unless social intervention discon-
> tinues or environmental shock disrupts the reproductive process.

Many of Jepperson's examples of institutions are illustrative of behavior
patterns: "the vacation, attending college, the handshake, formal expression of grief in bereavement, and voting." These examples, and the definition that underlies them, take us away from our interest in the *structures* that reciprocally connect individual beliefs and behavior with
collective outcomes.

An important aspect of the sociologists' definition is that institutions are the accumulation of historical actions that become embedded in
our social structures (March and Olsen make a similar claim). History,
then, is more than a description of past events; it is a central part of
analyzing any contemporary institution and its performance. This concern for the history of an institution as part of any analysis is recognized
and reflected in many of the essays. In its broad form, however, the
sociological definition does not give primacy to the explicit choices
reflected in institutions and in debates about institutional reform that are
an important theme in the program and in the writings of political scientists and economists.

We do not claim that one definition of an institution is more legitimate than another. These essays will not provide a unifying concept of an
institution, and that is not our intent. Nor is it clear that such a concept is
needed, so long as people understand how they, and we, are using the

term. We simply wanted to identify the uses of the term *institution* and the different objectives people have in mind when studying institutions before presenting our definition and analysis. This summary also points out where the essays converge with and diverge from other uses of the term and with other institutional analyses.

Structure

Our definition and analysis of an institution begins with the structure and design of the organizations that constitute the institution. Institutions require organizations. One major responsibility of institutions is to aggregate individual actions to reach collective outcomes. This aggregation must take place within some organizational structure, otherwise we are left with a large mass of unconnected individuals — the gas molecule metaphor. Organizations also provide the settings in which people interact, learn, and communicate their ideas and beliefs, socialize others, and perform integrative functions. Organizations, however, come in many varieties and with many properties. The purpose of this section is to suggest some of the organization structure variables that differentiate institutions and become a part of our means to explicitly aggregate, mold, and control behavior.

Unfortunately, it is hard to describe the wide range of organizations in a generic way. We would like to compare public and private bureaucracies, legislatures, interest groups, and voluntary social organizations with a common language. But such a language does not now exist, which forces us to be more descriptive and illustrative than desirable.

Zald, in arguing for the importance of combining history and the study of organizations, classifies organizations by their form, their purpose, and their incentive system. The ways control and authority are packaged constitute major aspects of form. Purpose, or function, generally describes an organization's objectives and the type of decisions it is expected to make. Incentive systems refer to the use of coercive, material, solidary, and purposive means to motivate members. Although Zald goes on to restrict the domain of his chapter to business organizations, these classifications are seen in other institutional structures as well.

How an organization structures authority and control of resources has substantial impact on outcomes. The more decentralized the control and the greater access subunits have to their own resources, the more independence the subunits have and the more likely any outcome is to reflect horizontal coalition building and bargaining among the separate elements. In an organization with a more hierarchical system of control, decisions and bargaining will flow vertically and place a higher premium on bureaucratic political behavior. And, as Zald illustrates with the modern corporation, hierarchically organized and functionally specialized organizations devote substantial attention and resources to monitoring and gaining compliance among subunits. Decision making in a market economy versus that in a centrally planned economy and the contrasts between policy making in a legislature compared to that in the executive branch illustrate these points.

Decentralized and hierarchically structured organizations may exhibit significant differences in adaptability, innovation, efficiency, and conflict resolution. Simulations have shown that decentralized organizations where subunits pursue local rather than global objectives perform better on global criteria than organizations structured so that all units try to pursue global objectives (Cohen 1984). Stafford and Robinson suggest that in ambiguous situations, as exist in industries depending on new product and process technologies, smaller, more flexible structures are required and, "any use of centralized directions is likely to be ineffective." However, they say, "large, stable bureaucracies can be compatible with success in heavy industry." Their example is the traditional U.S. automobile industry.

Function and responsibility, and the constraints they create, are major factors in defining an institution. Among public organizations, where such constraints are stricter, major variations in function concern the boundaries of the government. These boundaries are defined by the government's jurisdiction, function, and geographic territory. The structure may be defined vertically, as in a federal system where certain functions are reserved for different levels of government. Other constraints are horizontal, in that they define the domain and responsibilities of different governments. For example, some governmental bodies are responsible for specific functions, such as schools, parks and recreation, sanitation, or public safety. In other areas these functions may be the responsibility of a single governmental body. Finally, governments have geographical restrictions. All of these parameters can be varied to create different governmental institutions that alter how governments perform.[1]

Last, the incentive systems available to and used by organizations will have substantial impacts on what they do and how well they do it. Material incentives are the ones most often associated with economic organizations. But as we expand the definition of economic organiza-

---

1. Differences in jurisdiction, function, and territory, and their consequences, are easily observed among the various forms of metropolitan government existing within the United States. Some metropolises have little regional governance. Others have some

tions to include interest groups working to alter the allocation and distribution of resources, other incentives become important. Walker indicates that the availability and use of solidary and purposive as well as material incentives have important implications for interest group behavior and success. Zald suggests that an important incentive for many organizations, most notably those confronting potential free riders, is the authority to coerce people into contributing to the organization's support. Governments have this power in that they can levy and collect taxes, thus forestalling free riding behavior. Other groups have managed to obtain similar powers, even though they are not formally classed as governments. Unions in states with required membership have this power, and are more powerful than unions in states without this provision. At the college level, public interest research groups on many campuses have comparable power in that students must contribute or exercise certain procedures to avoid contribution or to obtain a rebate on dues. The ability to use this incentive greatly alters the strength and activities of these interest groups.

The important question is how organizational differences affect the behavior of institutions and ultimately the use and distribution of resources in an economy. We can say unequivocally that these structural variations produce different institutions and different results.

Formal Rules

The second of the terms defining and differentiating institutions concerns the formal rules that determine how decisions will be made, and that govern individual and organizational behavior. Different formal rules are central to the definition of an institution and to the design and choice of institutions for policy purposes. Chamberlin's essay provides a comprehensive discussion of the types of rules, the criteria for comparing rules, and the impact of rules on social outcomes.

Most of the work on the rules governing decision making has focused on voting rules. As Chamberlin points out, "Voting rules are among the simplest forms of institutions. They take individual preferences and process them to arrive at a social choice." Majority rule is a

---

metropolitan-wide, single function agencies, usually in such fields as transportation and waste water treatment. These are usually administrative units without elected officials. The Twin Cities, by contrast, have a metropolitan council that has a strong influence over the single function administrative agencies. Last, some metropolitan areas have created regional governments integrating a range of areas and services. All these arrangements produce quite different institutions, with quite different outcomes in terms of the level and distribution of services.

commonly known and used decision rule, though there are many others. For example, the wire service college football and basketball polls use a Borda voting system, where participants rank their preferences and the option with the highest average rank is selected.

Voting rules, taken by themselves, have a number of serious limitations as social institutions. Chamberlin points out that except for very limited situations, there is no voting rule that gives a stable, predictable collective outcome. Results will vary with the options offered, with the order in which alternatives are considered, and with the individual behavior induced by the voting rule. This latter point is particularly troublesome, in that individuals' behavior and whether they act according to their "true" preferences become a function of the rules being used. Some rules encourage more strategic behavior than others.

A second limitation to most voting systems is that they are difficult to implement except among small groups of people. Tiny New England towns, some social organizations, and academic departments can use direct voting, but this method quickly becomes infeasible in larger settings. This difficulty has led to a number of restrictions on participation, creating legislatures and executives who make and implement decisions. The hope is that these organizations, and the people that direct them, will take actions that "represent" the interests of their larger public.

Chamberlin points out that we have much less understanding of how formal rules alter the performance of representative entities. Recent work has expanded our knowledge of decision rules operating within legislatures, such as parliamentary rules (see Shepsle 1986, and the references cited therein). This work largely shows how procedural rules restrict options and allow majority voting to yield a decision. Frequently these rules advantage the status quo and imply that one needs more than a simple majority to agree on the need for change and its direction in order to change policy.

Our understanding of how the performance of a legislature, as an entity, varies with changes in the rules regarding representation is still quite limited. Variations in the number of representatives per district, in the rules for their selection, and in the number, size, and composition of districts may dramatically alter resulting legislation. Rules governing the number of representatives per district and their selection are critical in defining a legislature's performance. These rules include majority voting with various criteria for runoffs, plurality voting, and proportional voting. These selection criteria give different relationships between individuals' interests, or preferences, representation patterns, and the ultimate legislated outcomes. Chamberlin and Courant (1983), for example, conclude that a legislature with members selected by proportional representation more closely approximates the deliberations among all members of society than do single member majority rule districts.

The rules setting the size and composition of legislative districts have a significant bearing on the legislature's actions and performance. The magnitude of the decennial conflicts over redistricting underscores the importance of these factors. First, these rules influence who the likely representatives will be, which in turn affects legislation (see Cain 1984 and 1985 for excellent discussions of different redistricting strategies and their likely affect on the composition of the legislature). Second, district boundaries determine how much of society's variation in interests exists within and between districts. If districts are internally homogeneous, so that all the variation in preferences exists between districts, then the legislature becomes the focus of the conflict and controversy, and its decision rules become critically important in determining the outcome. If, on the other hand, the districts are internally heterogeneous, but cross-sectionally similar, most of the conflict and decision making may be dealt with in the selection process, to the extent that the selection process produces similar results in each district. The limiting case of a heterogeneous district is at-large representation where all individuals are combined into one district. In this case, the selection process is obviously a significant determinant of outcomes.

To illustrate the point about differences in the amount of conflict within and between districts, consider the history of how the U.S. Congress dealt with such issues as civil rights during the 1950s and 1960s, the energy crises of the 1970s, the ERA, the environment, and labor legislation. In the civil rights and energy cases, regional differences created far greater conflicts between than within districts, and Congress was unable to develop any effective legislation in these areas until there were massive changes in public attitudes or external circumstances. With the ERA, environment, and labor issues, there were relatively greater variations in interests within districts, particularly at the state level, than differences between districts. In these areas, Congress was able to fashion working compromises and coalitions that could pass relevant legislation. This legislation did not meet all demands, but Congress did set policy in these areas. All these issues had very intense partisans on both sides, so that differences in the intensity of feelings does not account for the different outcomes. The differential ability of Congress to function is more related to the distribution of these intense participants among and within districts.

Executives, public and private, are agents acting on behalf of different interests and individuals. The rules for selecting executives are also quite varied and will affect the character, decisions, and agenda of the

executive. Some of the variations match the ones just described for legislators, such as majority or plurality voting, but there are others. Variations in selection rules are most evident at the municipal level, where
elections may be partisan or nonpartisan, entail various types of primary
systems, occur at a variety of intervals, and are subject to different
campaign rules. Selection of the executive by a party caucus or by the
legislature provides another, more dramatic alternative. All of these variations will alter the relative power of the elected executive vis-à-vis the
legislature and the permanent bureaucracy, the types of issues and interests that are most influential, and the ability of the executive to implement policies.

Politicians would not be surprised at the statement that the method
of selecting executives matters, but we can also cite two different academic studies to illustrate the point. Both are drawn from the state and
local level where such variations exist. Hawley (1973) uses evidence from
the San Francisco area to conclude that the use of nonpartisan ballots
increases the probability that Republicans will be elected and that more
conservative policies will be pursued. Gormley (1983) analyzed the rate
setting decisions of state public utility commissions and concludes that
the nature of political participation, the cost of electricity, and the distribution of those costs differed between elected and appointed
commissions.

An important parallel exists in the selection of private and public
executives. In publicly held firms, executives are also elected by boards
of directors, who themselves are elected by the public shareholders.
Although these elections do not establish the type of control experienced
by most public officials, and we may even doubt their ability to establish
control at all, they fit our institutional definition nonetheless, and we can
evaluate their performance as we do other executive selection procedures.

This is not a comprehensive enumeration of the many rules that
define and differentiate public and private institutions or of the evidence
that rules matter. The examples offered are intended to illustrate what is
meant by formal rules and how they affect institutions and to point out
some of the more important distinctions.

Norms and Social Relations

The third institutional component comprises the norms, or informal
rules, that guide behavior. Every society has many norms that govern
individual and organizational actions. These are important in modeling
institutional behavior and its consequences. Institutions that function

one way with a given set of underlying norms may function quite differently with a different set. For example, both markets and democratic
institutions assume norms that give primacy to individual autonomy and
rationality. In another culture, with different norms, the rules and organizations that create these two institutions may produce quite different
results.

A norm central to many institutions is that of individualistic goal-
seeking behavior, described in its most sophisticated form by economists
and decision theorists as constrained maximization. Monetary goals,
e.g., income, profits, or revenues, are usually presumed, though goals
may also be political power, status, or recognition. Analysis of market
institutions and predictions about their performance are predicated on
the dominance of this norm among consumers and firm owners. Many
descriptions of behavior in the public sector also assume this underlying
norm. Elected officials are presumed to maximize the likelihood of
reelection or the satisfaction received from combining that likelihood
with personal objectives, such as influence or policy preferences. Bureaucrats are assumed to be maximizing their budgets. Many of the relationships we create in the public sector, such as legislative oversight, competitive parties, elections, and the separation of powers, are there to offset
this same presumed goal-seeking behavior on the part of public sector
officials.

Norms other than individualistic goal seeking are important and
observed in public and private organizations. European civil servants are
oriented toward the technical aspects of implementing public programs,
"preferring tranquility, predictability, manageability, and tidiness"
(Aberbach, Putnam, and Rockman 1981, 93). In the United States, by
contrast, senior civil servants "are much more oriented to traditionally
political roles such as advocacy, representation, and partisanship than
are their European peers" (Aberbach, Putnam, and Rockman 1981, 99).
In some economies, behavior within firms is governed more by procedures and a cooperative norm than by the competitive norm typical in the
United States. Japan has been described as "capitalism without the Western ideology of individualism and economic freedom" (Ozaki 1984, 51).
These variations in norms produce different institutions and political
economies.

One important norm for all institutions concerns the strategies
people are likely to pick in prisoner dilemma games. In societies where
cooperative strategies are more prevalent, political institutions, interest
groups, markets, and the relations between these organizations will be
quite different than in societies where people follow competitive strategies. Walker discusses the barriers and dilemmas that interest groups

potentially face from free riders. Although groups use a number of possible strategies to overcome this problem, a basic fact is that some people will behave cooperatively rather than try to be the free rider, permitting these groups to form and be active. Walker also suggests that this cooperative behavior is more prevalent among different social groups, producing a definite bias to interest group activity and resulting policies (see Wilson 1973 for evidence on this point among groups within the United States, and Almond and Verba 1965 for a classic work focusing on these differences internationally).

One very important place to observe the presence or absence of a cooperative norm is in the adherence to formal rules. In some cultures rules are routinely respected and thus effectively guide behavior. In others, there is much less respect for rules and they provide far fewer constraints on behavior. If people routinely reject rules set in place to govern individual and organizational behavior, no institution following our definition can be effective, or even exist. Societies establish organizations specifically to enforce rules and to punish deviant behavior, but even these organizations require a degree of cooperation to function, regardless of how powerful they may be. The propensity to act cooperatively in this and other settings surely varies among cultures, socioeconomic groups, and institutional settings, so that one must be careful to recognize these differences when studying and evaluating institutions.

Corcoran and Courant provide a striking example of how norms are critical determinants of outcomes within a given set of rules and structures. They explain an important part of female-male earnings differences by the different socialization of boys and girls. Specific jobs are characterized as primarily male or female jobs. The occupations girls and boys identify with and prepare for are strongly influenced by these characterizations and by the experiences of people close to them. The presence of these norms leads to substantially different outcomes than one would observe if behavior were guided by an earnings maximization norm. In addition to the obvious differences in female and male earnings, these socially created and reinforced norms create distinct "women's" and "men's" jobs and job markets, with little crossover, in spite of significant wage differences in the two markets. The presence of these pervasive norms means that efforts to explain earnings differences by differences in skills, work experience, or outright discrimination are inadequate. Corcoran and Courant's findings also indicate that strategies designed to eliminate wage differences that focus only on overt discrimination are not sufficient.

Many, many different norms are relevant to the study of institutions. We cannot attempt a complete enumeration of norms or of their place in institutional studies. We do argue that norms are central to the definition of an institution, offer some illustrations to reinforce this point, and suggest they need to be a central part of research on institutions. (The study of norms, and how they are developed, occupies a major place in some social science disciplines, such as sociology, but has received too little attention in others, such as economics.)

Relations Among Institutions

The relations among the organizations that constitute our institutions are a critical aspect determining their performance. A prominent view, at least in the United States, is that the relationships should be competitive and structured so there are stringent limits on how large and influential any organization can become. Inherent in this view is a belief that the dominant norm among those in the public and private sectors is one of individuals maximizing their material or political resources. Thus, we have competitive markets where the presence of many small firms all trying to maximize their own profits presumably prevents any one or a set of firms from dominating the market and setting prices and output. Explicit rules prohibit cooperation and collusion among firms to fix prices and output so that the competitive market is maintained. In situations where a single firm or a small set of firms comes to dominate a market, it is presumed that an adversarial government will check the power of the firm or the cartel.

Governments are designed so that power is shared by different branches that compete with and control each other. Rules define the relations among governmental organizations that share functions and territory, and among governmental and private organizations. The checks and balances embodied in the U.S. federal government exemplify these types of rules. The controversies and court cases about presidential and congressional veto authority are debates about the rules governing the behavior of these public organizations. Presidents have routinely asked for line item vetoes over parts of the budget, an authority given to many state governors. Conversely, Congress has tried to create a legislative veto over the actions of federal bureaucracies, which has been successfully challenged in court. Adoption of or changes in these veto powers will dramatically alter the relative power of the executive and legislative branches and the ability of each to control the other.

Aberbach's analysis and evaluation of congressional oversight of executive agencies at the federal level clearly illustrates both the theory and practice of control through competition. The executive and legislative branches were constitutionally separated, in contrast to a parliamentary system, given different electoral bases, and shared authority over programs. This shared authority is particularly evident in the relations between agencies and congressional committees. These relations also limit presidential authority to control the bureaucracy and to implement agendas. This design is predicated on the assumption that individuals strive for political power and resources, and thus come into competition with each other. Aberbach provides evidence for the success of this system and its underlying assumption. He finds there is considerable and effective congressional oversight of the bureaucracy, and that this success is driven by the desire of congressional members to exert, and to be seen to exert, influence. Although oversight is only one relatively small aspect of federal legislative-executive relations, and although those relations are only one example of relations among institutions, it clearly typifies the basic strategy we have followed in such interinstitutional relations.

The competitive relationships just described are not the only, or in some instances the preferred, way of structuring institutions. For example, Japanese competition is described as

> real, but the government and the private sector also possess the mechanisms to avoid "disruptive" and "excessive" competition. Such limits on competition include product specialization agreed on within a set of competing firms and the often-cited cartels to regulate capacity expansion during booms and cut-back arrangements in downturns. . . . In this setting, in which business collaborates as well as competes, the government appears as a marketplace actor. . . . (Zysman 1983, 237)

This mix of competition with collaboration and cooperation is attributed to the rules and structure established by government agencies. These relations create economic institutions that are quite different from those observed in the United States. In fact, as Stafford and Robinson argue, much of the debate about whether the United States should adopt an industrial policy is a question of whether this country needs "wide-ranging changes in our social institutions to achieve sustained economic growth." Those advocating these changes would have U.S. institutions resemble Japanese and some European institutions.

Stafford and Robinson suggest that institutions that promote less competitive and more cooperative relationships among firms and between government and industry may promote economic growth. A prime example of such cooperation is the establishment of research consortia, which require governmental approval as they would otherwise violate the antitrust rules promulgated to prevent cooperation. The areas Stafford and Robinson suggest as appropriate for cooperation have some of the attributes of publicness used to justify nonmarket institutions in other contexts. With R&D, for example, an individual firm cannot capture all the benefits of technological innovation because other firms learn from its experience and copy the innovation. The research consortia would pool contributions from all firms and share the results among the members. Research consortia created in the computer field and in the textile industry are cited as models (Stafford 1988, 4). In the latter case, the agreements explicitly involved labor unions as well as the firms within the industry operating under a government agreement to permit collaboration. Stafford and Robinson say similar arrangements regarding education, retraining, and income security can prove productive. These collaborative arrangements produce alternative economic institutions. Stafford and Robinson suggest that these more cooperative institutions may compete internationally better than the traditional competitive structure.

There are many ways of structuring relations among institutions. These involve some mix of competitive and cooperative arrangements. Unfortunately, we too often think only of purely competitive or purely cooperative possibilities. Stafford and Robinson point out that some blending of the two may work better. Recognizing the many possibilities and the fact that no single model will work best in all situations will lead to more imaginative and productive institutions. This is one area where public policy is literally a matter of institutional choice. Analyses of institutions will improve these choices.

Institutional Dynamics and the Importance of History

Institutions both aggregate the views and actions of individuals to produce collective outcomes and structure the way individuals think, develop preferences, and act in given situations. Combining these processes of aggregation and socialization introduces important dynamic characteristics into our study of institutions. Furthermore, the institutions themselves become subject to change once we consider that both the institutions in which people live and the outcomes of collective action lead to changes in preferences and actions, to altered norms, and certainly to efforts to change rules and structure. We want to point out some of these dynamic effects and their implications. Interest in these dynamics and in the types of models their presence requires is a relatively unexplored aspect of institutional research, and this section can only point to topics for study. Development of such models will radically alter the view of institutions held by social scientists.

Institutions as Socializing and Aggregating Agents

Many social science models assume a hierarchical structure. For example, the basic economics model treats individual tastes, incomes, technologies, and resources as given, and then proceeds to model price and quantity outcomes in a market, neglecting the question of how tastes, incomes, and so forth might change as a consequence of the outcomes, or even as a consequence of being in a particular market setting in the first place. Similarly, some policy analysts conceive of the policy process as flowing from decisions about priorities, to the selection of options, to the implementation of specific programs, and then to the evaluation of those programs. In reality, tastes, incomes, and technologies are altered by the workings of the market, and the selection and implementation of public policies change the structure that led to the policy choices in the first place. We want to discuss both the likely places for these nonrecursive links and their consequences for efforts to model and evaluate institutions.

One obvious departure from the hierarchical structure is the effect of institutions on values and beliefs, or what we refer to as norms. Corcoran and Courant, besides showing the importance of norms, argue that the functioning of the labor market itself in the United States contributes to the socialization of girls and boys. Employers use gender as an easy and cost effective means to assess occupational preparation and orientation of job candidates, assuming that men are more likely trained for male jobs and that women are more prepared for female jobs. This selection bias, even when grounded in observable average differences, contributes to the role identities and expectations central to the socialization of girls and boys. This socialization leads to the acquisition of certain skills and work expectations that greatly contribute to the separate labor markets for women and men. Thus it is not just the individual experiences of girls and boys, but those experiences combined with the institution we call a labor market that produces the outcomes observed in the workplace.

The difference in the norms of European and U.S. civil servants cited earlier provides another example of how institutions significantly shape norms and how together they affect collective outcomes. The difference in norms is that U.S. bureaucrats are more political and more oriented toward advocacy and partisanship than their European peers. Why do these differences exist? "To answer this question requires that we begin with institutions . . ." (Aberbach, Putnam and Rockman 1981, 95). The U.S. federal government, designed to insure that no faction could dominate, exists with many veto points and with fragmented accountability within and between branches. Consequently, civil servants are accountable to multiple "masters," from which they develop the entrepreneurial, political roles. Thus, the institutional structure of the U.S. government is largely responsible for the particular bureaucratic norms observed, and the combination of these norms and the institutions is responsible for the nature and consequences of U.S. federal policy.

Chamberlin suggests two other ways in which individual characteristics and actions are affected by institutional settings. The first is the amount and type of strategic behavior promoted by formal decision rules. In this case, the institution presumably does not alter individual preferences, but does affect whether those preferences are revealed and what behavior individuals follow in trying to achieve their preferred outcomes. Chamberlin's second point is that different institutions may elicit different aspects of individual preferences in making certain decisions. Some political institutions may encourage people to place greater weight on their utility for public goods and collective values relative to private interests. For example, behavior reflecting public goods preferences may be more evident in a town meeting with face-to-face discussion among the conflicting parties than in a referendum where actions are isolated and private. Chamberlin also suggests that people may learn about their preferences in political institutions that encourage debate and interaction relative to more atomistic settings. His suggestions strongly point to the interaction between institutions and individual characteristics and behavior and the nonrecursive nature of social decisions.

History and the Study of Institutions

Only by studying the development of institutions in their historical context can we fully capture the dynamic roles and properties of institutions in society. History provides the evidence of change and the information for examining how and why change occurs. History also forces consideration of more dynamic models where institutional change becomes part of our theory of institutions. Zald's plea for more integration of historical analysis and organization theory is a forceful argument for the need to consider both history and organization theory in the study of organizations. One cannot understand or theorize about organizations without an understanding of their history and the context in which they were formed. His argument applies to other social science areas and needs to be made about institutions broadly, not just about organizational structure. The dynamics of how institutions change and of how these changes affect society are particularly, and only, evident in historical perspective.

The magnitude of possible institutional change and its social implications is very evident in the contrast between the family implicitly described by Corcoran and Courant and the early American family described by Vinovskis. Corcoran and Courant analyze the occupational socialization provided by the role models in today's family but do not offer an explanation for how these role models arose or how they might be different. Vinovskis offers a different and changing picture of the American family, its impact on various institutions, and the consequences of institutional change for family structure. He describes how, in the earliest years, the father was responsible for catechizing and educating children. This role changed over time, as mothers came to be responsible for these functions. During this same period, religion (though not the church hierarchy) became a more female activity and teaching (but not school administration) became a more female occupation. These changes surely contribute to the role models and socialization that Corcoran and Courant observe.

McDonald presents an important theory and description of changes in the size, functions, and location of the public sector, or state, in the United States. His story is very much one of the dynamics of political institutions as means to aggregate individual preferences, as forces that influence the structure and articulation of these preferences, and as collections of actors with their own ability to alter outcomes. This country has always had active governments, but for a long time they existed at the local and state and not the federal level. Accompanying these governments have been conflicts and choices about their functions, size, and structure. The choices implicit in these conflicts are interdependent, in that the types of functions to be performed affect institutional choice at the same time that institutional choices affect the structure of interest groups and future choices about the functions to be performed.

The progressives campaigned against partisan politics and for various reform measures, such as Australian ballots and more stringent registration requirements, that created new, or at least different, political institutions. Their intent was to reduce the power of those who opposed the expansion of local government, lessen government's use of divisible rewards, and reintroduce a genuine political community. These reforms created governments largely responsible for provision of indivisible, or collective, goods. In order for these reform governments to maintain themselves and to expand the provision of collective goods, they had to become active promoters of interest groups that could help create and mobilize voters who shared these preferences. Thus, the governmental institutions the reforms created were not just a means to aggregate individual preferences, but became active participants in the expansion of local and state governments. One can surely see the continuation of the interaction between individual's interests, institutional structure, and government actions that McDonald recounts in the current debates over privatization (see Pack 1987).

McDonald's description also offers a historical view of the interest group behavior described by Walker and shows its dynamic consequences. Walker shows how dependent many interest groups are on government support to overcome the free rider problems faced by groups promoting public goods and dependent upon nonmaterial incentive systems. McDonald suggests that government officials contribute to the formation and maintenance of these interest groups to maintain their organizations. The consequence of this mutual dependency is a continual choice for public, as opposed to private, goods, and for public provision of those goods rather than reliance on private markets. In this case, the choice of an institution, individual preferences, and outcomes are inextricably intertwined.

Conclusion

The view of institutions and their role in society that emerges from these essays is both complicated and preliminary. The study of institutions has not been a central scholarly activity for the past several decades, though it once was central to the social sciences. Much attention has been paid to studying individual values, beliefs, tastes, and behavior in the belief that this knowledge would lead to an understanding of how society performed. McDonald describes this emphasis, and the scholarly beliefs it expresses, in some detail. Coincidently, there was considerable analysis of aggregate performance, such as in macroeconomics, but these efforts paid little attention to the actions of the units that composed the aggregates. We are now seeing a greater emphasis on, and a return to, interest in exactly how individual actions cumulate to produce macrolevel outcomes and how the social and political structures we refer to as institutions guide, constrain, and formulate individual values, beliefs, and behaviors. These essays provide two broad clues as to how that interest can be productively pursued.

Institutions both aggregate and socialize. Scholars cannot restrict their perception to only one of these roles. In predicting the likely outcomes with different institutions, one must consider the likely changes in values, beliefs, and behavior that result from the nonrecursive process, which may ultimately alter choices and behaviors in new ways. The impact of various policies on the distribution of wealth and political influence will also alter subsequent choices. Likewise, in analyzing how institutions affect individual beliefs and behavior it is necessary to consider how those institutions affect collective outcomes, which also affect individual beliefs and behavior. The presence and importance of these dynamic, or nonrecursive, elements in our institutional description pose considerable challenges to scholars. The use of careful historical studies, extensive time series, and analyses based on periods of social, economic, and institutional change become critical to the understanding and assessment of institutions.

The study of institutions requires an interdisciplinary approach. It is both foolish and arrogant to believe that any one discipline has the right approach to understanding and analyzing institutions. It is equally true that each discipline has important insights to contribute. Models of preference aggregation from economists and political scientists, an understanding of norms and beliefs from sociologists and psychologists, a demonstration of the way change occurs and its consequences from historians, theories of organizations from sociologists, and descriptions of political processes by political scientists are all examples of the necessary ingredients for a study of institutions. A synthesis of the concepts from these, and other, disciplines will lead to effective understanding and teaching about institutions. The integration of history with organization theory and the other social sciences, the blending of models of markets with those of the development of norms, the use and extension of economic models to understand and evaluate political decision rules, and the ability to view economic development as a problem in organizational behavior—all illustrate the necessity and power of such syntheses. Corcoran and Courant's frequent description of themselves as a political scientist and an economist doing sociology is an honest statement of how work must proceed. The promotion and support of this interdisciplinary scholarship may itself require new academic institutions to be successful.

With intensive, creative, and risky scholarship of the type presented here and represented by other recent writings on institutions, we will likely fulfill McDonald's concluding paragraph and his predicted "(Re)Turn to Institutions."

REFERENCES

Aberbach, Joel D., Robert D. Putnam, and Bert A. Rockman. 1981. *Bureaucrats and Politicians in Western Democracies.* Cambridge, Mass.: Harvard University Press.

Almond, Gabriel A., and Sidney Verba. 1965. *The Civic Culture.* Boston: Little, Brown & Co.

Cain, Bruce. 1984. *The Reapportionment Puzzle.* Berkeley: University of California Press.

_____. 1985. "Assessing the Partisan Effects of Redistricting." *American Political Science Review* 79:320–33.

Chamberlin, John R., and Paul N. Courant. 1983. "Representative Deliberations and Representative Decisions . . ." *American Political Science Review* 77:718–83.

Cohen, Michael D. 1984. "Conflict and Complexity: Goal Diversity and Organizational Search Effectiveness." *American Political Science Review* 78:435–51.

Gormley, William T., Jr. 1983. *The Politics of Public Utility Regulation.* Pittsburgh: University of Pittsburgh Press.

Hawley, Willis D. 1973. *Nonpartisan Elections and the Case for Party Politics.* New York: John Wiley & Sons.

Jepperson, Ronald L. 1989. "Institutions, Institutional Effects, and Institutionalism." In *The New Institutionalism in Organizational Analysis,* ed. Walter W. Powell and Paul J. DiMaggio. Chicago: University of Chicago Press.

March, James G., and Johan P. Olsen. 1984. "The New Institutionalism: Organizational Factors in Political Life." *American Political Science Review* 78:734–49.

_____. 1987. "Popular Sovereignty and the Search for Appropriate Institutions." *Journal of Public Policy* 6:341–70.

Ozaki, Robert S. 1984. "How Japanese Industrial Policy Works." In *The Industrial Policy Debate,* ed. Chalmers Johnson. San Francisco: Institute for Contemporary Studies.

Pack, Janet R., ed. 1987. *Journal of Public Policy and Management* 6:523–696.

Powell, Walter W., and Paul J. DiMaggio. 1989. *The New Institutionalism in Organizational Analysis.* Chicago: University of Chicago Press.

Riker, William H. 1980. "Implications from the Disequilibrium of Majority Rule for the Study of Institutions." *American Political Science Review* 74:432–47.

Shepsle, Kenneth A. 1986. "Institutional Equilibrium and Equilibrium Institutions." In *Political Science: The Science of Politics,* ed. Herbert F. Weisberg. New York: Agathon Press.

Stafford, Frank P. 1988. "A Model of Harmony." *Michigan Today* 20:4–5.

Wilson, James Q. 1973. *Political Organizations.* New York: Basic Books.

Zysman, John. 1983. *Governments, Markets, and Growth.* Ithaca: Cornell University Press.

CHAPTER 2

Sex-Role Socialization and Occupational Segregation: An Exploratory Investigation

Mary E. Corcoran and Paul N. Courant

It is well known that women earn less than men. For all of the rhetoric and research that takes this fact as a starting point, its causes are not well understood. In this chapter we advance the claim, based on our reading of the existing economic, sociological, and psychological literature, that events that occur before entrance into the labor market (some of which might best be termed "socialization," and others "pre–labor market discrimination") are likely to be important parts of a convincing explanation of observed wage differences between men and women.

The basic story that we have in mind is a simple one. Men and women are treated differently and exhibit different behaviors (e.g., choices of occupation) in the labor market. Pre–labor market decisions, made both by children themselves and by such socializing agents as parents and teachers, will be undertaken in recognition of labor market differences—that men and women face different constraints and opportunities (on average) suggests that the optimal training given to boys and girls will also differ (on average). Once these boys and girls reach adulthood, then, they will differ (again on average) in their tastes, values, and training, leading to differential treatment and behavior in labor markets, and again rationalizing differential socialization and training of boys and girls. The feedback system (some might say "vicious circle") outlined in

This project was partially funded by the Institute for Research on Poverty Small Grant Program supported by the Department of Health and Human Services. We are especially grateful to Deborah Laren for handling the computer work on this study, for helpful suggestions about the analysis plan, and for editing advice. We also want to thank Martha Hill and Michael Ponza for giving us a copy of their parent-child datafile from the Panel Study of Income Dynamics, for allowing us to use their computer programs, and for providing considerable advice. We are grateful for helpful comments from Gary Solon, from participants in the University of Michigan Program in American Institutions Seminar, and from participants in the the University of Michigan Public Finance Seminar. None of the above individuals or institutions is responsible for any opinions expressed in this essay.

this paragraph is strengthened by the presence of widely held social norms regarding sex-appropriate behavior and by institutional labor market practices that are consistent with these norms. Further, this feedback system, by lowering the benefits of challenging discrimination for both workers and employers, creates situations in which the ability of competitive forces to eliminate sex-based economic discrimination is weakened.

The preceding story may be simple, but the data requirements for testing it are (as we discuss later) enormous. Thus our goal here is more modest. Having made (in what we hope is a persuasive way) the claim that pre-labor market phenomena and the presence of social norms regarding sex roles may be important parts of an account of male-female pay differences, we report on two empirical exercises that indirectly tend to confirm it. We conclude that although we are a long way from making precise quantitative estimates of pre-labor market effects on labor market outcomes, there is good reason to believe that such effects are large enough to warrant a serious research effort on the topic.

Economic Explanations of the Wage Gap

Consider what for most economists is the preferred explanation of low female wages — that women on average have lower skills (human capital) than men and that these skill differences are the source of the male-female wage gap. These skill differences are voluntary and arise because of women's familial responsibilities (Mincer and Polachek 1974; Mincer 1978). Past empirical tests of this explanation have consistently reported that while there exist large differences in men's and women's work histories, training, and labor force attachment, these differences typically account for about one-third of the wage gap between white women and white men (Duncan and Corcoran 1984; Treiman and Hartmann 1981; Corcoran 1978, 1979; Oaxaca 1973; Corcoran, Duncan, and Ponza 1984). This leaves two-thirds of the wage gap unexplained. This residual is invariably attributed to labor market discrimination, pre-labor market discrimination, or socialization, with no explicit modeling of how these processes operate (Treiman and Hartmann 1983; Duncan and Corcoran 1983).

The "pure discrimination" explanation, as proposed by Becker (1957), is that employers may prefer one group of workers (men to women) and that employers would be willing to pay a premium to indulge their preferences. Arrow (1972a, 1972b) has shown that if employers vary in their preferences, then market forces ought to reduce and eventually eliminate group wage differences over time, although such complicating factors as customer, coworker, and statistical discrimination might slow this process down. How long the process "should" take is an empirical question, but we find it remarkable and implausible that the market does not seem to exploit the opportunities for profit implicit in a 20 to 25 percent wage gap (corrected for skills). Without detailed and testable modeling of the ways in which different kinds of discrimination are sustained in the presence of competitive forces, discrimination seems to us to have the same explanatory power as "not known."

According to the third explanation, the crowding hypothesis, there are two kinds of occupations: "male" and "female" (Bergmann 1974; Blau 1984; Blau and Hendricks 1979; Stevenson 1975). There are far fewer female occupations than male occupations. Women tend only to enter female occupations. This raises the supply of workers to female occupations and lowers the supply of workers to male occupations. This oversupply of workers to female occupations artificially lowers wages in these jobs. Similarly, wages are artificially raised in male occupations.

Blau (1984) and Strober (1984) argue that while the crowding explanation is descriptively veridical, there is no widely accepted economic explanation that fully delineates the processes that maintain the sex segregation of occupations in the face of competitive forces.[1] By itself, crowding is neither a discrimination nor a sex-role socialization story, but could be either or both. Employers could deliberately steer workers into sex-appropriate jobs (labor market discrimination) either because of their own tastes or those of male workers; schools and career counselors could restrict girls' opportunities to develop male job skills and to enter male jobs (pre–labor market discrimination); or girls because of early sex-role socialization might voluntarily choose to develop skills and to select jobs that are consistent with traditional sex roles.

Both sex segregation and the large residual wage gap are consistent with labor market discrimination, premarket discrimination, and socialization. None of the existing empirical work to date allows us to distinguish among these possibilities. It is our intention that the analysis in this essay provide a framework that will permit us to do so. We begin by discussing how sex-role socialization might influence women's labor market outcomes. Then we outline a modeling strategy that allows sex-role socialization and other pre–labor market differences in treatment of boys and girls to affect both workers' and employers' economic behaviors. In

---

1. A number of scholars have proposed partial explanations of the sex-segregation of jobs. See, for instance, Bonacich 1972; Edwards 1975; Kessler-Harris 1982; Matthaei 1982; Strober 1984.

the next section, we present an empirical investigation of possible family socialization influences on the sex-typicality of women's jobs and on husbands' and wives' wages. In the last section, we discuss the implications of our empirical results.

Socialization and Occupational Choice

In an extensive review of the literature, Eccles and Hoffman (1984) suggest that sex differences in socialization might affect occupational behavior in at least four ways.[2] First, socialization may lead women to be more fearful, more anxious, or less confident than men (Parsons, et al. 1976; Horner 1972; Tangri 1971; Nicholls 1975). Horner's work on "fear of success" is in this tradition. Second, sex-role socialization may directly affect workers' skills and personality traits (Hoffman 1972; Chodorow 1978; Parsons and Goff 1980). Some researchers argue, for instance, that girls are encouraged to be more dependent, more person-oriented, and less able mathematically than boys. Third, children may internalize traditional notions of sex roles, accept these cultural sex-stereotypes as fact, and eventually choose occupations that conform to these stereotypes (Bem and Bem 1970; Marini 1980; Tittle 1981). Fourth, sex-role socialization may affect the values men and women attach to different activities so that workers of both sexes tend to value "sex-appropriate" activities (Stein and Smithells 1969; Stein, Pohly, and Mueller 1971). Thus, women may value person-oriented tasks more than men do even if there were no sex differences in ability to perform such tasks.

The first two sets of phenomena are really human capital arguments. In both cases women differ from men in ways that may (on average) reduce these women's potential value in the labor market.[3] Such sex differences in human capital may or may not have been caused by discrimination. (Even when they have, the discrimination takes place before entry into the labor market.) The third and fourth findings suggest that equally qualified men and women may evaluate the same job characteristics quite differently when choosing jobs. They are thus "taste" explanations when considered from the perspective of the labor market. Following the economic tradition that takes adults' tastes as given, such an explanation, at least at the stage of the labor market, identifies at least some part of the wage gap as a compensating wage

---

2. The following paragraph summarizes and paraphrases a far more extensive discussion by Eccles and Hoffman, pp. 375ff.

3. Note that such differences are not accounted for in the empirical implementations of the human capital model described earlier.

differential. Note that human capital and taste differences may interact. Women may (on average) choose training that is consistent with their tastes for certain types of jobs. Having done this, they will have different human capital attributes from men (on average) when they enter the labor market.

Modeling Strategy

We start by restating two facts from the preceding sections. (1) On average, men and women perform differently in the labor market, and the differences are not fully accounted for by differences in measured human capital attributes. (2) On average, there are differences in the upbringing of boys and girls, and these differences tend to be consistent with traditional notions about appropriate sex roles. The main thesis of this essay is that (1) may be largely accounted for by (2). The purpose of this section is to outline the processes that could lead to such a result. The discussion assumes that we start in a world where facts (1) and (2) are true. Thus the dead hand of history leaves us in these circumstances, and the question now at hand is whether and how these circumstances can replicate themselves over time.

We reject the simplest explanation, that of direct discrimination against women on the part of employers, for the reasons given earlier. Direct discrimination can and probably does play some role and we discuss it further below, but it seems highly implausible that skill-corrected wage differences of 20 to 25 percent in a (roughly) competitive labor market can be accounted for by discrimination alone. Instead, we follow two other lines of inquiry. The first is based directly on the idea that men and women may value (on average) different types of labor market behaviors differently. The second embeds the first in models based on the literatures on screening (Spence 1973; Bergstrom 1978) and statistical discrimination (Aigner and Cain 1977). Taken together, these approaches add a supply side to the labor market, and this supply side tends to generate distributions of tastes and skills that differ by sex in ways that make differential treatment on the demand side persist even where there are no intrinsic differences between men and women at birth. Our purpose in using these kinds of explanations of differences in labor market outcomes of men and women is not to justify the differences as being in some sense warranted by economic reality. Rather, it is to provide a framework that permits pre–labor market training and socialization to interact with labor market performance, and that also allows us to consider the strength of the market and social forces that stand in the way of the attainment of equal outcomes. Only by delineating such forces can we formulate social policy that would be effective in changing them.

"Simple" Socialization

The pure socialization explanation of wage differences is straightforward.[4] Assume that individual workers (or potential workers) care about both income and other attributes of jobs. Further, assume that some of the attributes that they care about, for at least some of the workers, involve traditional notions of sex appropriateness and that jobs vary in the extent to which their requirements are traditionally male or female in character. A given worker may not care about sex appropriateness, but then again he or she may care about it. On average, women will be willing to give up some income in return for job attributes that are more consonant with traditional female roles, and men will have a preference for traditional male roles. Note that attributes of the job may include such elements as the sex ratio of current employees, the extent of perceived coworker prejudice, and the degree to which such prejudice would directly affect the worker.

If jobs with attributes that tend to be valued by women more than men are relatively scarce, then it is easy to tell a story consistent with Bergmann's (1974) crowding hypothesis that would explain why jobs that are largely filled by women pay less, for a given vector of measured human capital attributes, than jobs that are mostly filled by men. All that is occurring is a market equilibrium with a compensating wage differential — women are paying (in lower wages) for doing things that they value.[5]

Screening by Sex

Statistical screening is based on the idea that economic agents will use information on the average characteristics of groups in assessing the expected characteristics of individual members of the groups. The most familiar type of screening occurs in insurance markets. Auto insurance rates are higher for teenagers, because on average teenagers are worse drivers than older people, even though some individual teenagers are

---

4. See Corcoran and Courant 1985 for a more formal presentation of the argument in this section.

5. This explanation does not provide an account of why women's jobs would be relatively scarce. However, *if* the workplace is organized in this way, it does explain why women would not all move into men's jobs and arbitrage the differences away. This is especially plausible if coworker prejudice is worth paying something to avoid.

surely better drivers than some adults. Men pay higher life insurance rates than women because on average men have higher mortality rates at all ages, notwithstanding the fact that many men outlive many women. The key feature here is that although some relevant information can be obtained about individuals (driving record, passage of a driver education course, weight, smoking behavior, etc.) and this information can be and is used, information about group membership is also relevant. Thus, rational insurance underwriters will use such information. In some sense, this is unfair to unusually careful teenagers or unusually healthy men, but failing to use such information would be unfair to adults on average and women on average.

The presence of group differences (on average) and imperfect measurement of individual attributes are both required for statistical screening to operate in labor markets. If, on average, men and women came to the labor market with identical skills, group membership would convey no information. If test scores, educational credentials, and so on were perfect measures of productive attributes in each individual case, group membership would convey no additional information in the labor market. One person with a 3.28 grade point from Hasty Pudding State and a combined GRE of 1130 would be known to be exactly like another. But neither of these conditions holds in practice. Both the training and tastes of men and women will differ, on average, when they enter the labor market (Eccles and Hoffman 1984), and we all know that the credentials that people have measure their productive attributes only imperfectly. (They do not even do such a good job of predicting success in graduate school, surely a simpler problem than predicting success in the labor market.)

Leaving aside differences in tastes, suppose that job-related attributes are distributed differently for men and women. Due to differences in upbringing and training (cf. the discussion of simple socialization above) women will be more likely to have developed skills that are consistent with effective performance of traditional roles. Now consider an employer's evaluation of a man and a woman who have identical paper credentials. Knowing that men and women have different distributions of attributes, and that credentials measure true attributes only imperfectly, the employer's expectation of the woman's true attributes conditional on her credentials will be that the attributes are more consistent with those of women in general than the man's true attributes. If traditional male attributes are more productive in the job under consideration, the employer will expect the man to be more productive in the job, and will offer pay accordingly. If the stated assumptions of this little example hold, competition will force this outcome — as long as men and women are drawn from different distributions of productive attributes *at the level of the labor market*, employers who treat men and women with the same paper credentials in the same way will be less efficient than those who take sex into account in making their offers.[6]

In practice, because the law prohibits paying the woman less than a man with the same training for doing the same job, there will be an obvious motive for the employer to do the kind of steering that is often cited as a cause of occupational segregation. Moreover, employer behavior of this sort is easily self-sustaining. A certain set of credentials admit men to one set of jobs and women to another. On average, men with these credentials are as productive as expected, and so are women, but the expectations for the two groups are different.[7] Finally, note that average differences in tastes for different kinds of work can reinforce this argument. If employers know that on average women (men) are more comfortable performing traditional roles, they will observe that productivity conditional on credentials is higher when they are placed in traditional roles. Again, employers will rationally tend to screen by sex.

Here we get into some issues of semantics that cannot be ignored. It is probably fair to say that anyone who is not trained in neoclassical economics would view the circumstances of the preceding paragraph as discrimination, pure and simple. After all, individuals whose measured characteristics are identical in every dimension save sex are treated differently by the demand side of the labor market. If that is not discrimination, what is? The answer lies in the fact that under the assumptions of the model men and women with equal measured characteristics will, on average, have different productive characteristics, because the distributions of productive characteristics from which they are drawn are different. Thus, sex conveys (in a statistical sense) information about the expected productivity of an individual, conditional on his or her other measured characteristics. From an economic perspective, acting on such information is not discrimination.[8] From a legal perspective, this is indeed discrimination (consider the recent court decisions requiring the

---

6. See Aigner and Cain 1977 for a discussion of the technical requirements needed to make this example "fly."

7. Spence (1973) constructs an example where education (paper credentials, in our terms) is valuable in predicting differences in productivity within groups, but is not used to compare across groups. The discussion here is consistent with that example, and adds a reason why the two groups might not be directly compared.

8. To the extent that a Spence-type signaling equilibrium were all that was operating, but average differences in productive ability vanished, there would indeed be economic discrimination, although there would also be forces tending to generate a market in the signals that would tend to make the discrimination disappear over time.

use of unisex life tables for computing annuities). Whether the outcome in the preceding paragraph is called "discrimination" or not is less important than the fact that under the assumptions of the model there will be no immediate market forces that will tend to eliminate the differences in circumstances between men and women. As long as men and women have different average abilities when entering the labor market and the information conveyed by paper credentials is imperfect, market forces will not tend to eliminate the different outcomes in labor markets. The forms that the different outcomes take appear to be complicated enough in practice so that legal remedies can be only partially effective and will in any event (in the narrow economic sense) cause inefficiencies of their own. The question, then, is whether there exist forces that will tend to improve signals and equalize average abilities.[9]

Socialization and Screening over Time—A Vicious Circle

Screening cannot be sustained unless the average differences between groups are sustained. Thus, if the relevant characteristics of women entering the labor market were to become, on average, the same as that of men, the kind of story outlined above could not obtain. But the potential obstacles to such an event occurring are considerable. Suppose for the moment that the parents of both boys and girls are concerned with raising their children in a way that will maximize the lifetime income prospects for their children. (Thus, suppose that all values concerning appropriate sex roles were suddenly to vanish. They will reappear later in the discussion.) Suppose further that parents believe (accurately) that a son and a daughter who have equal innate abilities and who pursue identical courses of preparation for the labor market will be treated differently once they get there. (Parents need not attribute this to historical differences in group means, but they know the facts when they see them.) Under these circumstances, socialization and training of children toward traditional male values and roles will yield higher expected lifetime earnings potential for boys than it will for girls, given equal potential abilities. This in itself does not imply that it would be irrational for parents to socialize and train their girls to traditional male values and roles. The outcome depends on the opportunities available to women

---

9. Having framed the question to include the possibility that the reliability of signals might be changed, we ignore the issue in the discussion that follows. However, if the logic of the argument here is correct, it is highly rational for women to go out of the way to acquire credentials that are considered highly reliable. In this interpretation, the dramatic increase in female attendance at law schools and business schools may say less about a taste for the relevant professions than about the value of acquiring (relatively) reliable signals.

whose tastes and talents are more traditionally female in character. But it does imply the possibility of a sustained equilibrium difference in average outcomes, based on differences in tastes and in average ability *at the level of the labor market*, where the differences in ability and tastes are replicated from generation to generation.[10] Such a sustained equilibrium is all the more likely, even in this most narrow economic model, when we remember that one route to income available to women is to marry men, and at least in some cases traditional female characteristics may increase the returns from this strategy.

Leaving the narrow economic model, and recognizing that in the majority of households there is a positive preference on the part of parents (and if not parents, teachers, counselors, peers) for children of both sexes to act in conformance with traditional sex roles, the difficulties involved in generating equal outcomes for men and women in competitive markets become multiplied.[11] Indeed (and this is what social norms are all about) there will, on average, be all sorts of noneconomic (and perhaps some economic) rewards for behaving in ways that are consonant with traditional sex roles. In more formal terms, most people will have an element of the utility function (with positive weight) that values such consonant behavior. Moreover, following the logic of Cohen and Axelrod (1984) even nontraditional women who do not have such a value to begin with may learn to place positive weight on it. Life is easier when you don't buck the system. (But note that the system here is not the labor market, it is social norms.)

The preceding discussion suggests the possibility that once there are differences in the treatment of boys and girls (and men and women) there may be powerful forces blocking the erosion of such differences. Even if all overt discrimination (in the sense of equal pay for equal work) is eliminated, if the environments in which boys and girls are raised are

10. Lundberg and Startz (1983) present a model of investment in education that exemplifies this kind of process. In their model, human capital investment is affected by group differences in labor market outcomes, which in turn generates such differences.

11. Indeed, widely held preferences for consonance with traditional roles and values will also have a direct effect in the labor market. If coworkers are more productive in a traditional environment, employers will be rationally leery of placing women in nontraditional roles, even if the women are known to be fully able to meet the technical requirements of the job. Further, such discrimination on the part of coworkers (or employers) can induce behavioral responses on the part of potential women employees. If there is an expectation of "hassle" of various kinds when a woman performs a nontraditional role, then it will be worth some pay reduction to take a position (a traditional position) that will offer a more pleasant environment. Here the expectation of discrimination induces a behavioral response that can be interpreted as a compensating wage differential — here the compensation is in exchange for avoiding painful circumstances.

different the outcomes of men and women will differ as well, provided that the training and values of men and women differ in ways that affect productivity and the psychic rewards from pursuit of different types of market and nonmarket work.[12]

In sum, socialization and other forms of pre–labor market differences in treatment between boys and girls can lead to an equilibrium in which men and women have different distributions of both tastes (values) and talents. As long as men and women differ on average, it will be costly for nontraditional members of either sex to choose to take nontraditional routes. Differences may then tend to persist from generation to generation. Women with nontraditional training and values can indeed enter the male labor market, but their credentials will mean less there than men's credentials will. Further, relatively traditional women will be willing to sacrifice economic rewards in order to obtain psychic ones in the female labor market. This latter behavior is optimal for those who engage in it, but has an externality that reduces the rewards available to nontraditional women by reducing the average productive characteristics (and hence value of credentials) of women in the male market.

Direct Discrimination

The preceding suggests ways in which men and women might have very different labor market outcomes without any direct discrimination. Although we have argued that direct discrimination is an inadequate account of differences of the magnitudes that we observe, it is worth pointing out that in the context of the kinds of processes we have discussed, direct discrimination can play an important role.

To begin with, ubiquitous tastes for discrimination are highly plausible if socialization is an important determinant of adult behavior. Precisely the same processes that lead women and men to value traditional roles and behaviors for themselves will lead them to value traditional roles and behaviors for each other. Thus it is plausible that coworkers,

---

12. See Loury 1981 for a discussion of a model in which, for blacks and whites, equal opportunity may not lead to equal equilibrium outcomes, in spite of equal intrinsic abilities at birth. The mechanism in Loury's model is that blacks and whites, due to segregation, grow up in different neighborhoods, and neighborhood characteristics matter to the acquisition of wealth-enhancing skills. In the context of the argument we make in this essay, the different "neighborhoods" for boys and girls are different patterns of socialization and training. The logic of the argument is essentially the same, with addition here that socialization may lead to men and women placing different psychological values on different types of work.

customers, and employers themselves would prefer an environment that is consonant with traditional values regarding sex roles.

Further, much of the preceding argument depends on the assumption that information about employees' true attributes is both imperfect and costly to obtain. The same will be true regarding information about employers' and coworkers' tastes. While it is highly plausible that there exist some workplaces in which employers do not care about traditional roles, and somewhat (although less) plausible that the same will be true regarding coworkers, it will be costly for a given potential employee to find such a workplace. Under these conditions, there will be room for some practice of direct discrimination, because the standard arbitrage mechanism that would lead to the erosion of discriminatory differentials in a competitive market will only operate to the extent that the gains from finding a nondiscriminating employer exceed the costs of search. If women employees expect discrimination in some types of work but not others, their reservation wages for the former will be lowered relative to those for the latter, even if some (hard to find) employers do not discriminate by sex for any type of job.[13]

Tests

In the context of the preceding, the standard human capital regression tells us very little about the sources of male-female pay differentials. Explanations that are based on differences in employee tastes for job attributes are indistinguishable from explanations that are based on employer or coworker discrimination. Further, the interaction between them makes it difficult to isolate either of the two classes of explanation empirically. Our intention thus far has been to show that it should be fairly easy to write down models in which many potentially important factors interact; but if we are to find out which of these factors are important in the labor market, we need empirically testable implications of socialization-based explanations that are different from discrimination-based explanations. We must turn to examination of processes that might generate the average differences in values and training that make the models go round.

The ideal way to disentangle the possibilities implicit in the preceding discussion would involve following a panel of children over time and

---

13. See Courant 1978 for a model of housing market discrimination that is constructed along these lines. Adaptation to search in a labor market is straightforward. See Akerlof 1985 for a more elegant generic form of such a model, in which the key assumption is that not all potential traders make contact with each other.

examining how their family environments and their school environments affected their sex-role attitudes and aspirations; how families, schools, attitudes, and aspirations influenced decisions about investment in education and training; and how families, schools, attitudes, aspirations, and human capital affected job choice and wages. At key decision points — choice of college major, first job, etc. — we would need to ask detailed questions about the factors that influenced those decisions — particularly about paths not taken. We know of no data that would allow us to take this approach.[14]

We can, however, use currently available data to take a preliminary look at whether socialization might be important. At this stage we are looking for evidence of two types of relevant phenomena: (1) direct links between the sex-role relevant labor market behavior of parents and that of their children's adult labor market behavior; and (2) labor market behavior on the part of adults that can be best explained as arising from the fact that men and women value traditional sex roles. Neither of these types of evidence would be as convincing as that which might be developed with the ideal data set discussed in the preceding paragraph, but it is worth noting that each is quite different from the other and finding examples of both would suggest that socialization can have powerful effects on the adult labor market outcomes of men and women.

For the first types of phenomenon, we use a sample of young adults aged 25–30 years in 1981 to see if family factors that have been shown to influence sex differentiation in attitudes and aspirations also affect occupational choice. For the second, we look at an unusual sample of couples — couples for whom wives' predicted hourly earnings exceed the husbands' predicted hourly earnings. If couples try to maximize income when making decisions about labor market work and family time, then these couples ought, on average, to have a nontraditional division of labor within the household and the wives' actual wages ought to exceed the husbands' actual wages.

Family Socialization and Sex-Typicality of Jobs

A key assumption of socialization-based explanations of male-female wage differences is that sex-role patterns learned in childhood will affect adult economic behavior. Psychological studies of children's socialization have identified the following family factors which tend to reduce sex-role differentiation on psychological dimensions such as attitudes or

---

14. And even here we would not have examined the operation of the labor market itself.

aspirations: being raised in a female-headed household, being raised in a family with children of one sex, and having nontraditional parents (for summaries of this research, see Eccles and Hoffman 1984; Marini and Brinton 1984). But no studies have yet established a link between early family socialization and women's actual labor market behaviors for a nationally representative sample of women.

We use a subset of young adults from the Panel Study of Income Dynamics (PSID) to test for such a link. The PSID provides fourteen years (1968–81) of data for a nationally representative sample of 762 girls aged 12–17 in 1968. These individuals were 25–30 years old in 1981.[15] All were children in their parents' homes in 1968 and had established their own homes by 1981. For each of these young adults the PSID provides measures of parental and family characteristics reported by the parents during the years the young adults lived in their parental homes and labor market information reported by the young adults after they had left home.

This PSID sample has both advantages and disadvantages for our purposes. Its strongest advantage is the richness of data on parents. Most importantly, the PSID provides measures of the nature, timing, and duration of mothers' labor market behaviors as reported by the mothers. Psychological theories of sex-role socialization strongly emphasize the importance of identification with and role-modeling of the same-sex parent. The PSID permits a direct test of whether girls emulate mothers' work behaviors.

Two disadvantages are the relative youth of the PSID sample and the lack of any direct measure of sex-role attitudes. At ages 25–30, many young adults are still launching their careers, and so this sample is not well suited for examining wages and wage growth. Therefore, we concentrate on examining only education and the sex-typicality of occupations for these young women. By ages 25–30, most young adults will have completed their schooling. And family socialization effects on the choice of sex-appropriate occupations should be strongest early on in workers' careers when young adults are leaving their parental family to establish their own households. The lack of a good measure of sex-role attitudes means that we cannot directly test a key prediction of socialization models—namely, that women who value traditional roles will be more likely to choose female jobs. Instead, we test whether family characteristics that have been shown to affect sex-role attitudes also affect the choice of a female job. This is a much weaker test.

---

15. This age range was chosen to insure representativeness. Most children remain living with parents until age 17, and most have left home by age 25. See Corcoran, Duncan, and Hill 1984 for a more extensive description of this sample.

Table 1 defines the variables we used in our analysis of the sex-typicality of young women's jobs held since leaving home.[16] We estimate regressions separately by race since it has been argued that different processes may govern sex-role socialization for blacks and whites (Barnett and Baruch 1968; Datcher 1983; Dorr and Lesser 1980; Eccles and Hoffman 1984).

We regress sex-typicality of children's work experience on three sets of predictor variables. First, we include as controls the following conventional background measures: family income, father's education, mother's education, father's occupation, and number of siblings. We have no strong a priori notions regarding the effects of these variables; we include them because they are generally related to the labor market experience of children.

The second set of predictor variables are three measures of mother's work outcomes: proportion of family income earned by mother, proportion of time worked by mother while the child was at home, and sex-typicality of mother's work experience. (See table 1 for definitions of these variables.) These first two variables are included to pick up the extent of mothers' labor market commitment, following past research that indicates that girls whose mothers have worked extensively have more realistic work expectations, plan to work more in the future, and have more knowledge of occupations than other girls (see Marini and Brinton 1984, 210–11, for a summary of this research). However, extensive maternal work need not mean that mothers are transmitting aspirations for nontraditional market work to daughters since most mothers, like most women, are employed in female jobs. An additional complication is that families where mothers work a lot and contribute a large proportion of family income are likely to have less time and fewer resources than families with similar levels of incomes where mothers do not work. This ought to dampen achievement outcomes for both sons and daughters. Probably the cleanest measure of mothers' sex-role relevant labor market behavior is the sex-typicality of jobs held by the mother.[17] We note, by the way, that "female" jobs are not characterized by low education, so the sex-typicality of mothers' jobs can affect daughters' job choices quite independently of standard human capital attributes of both mothers and daughters.

---

16. There is relatively little missing data on the predictor and variables used in these analyses since parents provided contemporaneous reports of their attributes. We deal with missing data on prediction variables by using pair-wise deletion when creating matrices for OLS regression. There is also relatively little missing data on outcome measures. Any cases with missing data on outcomes are dropped from analysis runs.

17. This could arise from tastes or steering into sex-typical jobs. In either case, it is readily observable by both researchers and daughters.

TABLE 1. Family Background Measures and Child's Outcome Measures

Variable Name	Definition
Conventional Background Measures	
Family income	Annual family income (in thousands of 1980 dollars) averaged over the years child lived at home
Father's education	Years of schooling attained by father as reported by the father[a]
Mother's education	Years of schooling attained by mother as reported by the mother[a]
Father's occupation	Duncan scores of father's one-digit census occupations averaged over the years child lived at home[b]
Number of siblings	Number of child's brothers and sisters
Measures of Mother's Work Behavior	
Proportion of family income earned by mother	Labor income earned by mother during the years child lived at home divided by total family income during that period
Mother's proportion time worked	Total time worked by mother during years while child lived at home divided by the product of the number of years child lived at home and 2,000
Sex-typicality of mother's work experience	The percent female in mother's occupation-industry categories averaged over the fourteen-year sample period.[c] Women who *never* worked during this time were assigned the sample mean[d]
Family Composition Measures	
Mother-only household	1 if child ever lived in a mother-only household before leaving home; 0 otherwise[e]
Duration in mother-only household	Number of years lived in a mother-only household[e]
Opposite sex sibling	1 if an opposite sex child aged 0–17 years lived in child's parental home in 1968; 0 otherwise
Opposite sex sibling and family income	Family income if there is an opposite sex sibling; 0 otherwise
Outcome Measure	
Sex-typicality of child's work experience	The percent female in child's occupation-industry categories averaged over the period after which the child had left home[f]

aThe child's report of parental education was used for cases with missing data on these variables.

bThe child's report of father's occupation was used for cases with missing data on this variable.

cIndustry is coded into two-digit categories for the years 1971–81. Occupation is coded into one-digit categories for all the years thereafter. For each occupation-industry subgroup, we calculated a measure of percent female. (See Corcoran, Duncan, and Ponza 1983 for a more complete description of this procedure.)

dA dummy variable indicating whether the mother never worked is included to control for possible measurement error.

eWe were unable to obtain information on these two measures for children whose fathers reported being in their second marriages in 1968 — about 15 percent of the sample. We included a dummy variable for second marriages to control for possible measurement problems in all analyses using these measures.

fThis variable is coded in the same way as sex-typicality of mother's work experience.

The third set of variables are four family composition variables: whether child had a sibling of the opposite sex, an interaction between family income and whether child had a sibling of the opposite sex, whether child ever lived in a mother-only family, and years lived in a mother-only family. Eccles and Hoffman (1984) argue that there may be less sex-role stereotyping of daughters in families without sons. Girls may do better when they are not compared or do not compare themselves to brothers, and parents may have higher aspirations for daughters when they have no sons. The opposite sex sibling measure will test for this. Eccles and Hoffman also argue that parents may be less likely to differentiate between brothers and sisters in families with abundant resources. We include the interaction term to see if there is more differentiation between brothers and sisters in low-income families. Sex-role socialization theorists have also argued that there should be less sex-role differentiation among children, particularly boys, raised in female-headed households since there is no male role model for boys and since women who head households often must take on nontraditional roles — e.g., provider or disciplinarian. However, as McLanahan (1983) points out, father absence could also affect children by reducing economic resources and parental time available to children within the family. Thus, the measures of father absence may influence outcomes through several very different processes, and the net effect could go either way.

Table 2 reports the results of estimating the sex-typicality of young women's work experience after leaving home. The results are quite consistent with predictions of sex-role socialization theories. Women whose mothers worked in female-dominated fields tend also to work in such fields. Effects are sizable and significant for both black and nonblack women, and effects for black women are 75 percent higher than those for white women. There are few consistent or significant effects of the other maternal work variables, suggesting that the kind of jobs mothers hold are more important than how much or whether or not they work. It may be that the maternal work variables affect other aspects of economic attainment such as labor force participation or wages. The conventional background and family composition measures are also insignificant, suggesting that social class and family structure have few effects on young women's taste for sex-appropriate work.

Division of Labor in Potentially Nontraditional Households

Another way to investigate sex-role socialization is to examine the wages and work behavior of husbands and wives in couples where the wives' predicted earnings exceed the husbands' predicted earnings. In such fam-

TABLE 2. Regression for Sex-Typicality of Work Experience of Young Women Aged 25 – 30, by Race

Variable Name[a]	Nonblacks	Blacks
Family income	−.0002	−.0002
	(.0010)	(.0022)
Father's occupation	−.0011	.0018*
	(.0007)	(.0007)
Father's education	−.0001	−.0021
	(.0040)	(.0029)
Mother's education	.0013	−.0053
	(.0042)	(.0039)
Proportion of family income	−.0946	−.0392
earned by mother	(.1114)	(.0863)
Mother's proportion of time worked	.0485	.0879
	(.0539)	(.0574)
Sex-typicality of mother's work	.1355**	.2522**
experience	(.0509)	(.0418)
Mother-only household	−.0501	−.0744**
	(.0351)	(.0283)
Duration in mother-only household	.0071[+]	.0054*
	(.0038)	(.0023)
Opposite sex sibling	−.0090	−.0227
	(.0410)	(.0420)
Opposite sex sibling and family	−.0002	−.0022
income	(.0011)	(.0022)
Number of siblings	.0007	−.0003
	(.0044)	(.0037)
Education	−.0083[+]	−.0070
	(.0050)	(.0055)
N	445	317
R^2	.063	.168

Note: Standard errors are shown in parentheses below the coefficients.

aControls are also added for mothers who never worked outside the home and fathers who were in their second marriage in 1968.

[+] Significant at the 10 percent level
*Significant at the 5 percent level
**Significant at the 1 percent level

ilies, wives have an absolute earnings advantage. According to Becker's (1974) production theory of marriage, the spouse with the higher wage rate ought to specialize in the market while the other spouse (the husband) ought to specialize in home production. Thus, if only economics matters, in most of these families the wives' actual wages should exceed husbands' actual wages and husbands should spend relatively more time than wives in home production.[18]

---

18. This assumes husbands and wives are equally talented at home production.

We used a sample of 3,066 pairs of married male household heads and wives in 1982 taken from the PSID to investigate this issue. Couples were excluded if either spouse was over 64 years old, a student, retired, or disabled. For each husband-wife pair, we constructed measures of predicted hourly wages for both husband and wife. The earnings functions used to construct these predicted wage measures estimated hourly wages as a function of education, age, age squared, whether lived in the South, and city size. The sample used for the men's equations were all employed men under 65 years who were not students, retired, or disabled. The sample for the women's equation were all employed women under 65 years who were not students, retired, or disabled, and *who had worked continuously since leaving school*. We restricted the sample to women who had continuous employment in order to estimate women's expected wage given that women do not stay at home for family responsibilities. We mean this to measure a woman's labor market opportunities upon completion of schooling.

Wives' expected hourly earnings exceeded husbands' expected hourly earnings for only 133 of the 3,066 husband-wife pairs (4.3 percent). These were very unusual couples; wives averaged about four years more schooling than did their husbands (12.8 versus 8.7). Wives' actual earnings exceeded husbands' actual earnings for only 33 of these 133 pairs (25 percent). This is far fewer than one would expect if families are solely income maximizers.

As a next step, we estimated the following equation for the 133 husband-wife pairs where the wives had higher expected earnings than their husbands.

$$p = a_0 + B_1 ed_h + B_2 exp_h$$
$$+ B_3 exp_h^2 + B_4 ten_h$$
$$+ a_1 ed_w + a_2 exp_w + a_3 exp_w^2$$
$$+ a_4 ten_w$$

where

p = 1 if wife's actual wage was larger than husband's wage
   = 0 otherwise
ed = years of school completed
exp = work experience prior to current employer
ten = years employed with current employer
h = husband
w = wife

Here the dependent variable is a dummy variable that takes on a value of 1 when the wife's wage exceeds the husband's wage. The predictor variables are measures of the husband's and wife's education, work experience, and job tenure.

Table 3 reports the results when the equation is estimated using ordinary least squares.[19] The results are no surprise. Only two of the eight predictor variables have significant coefficients: wife's and husband's job tenure. The higher the wife's job tenure, the more likely her wage will exceed her husband's wage. The higher the husband's job tenure, the less likely his wife's wage will exceed his wage.

Since job tenure of both spouses seems to be a key factor in predicting which spouse will have higher wages, we regressed job tenure on potential experience (age − education − 6) and on number of children under age 14 separately for husbands and wives. Table 4 reports the results. For wives, number of children strongly predicts job tenure. For each child under age 14, a wife's job tenure drops by 0.58 years. There is no effect of children on husband's job tenure. Thus, even in families where wives have higher predicted earnings than husbands, children reduce wives' job tenure but have no effect on husband's job tenure. This, in turn, reduces the chances that wives will actually attain higher

TABLE 3.   Regression for Dummy Variable Measuring All Husband-Wife Pairs Where Wife's Wage Exceeds Husband's Wage

Variable Name	
Husband's education	.0166
	(.0288)
Wife's education	−.0134
	(.0246)
Husband's experience prior to current job	.0038
	(.0127)
Husband's experience, squared	−.0002
	(.0003)
Wife's experience prior to current job	.0137
	(.0178)
Wife's experience, squared	−.0002
	(.0008)
Husband's job tenure	−.0243*
	(.0082)
Wife's job tenure	.0603*
	(.0130)
R^2	.219

Note: Standard errors are shown in parentheses below the coefficients.
*Significant at the 1 percent level

---

19. The same pattern of results is obtained when this model is estimated using probit analysis.

earnings than their husbands. This behavior, of course, is completely consistent with the proposition that one or both partners values traditional sex roles. Indeed, in this case, there is a clear monetary value placed on traditionality.

Conclusions

Our major theoretical finding is that in order to distinguish between socialization and discrimination as explanations for male-female pay differentials, one must look at each of the processes, rather than just the outcome, as is implicitly the case in the standard human capital regression. Further, the models we outline suggest that if socialization and other forms of pre-labor market differential treatment are important to begin with, labor market incentives will not tend to make them go away. In this essay, we have tried to look at both the process of socialization and the possibility that households train boys and girls differently, although our effort to look at socialization has been hampered by the fact that the data we used contained no information on the attitudes of respondents in the sample. Indeed, having gone on at length about how a vector of sex-appropriate characteristics and tastes regarding them might operate in the labor market, the only measure we have of sex-appropriateness is the percent female in mothers' occupations, and even this is not a pure taste variable.

The gap is important. The literature on sex-role socialization and occupational choice suggests that various family behaviors should influence occupational aspirations and the valuation of traditional sex roles, and that these in turn should affect behavior. The first link, that between family behavior and aspirations and attitudes has been the subject of an extensive literature in psychology. The second link remains unexplored; what we have done here in our examinations is to jump from family circumstances to adult behaviors directly. Even that jump was complicated by the fact that our measures of family background (e.g., presence or absence of a father) could plausibly lead to any of a number of

TABLE 4. Regression for Job Tenure of Each Spouse

Variable Name	Husbands	Wives
Potential experience	.2303*	.0862*
	(.0333)	(.0227)
Number of children under age 14	-.0791	-.5849*
	(.3901)	(.2007)
R^2	.271	.159

Note: Standard errors are shown in parentheses below the coefficients.
*Significant at the 1 percent level

behaviors. In order to get much further, we will need longitudinal data that has information about attitudes (of both parents and children) as well as about economic outcomes. We are currently exploring other data sets and contemplating generating new ones in order to continue this work.

In spite of the absence of attitude measures, our empirical results tend to confirm the idea that pre–labor market differences between boys and girls may be important. That the sex-typicality of mothers' occupations influences that of daughters' tends to indicate that sex-role socialization matters in the labor market behavior of women. As it stands, we find this result to be suggestive of a process at work rather than a description of the process or a good measure of its power. With better measures of the ways in which the upbringing of boys differs from that of girls, we would expect to see more of an effect, rather than less.

Finally, the finding that consistency with traditional sex roles regarding childrearing versus market work seems to be more important in determining household division of labor than income maximization also supports the idea that at the level of the labor market different tastes (presumably arising from socialization) account for some of the differences between the behavior of men and women. In a way, the result is not surprising — it is universally known that women do most of the childrearing. Yet it is hard to account for either the finding or its plausibility unless one believes that there are powerful forces at work leading members of both sexes to perform traditional roles. That the outcome of these forces is readily observable in this case suggests that they may also be at work in other cases that are relevant to differences in pay between men and women.

We began by arguing that differences between men and women that arise from their upbringing in a society in which boys and girls are treated (and behave) differently might be an important part of an explanation of male-female pay differentials. Our findings here suggest that this indeed may be the case, although in order to find out how the process works and how important it is, a great deal of work remains to be done.

REFERENCES

Aigner, D., and G. Cain. 1977. "Statistical Theories of Discrimination in Labor Markets." *Industrial and Labor Relations Review* 30(2): 175–87.
Akerlof, G. A. 1985. "Discriminatory, Status-Based Wages among Tradition-

Oriented, Stochastically Trading Coconut Producers." *Journal of Political Economy* 93(2): 265–76.

Arrow, K. 1972a. "Models of Job Discrimination." In *Racial Discrimination in Economic Life,* ed. A. H. Pascal. Lexington, Mass.: D.C. Heath and Co.

———. 1972b. "Some Mathematical Models of Race in the Labor Market." In *Racial Discrimination in Economic Life,* ed. A. H. Pascal. Lexington, Mass.: D.C. Heath and Co.

Barnett, R. C., and G. K. Baruch. 1968. *The Competent Woman.* New York: Halstead Press.

Becker, G. S. 1957. *The Economics of Discrimination.* Chicago: University of Chicago Press.

———. 1974. "A Theory of Marriage." In *Economics of the Family: Marriage, Children, and Human Capital,* ed. T. W. Schultz. Chicago: University of Chicago Press.

Bem, S. D., and D. J. Bem. 1970. "Case Study of a Nonconscious Ideology: Training the Woman to Know Her Place." In *Beliefs, Attitudes, and Human Affairs,* ed. D. J. Bem. Belmont, Calif.: Brooks/Cole.

Bergmann, B. R. 1974. "Occupational Segregation, Wages and Profits When Employers Discriminate by Race or Sex." *Eastern Economic Journal* 1:103–10.

Bergstrom, T. C. 1978. "A Model of Bayesian Racial Prejudice and the Acquisition of Skill." University of Michigan. Typescript.

Blau, F. D. 1984. "Occupational Segregation and Labor Market Discrimination." In *Sex Segregation in the Labor Force: Trends and Prospects,* ed. B. F. Reskin. Washington, D.C.: National Academy of Science Press.

Blau, F. D., and W. E. Hendricks. 1979. "Occupational Segregation by Sex: Trends and Prospects." *Journal of Human Resources* 14(1): 197–210.

Bonacich, E. 1972. "A Theory of Ethnic Antagonism: The Split Labor Market." *American Sociological Review* 37:547–59.

Chodorow, N. 1978. *The Reproduction of Mothering.* Berkeley, Calif.: University of California Press.

Cohen, M., and R. Axelrod. 1984. "Coping with Complexity: The Adaptive Value of Changing Utility." *American Economic Review* 74(1): 30–42.

Collins, R. 1972. "A Conflict Theory of Sexual Stratification." *Social Problems* 19(4): 3–21.

Corcoran, M. 1978. "The Structure of Female Wages." *American Economic Review* 68(2): 165–70.

———. 1979. "Work Experience, Labor Force Withdrawals and Women's Earnings: Empirical Results Using the 1976 Panel Study of Income Dynamics." In *Women in the Labor Market,* ed. C. B. Lloyd, E. Andrews, and C. L. Gilroy. New York: Columbia University Press.

Corcoran, M., and P. Courant. 1985. "Sex-Role Socialization and Labor Market Outcomes." *American Economic Review* 75(2): 275–78.

Corcoran, M., G. Duncan, and M. Hill. 1984. "The Economic Fortunes of Women and Children." *Signs* 10(2): 242–48.

Corcoran, M., G. Duncan, and M. Ponza. 1984. "Work Experience, Job Segregation and Wages." In *Sex Segregation in the Labor Force: Trends and Prospects,* ed. B. F. Reskin. Washington, D.C.: National Academy of Science Press.

Corcoran, M., and C. Jencks. 1979. "Effects of Family Background." In *Who Gets Ahead,* ed. C. Jencks et al. New York: Basic Books.

Courant, P. N. 1978. "Racial Prejudice in a Search Model of the Urban Housing Market." *Journal of Urban Economics* 5(3): 329–45.

Datcher, C. 1983. "Race/Sex Differences in the Effects of Background on Achievement." In *Five Thousand American Families,* ed. G. Duncan and J. Morgan. Ann Arbor, Mich.: Institute for Social Research.

Dorr, A., and G. S. Lesser. 1980. "Career Awareness in Young Children." In *Women, Communication, and Careers,* ed. M. Grewe-Partsch and G. J. Robinson. Munich and New York: K. G. Saur.

Duncan, G. J., and M. Corcoran. 1984. "Do Women Deserve to Earn Less than Men?" In *Years of Poverty, Years of Plenty,* ed. G. J. Duncan et al. Ann Arbor, Mich.: Institute for Social Research.

Eccles, J. P., and L. W. Hoffman. 1984. "Sex Differences in Preparation for Occupational Roles." In *Child Development and Social Policy,* ed. H. Stevenson and A. Siegel. Chicago: University of Chicago Press.

Edwards, R. 1975. *Contested Terrain: The Transformation of the Workplace in America.* New York: Basic Books.

Filer, R. K. 1983. "Sexual Differences in Earnings: The Role of Individual Personalities and Tastes." *Journal of Human Resources* 18(1): 82–99.

Hoffman, L. W. 1972. "Early Childhood Experiences and Women's Achievement Motives." *Journal of Social Issues* 28:129–56.

Horner, M. 1972. "Toward an Understanding of Achievement-Related Conflicts in Women." *Journal of Social Issues* 28:157–75.

Jusenius, C. L. 1977. "The Influence of Work Experience, Skill Requirement, and Occupational Segregation on Women's Earnings." *Journal of Economics and Business* 29(2): 107–15.

Kessler-Harris, A. 1982. *Out to Work: A History of Wage-Earning Women in the United States.* New York: Oxford University Press.

Loury, G. 1981. "Is Equal Opportunity Enough?" *American Economic Review* 71(2): 122–26.

Lundberg, S. J., and R. Startz. 1983. "Private Discrimination and Social Intervention in Labor Markets." *American Economic Review* 73(2): 340–47.

Malkiel, B. G., and J. A. Malkiel. 1973. "Male-Female Pay Differentials in Professional Employment." *American Economic Review* 63(4): 693–705.

Marini, M. M. 1980. "Sex Differences in the Process of Occupational Attainment: A Closer Look." *Social Science Research* 9(4): 307–61.

Marini, M. M., and M. C. Brinton. 1984. "Sex-Typing in Occupational Socialization." In *Sex Segregation in the Workplace: Trends, Explanations and Remedies,* ed. B. F. Reskin. Washington, D.C.: National Academy of Science Press.

Matthaei, J. A. 1982. *An Economic History of Women in America: Women's Work, the Sexual Division of Labor, and the Development of Capitalism.* New York: Schocken Books.

McLanahan, S. 1983. "Family Structure and the Reproduction of Poverty." Institute for Research on Poverty, University of Wisconsin. IRP Discussion Paper no. 7208A83.

Mincer, J., and S. Polachek. 1974. "Family Investments in Human Capital: Earnings of Women." *Journal of Political Economy* 82(pt. 2): S76–S108.

————. 1978. "An Exchange: Theory of Human Capital and the Earnings of Women: Women's Earnings Reexamined." *Journal of Human Resources* 13(1): 118–34.

Nicholls, J. G. 1975. "Causal Attributions and Other Achievement-Related Cognitions: Effects of Task Outcomes, Attainment Value, and Sex." *Journal of Personality and Social Psychology* 31:379–89.

Oaxaca, R. 1973. "Male-Female Wage Differentials in Urban Labor Markets." *International Economic Review* 14(3): 693–709.

————. 1977. "The Persistence of Male-Female Earnings Differentials." In *The Distribution of Economic Well-Being,* ed. F. T. Juster. Cambridge, Mass.: Ballinger Publishing Co.

Parsons, J. E., and S. B. Goff. 1980. "Achievement Motivation: A Dual Modality." In *Recent Trends in Achievement Motivation: Theory and Research,* ed. L. J. Fryans. Englewood Cliffs, N.J.: Plenum.

Parsons, J. E., D. N. Ruble, K. L. Hodges, and A. W. Small. 1976. "Cognitive-Developmental Factors in Emerging Sex Differences in Achievement-Related Expectancies." *Journal of Social Issues* 32:47–61.

Roos, P. A., and B. F. Reskin. 1984. "Institutional Factors Contributing to Sex Segregation in the Workplace." In *Sex Segregation in the Labor Force: Trends and Prospects,* ed. B. F. Reskin. Washington, D.C.: National Academy of Science Press.

Spence, M. 1973. "Job Market Signaling." *Quarterly Journal of Economics* 87(3): 355–74.

Stein, A. H., S. R. Pohly, and E. Mueller. 1971. "The Influence of Masculine, Feminine, and Neutral Tasks on Children's Achievement Behavior, Expectancies of Success and Attainment Values." *Child Development* 42:195–207.

Stein, A. H., and T. Smithells. 1969. "Age and Sex Differences in Children's Sex-Role Standards about Achievement." *Developmental Psychology* 1:252–59.

Stevenson, M. H. 1975. "Relative Wages and Sex Segregation by Occupation." In *Sex, Discrimination, and the Division of Labor,* ed. C. Lloyd. New York: Columbia University Press.

Strober, M. H. 1984. "Toward a General Theory of Occupational Sex Segregation: The Case of Public School Teaching." In *Sex Segregation in the Labor Force: Trends and Prospects,* ed. B. F. Reskin. Washington, D.C.: National Academy of Science Press.

Tangri, S. S. 1972. "Determinants of Occupational Role Innovation among College Women." *Journal of Social Issues* 28(2): 177–99.

Tittle, C. K. 1981. *Careers and Family: Sex Roles and Adolescent Life Plans.* Beverly Hills, Calif.: Sage Publications.

Treiman, D. J., and H. I. Hartmann, eds. 1981. *Women, Work, and Wages: Equal Pay for Jobs of Equal Value.* Washington, D.C.: National Academy Press.

CHAPTER 3

American Institutions and the Study of Family Life in the Past

Maris A. Vinovskis

One of the most important institutions in Western society is the family. Yet historians did not pay much attention to the family before the mid-1960s. Instead, most historical accounts focused on political, economic, or diplomatic developments with particular emphasis on the experiences of national or local leaders. Today the situation is quite different as the study of American family life in the past is one of the most popular areas for historical research and the lives of ordinary people are studied as much as those of elites (Degler 1980; Gordon 1978; Ryan 1982).

The sudden emergence and rapid growth of the field of family history spawned a variety of research approaches and perspectives. Few attempts (Vinovskis 1977, 1988) have been made to assess the strengths and weaknesses of different strategies for studying family life or to integrate the findings from these studies into the mainstream of American history. Particularly lacking are efforts to relate the development of the family to changes in other American social institutions such as schools and churches.

As an introduction to the recent approaches to family history, this essay will first trace the evolution of analytic strategies employed in studying family history from the use of mean household size to the reliance on life course analysis. There is still a major debate among scholars today on how to study family life. Some argue that one should look at the family as a whole by using a model of the family cycle. Others regard this approach as inadequate and misleading and advocate looking at the life course of individuals embedded within the context of their family life. While the latter approach seems more promising, it needs to be supplemented by more attention to the effects of changes in social organizations and norms on the life course.

After considering alternative ways of studying families, we will turn to a specific example of how one can take a broader, institutional approach to the study of the life course in the past. The changing relationship between the family and other social institutions in the education of children will be considered. Next an analysis will be made of how changes in the perception of the intellectual capabilities of young children in the early nineteenth century affected how, where, and when they were educated. Finally, the emergence of age-grading as a new norm in education will be investigated by considering the institutional and intellectual factors that promoted it in the late nineteenth century.

From Household Size to the Life Course

Historians and other scholars directed their attention to the American family in the late 1960s and early 1970s. The studies (Demos 1965, 1970; Greven 1966, 1970; Lockridge 1966, 1970) initially concentrated on colonial New England and were part of a larger effort to reconstruct everyday life in local communities using such new techniques as family reconstitution.[1] Rather than employing any particular overall framework for analyzing family life, these historians were content to calculate basic demographic indices on the ages of marriage, number of births, and the expectation of life.[2] Some historians employed the concept of generations to organize their data on families. Greven (1970), for example, studied the first generation of settlers to Andover, Massachusetts, in the mid-seventeenth century and traced their descendants in the community through the fourth generation. While generations as an analytical construct sometimes can be used effectively to investigate the transfer of wealth or property from parents to their children, usually it is too imprecise to be helpful.[3]

As the small number of American colonial family historians were

1. Investigations of family life in the past have now shifted to the colonial South (Lewis 1983; Smith 1980) or the nineteenth century (Censer 1984; Hareven 1982b; Lebsock 1984). Whereas the family life in colonial New England received a disproportionate amount of attention initially, today few scholars are analyzing it, despite the need for additional research (Moran and Vinovskis 1982).

2. A few (Greven 1966, 1970) tried to relate the timing of marriage to the manner of transmitting property from parents to children, but even these attempts were often badly flawed methodologically, as most young historians had not received any formal social science training in research design or the use of statistics. Unfortunately, there have been few sophisticated studies of the process of inheritance in colonial America. For example, see Smith 1973.

3. In Andover, for example, by the third and fourth generations, many of the individuals in those two categories were born at the same time and probably did not even realize that they belonged to different generations (Vinovskis 1977). Scholars often misuse the word *generation* by confusing it with different age-cohorts (Mannheim 1952) or developmental stages (Eisenstadt 1956). Kertzer (1982) provides a very useful critique of the way the concept of generations has been used and misused by scholars.

groping for ways of organizing and interpreting their scattered demographic data, their European counterparts launched an ambitious and a much more coordinated project to analyze family life. Led by Laslett (1972) and the Cambridge Group for the Study of History of Populations and Social Structure, English historians tried to show that at least by the sixteenth century, the Western family usually consisted of parents and their unmarried children (the nuclear family) rather than three generations living together (the extended family).[4]

Despite the initial and rather uncritical enthusiasm for the use of mean household size to characterize families in the past, a few scholars began to question the meaning and usefulness of this approach. The most damaging attack on the use of mean household size came from Berkner (1972) who challenged the use of any static, cross-sectional index to characterize family life. Since families and households gain and lose members over time, Berkner argued that one needs a more dynamic, developmental approach to family life.[5] The debates over the appropriateness and validity of using mean household size led to its gradual abandonment by almost everyone despite its prominence and popularity among many leading family historians in the late 1960s and early 1970s.[6]

European family historians took the lead in both advocating and then rejecting the use of mean household size, but they have been surprisingly slow to develop a more dynamic framework for analyzing family life.[7] American family historians (Hareven 1974, 1978a, 1978b; Katz, Doucet, and Stern 1982) instead are taking the lead in finding alternative ways of studying the family.

---

4. In the sixteenth and seventeenth centuries, the terms *family* and *household* were used interchangeably, so there is often some confusion about the meaning of these terms when we encounter them in the historical documents. For an overview of the changing meaning of family and household as well as a modern definition of them, see the volumes produced by the Cambridge Group for the History of Populations and Social Structure (Laslett 1972; Wall, Robin, and Laslett 1983).

5. Reacting to these criticisms, Laslett and his colleagues (Wachter, Hammel, and Laslett 1978) turned to demographic simulation models to refute the notion that a high proportion of English households were extended in the past if one uses a development perspective. Although Laslett (1977) is correct in pointing to the prevalence of nuclear households throughout much of Western Europe, he has exaggerated their existence in areas such as central Italy and southern France (Kertzer 1984).

6. Despite the strong criticisms of mean household size, a few historians (Morgan and Golden 1979) continue to use it.

7. Using the ideas of the Russian economist Chayanov (1966), some (Czap 1983; Wall 1983) have tried to model family and household changes in terms of the number and ages of workers and consumers in the home. But most of these attempts have been rather limited in scope and usefulness. Berkner's (1972) alternative to the mean household size, for example, simply depicts the cyclical changes in the family according to whether the desig-

There is a fundamental division among American historians today on how to study family life. Some focus on the family as a whole and use a family cycle approach which in large part traces changes in the composition of family units over time. Others reject the study of the family as a whole and concentrate on individuals using life course analysis. Although most practitioners seem to be unaware of the difference between those who study the aggregate family and those who analyze the individual family members, this important distinction implicitly separates the research strategies of those who use a family cycle model from those who employ life course analysis.

The family cycle approach, borrowed from sociologists like Duvall (1967) and Hill (1964), seems very attractive at first glance to historians trying to organize their data to take into account changes in family circumstances.[8] Yet the family cycle models proposed by Duvall (1967) and Hill (1964) are limited because they mainly reflect changes in childbearing or childrearing reflecting only the experiences of the oldest child. Any model that describes the important changes in family life only on the basis of the family's responses to the birth and experiences of the eldest child is particularly limited historically because families in the past had many more children than families today. Efforts (Rodgers 1962) have been made to expand the Duvall and Hill family cycle models to include changes in the experiences of the youngest as well as the oldest child, but this led to an unwieldy 24-stage family cycle model. Indeed, the fundamental weakness of the family cycle approach is that it only captures a very small part of the important experiences of the family, such as childbearing or childrearing, but does not address other potentially significant factors such as career changes. Nor do the family cycle models lend themselves to a situation where an increasingly large proportion of families are single-parent households at some time, for the models do not take into consideration any variation in the timing and sequencing of these stages. As a result, although a few sociologists (Hudson and Murphy 1980; Velsor and O'Rand 1984) still continue to use family cycle models, most (Elder 1978, 1981a, 1981b, 1983; Nock 1979, 1981; Spanier, Sauer, and Larzelers 1979) have abandoned this approach as conceptually limited and impractical in most applications.

---

nated heir and his bride are living together. Berkner does make a useful distinction between changes in the household. To document the stages of the household cycle, Berkner employs the age of the male head of the household (ages 18–27, 28–37, 38–47, 48–57, and 58–90). One of the problems of many of these schemes using the age of the male head of household is that they seem to use different age-categories rather arbitrarily.

    8. According to these family sociologists (Duvall 1967; Hill 1964), the family can be subdivided into eight or nine stages that reflect the major changes in family life.

If the sociologists of the family are expressing serious doubts about the usefulness of family cycle models, several American family historians (Chudacoff 1978a, 1978b; Hareven 1974, 1978a, 1978b, 1982a; Katz, Doucet, and Stern 1982; Ryan 1981; Wells 1985) are embracing them enthusiastically. Hareven (1974), who introduced the family cycle to historians, continues to endorse it even though her own work (1982b) is now shifting to a life course perspective. Interestingly, although Hareven called for historians to create their own family cycle model more than a decade ago, she has neither developed nor found a satisfactory one. Many other historians (Ryan 1981; Wells 1985) use family cycles in their writings and research, but do not seem to understand fully either the implications or the limitations of this approach.

The most detailed family cycle model developed by historians is the one by Michael Katz and his associates (Katz, Doucet, and Stern 1982) in a study of family life in Hamilton, Ontario, and Buffalo, New York, in the mid-nineteenth century (see table 1). Unlike other American family historians, these scholars seem unaware of the work of Duvall (1967) or Hill (1964) and concentrate on depicting the financial strain on the family by the presence or absence of children in a twelve-stage family cycle model.

There are numerous shortcomings in this particular family cycle model. Although the stated purpose of the model is to reflect the economic well-being of the family over time, the use of the age of the wife rather than of the husband to index changes is questionable. Since few married white women worked outside the home in the nineteenth century and those that did earned relatively low wages (Mason, Vinovskis, and Hareven 1978), the husband's occupational career better reflects the economic circumstances of the family. The model only takes into account

TABLE 1.   A Twelve-stage Model of the Family Circle

Stage I	Young (wife under 25), no children
Stage II	Young (wife under 25), all children aged 1–6
Stage III	Early Midcycle (wife 25–34), no children
Stage IV	Early Midcycle (wife 25–34), all children aged 1–14
Stage V	Late Midcycle (wife 35–44), no children
Stage VI	Late Midcycle (wife 35–44), all children aged 1–14
Stage VII	Late Midcycle (wife 35–44), at least one male child 15 or over
Stage VIII	Late Midcycle (wife 35–44), all children 15 or over female
Stage IX	Late Cycle (wife 45 or over), at least one male child 15 or over
Stage X	Late Cycle (wife 45 or over), all children 15 or over female
Stage XI	Late Cycle (wife 45 or over), no children
Stage XII	Late Cycle (wife 45 or over), other

Source: Katz, Doucet, and Stern 1982.

the presence or absence of children in certain age groups but does not calculate the total number of children in any category or overall, even though this might be a more accurate index of the contribution or cost of children. The model also does not distinguish between children who are in school or at work and therefore does not provide much information about the actual income of the family.[9] In addition, unlike Duvall's (1967) family cycle model, this one minimizes the importance to the family of the entry into or exit from school of any of the children. As in most other family cycle models, there is no attempt to incorporate individual career trajectories or changes in the assets of the family over time.

Katz, Doucet, and Stern's (1982) family cycle model is based upon the assumption of a two-parent family and does not reflect the particularly great financial stress placed upon many nineteenth-century families by the death of the male breadwinner. By seemingly ignoring the problem of marital disruption from either death in the nineteenth century or divorce in the twentieth, this approach underestimates the economic and emotional disruption that many family members experienced in the past.[10] Finally, since being present in one of the twelve stages may preclude membership in another, this family cycle model describes only some of the stages that any particular family may experience.

The family cycle approach seems to be gaining a surprising number of adherents among American family historians today. As this discussion has indicated, such an approach is a very questionable strategy for studying family life in the past because by its very nature it will be quite limited and insensitive to variations in the timing and sequencing of life events. While one might construct a family cycle model to illuminate some particular research question, we should give up any hope of ever developing a more general family cycle model appropriate for most historical analyses.[11] Indeed, in most situations we are probably better advised to devote

---

9. For alternative attempts to derive estimates of the work and consumption ratios of families using the federal manuscript censuses, see Haines 1981; Kaestle and Vinovskis 1978, 1980; and Mason, Vinovskis, and Hareven 1978.

10. Katz and his associates note that "the family cycle ended with dissolution, most often the result of death. In fact widowhood formed a significant part of the life cycle of women" (Katz, Doucet, and Stern 1982, 290). This implies that the family cycle ends with the death of either spouse. Yet in a later discussion they estimate the percentage of female-headed households in each of their twelve stages. Since a high proportion of households are female-headed in stages seven through twelve, one wonders how accurately their stages portray the actual economic circumstances of the family as this model does not take into consideration the presence or absence of the husband.

11. One of the major difficulties in using any family cycle model is following the family over time once individuals leave the household. When someone leaves the home, it is

our energies to analyzing changes in the lives of individuals within the context of their families as well as within the broader social and historical setting in which they lived, rather than trying to model changes in families as a whole over time (Kertzer 1984; Vinovskis 1977, 1988).

The weaknesses inherent in any family cycle model led many psychologists and sociologists to turn to the life course perspective, which follows individuals over time rather than families or households. While the family cycle models are usually easy to understand and describe since they consist of only a few well-defined stages, the life course approach is much more complex because it is really more of a perspective than a simple prescription for analysis. A useful summary of the life course is provided by Elder (1978), one of its most articulate proponents among sociologists who has greatly influenced the work of American family historians during the past ten years.

> The life course refers to pathways through the age-differentiated life span, to social patterns in the timing, duration, spacing, and order of events; the timing of an event may be as consequential for life experience as whether the event occurs and the degree or type of change. Age differentiation is manifested in expectations and options that impinge on decision processes and the course of events that give shape to life stages, transitions, and turning points. Such differentiation is based in part on the social meanings of age and the biological facts of birth, sexual maturity, and death. These meanings have varied through social history and across cultures at points in time, as documented by evidence on socially recognized age categories, grades, and classes . . . . Over the life course, age differentiation also occurs through the interplay of demographic and economic processes, as in the relation between economic swings and the timing of family events. Sociocultural, demographic and material factors are essential elements in a theory of life-course variation. (Elder 1978, 21–22)

Life course analysis is particularly useful for historical investigations because it focuses on the transitions in the lives of individuals within the changing contexts of their families, neighborhoods, and historical time periods rather than trying to study the aggregate family over time. This perspective is now being used by many American family historians because it provides flexibility for studying individuals within very

---

not always clear how to handle these new groupings using the family cycle approach (Kertzer and Schiaffino 1983).

different family systems and takes into account the potential importance of deviations in the timing, duration, and sequencing of events in the lives of individuals that deviate from the cultural norms of that society. Furthermore, rather than studying the individual or the family in isolation from other organizations, the life course perspective challenges the researcher to study the interactions between individuals and social institutions such as schools and churches over time.

The life course approach has been described in many other essays (Elder 1978, 1981a, 1981b, 1983; Hareven 1977, 1978a, 1978b, 1982a, 1982b; Vinovskis 1977, 1983, 1988) and need not be discussed at length here. One should recognize, however, that much of the virtue of this framework for analysis lies in its ability to encourage scholars to formulate their questions from a broader and more historical perspective. It does not attempt to provide a comprehensive or detailed plan for designing anyone's specific research project. Furthermore, the type of rich, longitudinal data on individuals over time envisioned by this approach often does not exist historically and therefore scholars are forced to improvise in order to patch together sufficient data to analyze the life course of individuals in the past.[12]

One of the major shortcomings of the life course approach in practice is that few scholars pay sufficient attention to how changes in social institutions and norms may affect the lives of individuals. Most analyses of the life course seem to assume implicitly that individuals experience personal changes within the context of static institutions and norms. Yet the historical record suggests otherwise. As we shall see in the next section, society is continually evolving and therefore individuals develop within a forever shifting configuration of institutions and norms that guide their particular pathways through time.

The Changing Roles of Families and Schools in the Education of Children

Having explored alternative ways of looking at family life in the past, we now turn to a brief overview of the roles of families and schools in the education of children. Rather than trying to survey overall trends in American education, we will only consider a few developments that illustrate the need to analyze the training of children from a broad perspective, including the interactions of families, social organizations such as

---

12. For a discussion of the problems of applying a life course perspective to the past, see Vinovskis 1988.

schools and churches, and changes in the cultural norms which guide and constrain behavior in this area.

When Americans think of the education of children today, they assume that most of it occurs within a classroom. In seventeenth-century English society, however, schools were only one of several social institutions assigned the task of training children, with churches playing a vital part in the socialization of the young. Even more important, especially among English Puritans, was the family, which had the responsibility for catechizing young children and teaching them to read the Bible in the home (O'Day 1982; Stone 1964, 1977).

When Puritans settled New England, they tried to recreate the same system of educating children that they had known in England. For them education was primarily a way of preparing children for their religious duties rather than a means of developing critical thinking (Axtell 1974; Murphy 1960). The father as the head of the household was assigned the primary responsibility for the religious training of the children in the home. Since males were more literate than females in mid-seventeenth-century New England and were considered more reliable religiously, the father was given the largest role in the education of young children (Auwers 1980; Lockridge 1974). The mother was expected to assist the father in bringing up the children, but he was clearly considered the central figure in the education of the young (Moran and Vinovskis 1986). The Puritans initially assumed that elementary education would begin in the home under the supervision of the church and that schools would be established mainly for preparing a small number of students for college and the ministry.[13]

The Puritan scheme for the education of the young in the home was built upon the premise that sons would continue to be as religious as their fathers who first settled New England. When the male descendants of these settlers inexplicably and unexpectedly chose not to join the church in the second half of the seventeenth century, the Puritans faced a difficult dilemma (Moran 1979; Moran and Vinovskis 1982). Who should catechize the children if many fathers were no longer sufficiently religious to be delegated that important responsibility?

The Puritans experimented with several alternatives. First, they tried to persuade males to become church members but failed to make much

---

13. The situation in the South was very different from that in New England, as the former was settled by Anglicans who encountered a very different set of circumstances in Maryland and Virginia. In this essay we will confine our attention mainly to New England. Although not much has been written about education in the colonial South, the interested reader should consult Carr and Walsh 1977, Cremin 1970, and Smith 1980.

headway as churches became increasingly feminized by the late seventeenth century. Ministers and schoolmasters were frequently delegated the task of catechizing children, but the Puritans still expected the family to provide the primary training. Reluctantly and hesitatingly, the Puritans turned to women, who continued to join the church in larger numbers than men, to assume the task of teaching and catechizing their own children (Axtell 1974; Moran and Vinovskis 1986).

The shift in the responsibility for the religious training of children from the father to the mother in the home had very important and unanticipated consequences in the long run. In order to teach children, it became necessary for women to become more literate themselves and provided a rationale and impetus for female education (Kerber 1980; Norton 1980, 1984). The role of the mother in the care and socialization of the child expanded, while that of the father contracted (Demos 1982; Vinovskis 1986). By the nineteenth century the mother was almost universally viewed as the "natural" caretaker of children with the father as a somewhat removed, but still powerful administrator of discipline in the home (Cott 1977; Ryan 1981, 1982). Increased literacy among women as well as their perceived ability to teach young children became so accepted that women gradually replaced men as common school teachers. By the time of the Civil War, it is estimated that one out of every five native-born white women in Massachusetts taught school at some point in their lives (Kaestle and Vinovskis 1980; Vinovskis and Bernard 1978).

Throughout most of the colonial period, it was assumed that the parents had the primary responsibility for educating their young children either in the home or in a private school. Children were taught in the home or in one of the local schools created as settlements became more populated, and many parents preferred to send their offspring to one of these small and impermanent private institutions. The community provided assistance only if the family was deemed incapable of teaching their own children and could not afford to send them to a private school. Parents unwilling to educate their own children in seventeenth-century Massachusetts were often called before the magistrates and fined for neglecting their duties (Cremin 1970; Kaestle 1983).

Many people today suspect that public schools have always been encroaching upon the responsibilities of parents by assuming a larger role for the education of children. We forget, however, that in the past it was often the parents who demanded that their children be allowed to attend public schools rather than taught at home or sent to a private school.[14] In the early nineteenth century, for example, the Boston School

---

14. While educators were reluctant to encourage young children to enter schools sooner, they usually were eager to persuade them to stay longer. Hence, much of the

Committee reiterated that parents should either teach their children at home or send them to a private school since one could not enter the public grammar schools unless they could already read and write (Wightman 1860). Yet the parents succeeded in forcing the Boston School Committee to reverse its policy and create public primary schools for all students.

So, during the colonial period there was a major change in the responsibility for catechizing children from the father to the mother as changes in church membership forced that society to reorganize its manner of educating its young. As colonial society became more developed and despite the impressive gains in male and female literacy, parents were no longer interested or willing to teach their children at home. Instead, public primary schools were created to teach children how to read and write, notwithstanding the opposition from many school officials who did not want to burden taxpayers with this new responsibility.

The changes in how children are educated points to the value of a life course approach. Rather than studying the family as a whole, which would not have revealed any major shifts, we have seen how changes in the roles of women in the family altered their responsibilities and thereby influenced the socialization of their children. Similarly, the development of social institutions such as schools provided parents with alternatives for educating their children and led to a reorganization of tasks within the family. Thus, changes within the family, often influenced by developments outside the family, affected the life course of individuals but would not necessarily have been revealed if we had only employed a family cycle approach.

The education of children is not only determined by the designation of those appropriate to teach them and the availability of facilities such as schools, but also by our perceptions of the intellectual capabilities of children. While it is difficult to establish exactly how a young child's mind works, adult perceptions of its functioning varied considerably historically and had a great impact on the design of social institutions that trained young children (Kagan 1984).

Some historians (Demos 1970; Zuckerman 1970) argue that colonial Americans did not see childhood as a separate and distinct phase of development. Instead, they claim that children were regarded as "miniature adults." More recent work (Stannard 1977; Juster and Vinovskis 1987), however, has established that the Puritans did differentiate between children and adults. Their conception of children was very dif-

---

conflict between parents and schools in the nineteenth century involve efforts by the educators to force teenagers to remain in school longer (Kaestle 1983).

ferent than that of today, as Puritans stressed the ability of very young children to learn to read. If colonial Americans saw the child as intellectually more capable than we do today, they did not always insist upon early childhood education. Yet numerous examples can be cited of three- and four-year-olds learning their catechisms and being taught to read the Bible in the seventeenth and eighteenth centuries.

In the early nineteenth century in Europe, special institutions were created for infants from poor or broken families to teach them how to read. The idea of these infant schools quickly spread to the United States in the 1820s and was quickly incorporated into many schools (May and Vinovskis 1976). At first, infant schools in America were also intended only for children from disadvantaged backgrounds, but once middle-class parents recognized their value, they demanded equal access for their own children lest the poor gain too much of an advantage. As the *Ladies' Magazine* reported:

> The interesting subject of Infant schools is becoming more and more fashionable . . . . We have been told that it is now in contemplation, to open a school for the infants of others besides the poor. If such a course be not soon adopted, at the age for entering primary schools those poor children will assuredly be the richest of scholars. And why should a plan which promises so many advantages, independent of merely relieving the mother from her charge, be confined to children of the indigent? (*Ladies' Magazine* 1829, 89–90)

The popularity of these infant schools is demonstrated by the fact that in 1840 nearly forty percent of all three-year-olds in Massachusetts were enrolled in a public or private school (May and Vinovskis 1976; Kaestle and Vinovskis 1980).

Some infant schools were reluctant to stress teaching children to read at such early ages, while others felt it was appropriate and important. Pressure from parents soon forced most infant schools to teach three- and four-year-olds to read since this was a highly visible and tangible way of demonstrating the benefits of early education. While some educators enthusiastically embraced infant education, others, especially teachers, were concerned that the presence of children ages two or three in regular classrooms was disruptive for older students as it was difficult to get these younger children to sit still the entire day. Yet the combination of the growing faith in the power of education to improve the lives of individuals as well as the intellectual heritage that young children were capable of learning to read at early ages made infant schools very popular among parents and the community.

The enthusiasm for infant schools did not last long. In the early 1830s medical experts began to question the advisability of teaching such young children, as doctors stressed the importance of balanced physical and mental growth. Amariah Brigham, a prominent nineteenth-century physician, attacked infant education in the early 1830s as dangerous to the future health of the child.

> Many physicians of great experience are of the opinion that efforts to develope [sic] the minds of young children are very frequently injurious; and from instances of disease in children which I have witnessed, I am forced to believe that the danger is indeed great, and that very often in attempting to call forth and cultivate the intellectual faculties of children before they are six or seven years of age, serious and lasting injury has been done both to the body and the mind. . . .
>
> I beseech parents, therefore, to pause before they attempt to make prodigies of their own children. Though they may not destroy them by the measures they adopt to effect this purpose, yet they will surely enfeeble their bodies, and greatly dispose them to nervous affections. Early mental excitement will serve only to bring forth beautiful, but premature flowers, which are destined soon to wither away, without producing fruit. (Brigham 1833, 15, 55)

Brigham's ideas were quickly disseminated to the public through articles published in popular magazines or in childrearing manuals. As a result, many middle-class parents who read these magazines or advice books, as well as the educators who followed the medical literature, strongly argued against allowing young children into the schools. Yet most parents were reluctant to withdraw their young children from the schools as their own views of child development were slow to change, and many mothers were still happy to have an opportunity to be relieved of the burden of supervising their youngsters at home. Furthermore, since most private and public schools were directly controlled by the parents in each local school district, neither the teachers nor the administrators possessed the authority necessary simply to prohibit children ages three or four from enrolling in schools. Nevertheless, the dramatic change in the way that the child's mind was perceived by experts and middle-class publicists gradually had an effect, so that by 1860 there were almost no children ages three or four enrolled in Massachusetts schools. Indeed, when kindergartens were introduced at that time in the United States, they were intended for older children and did not try to teach them to read (May and Vinovskis 1976; Kaestle and Vinovskis 1980).

The rise and fall of the infant school movement in nineteenth-century America illustrates the importance of how changes in our view of the intellectual capabilities of the child may influence the way we try to educate them. The infant school episode also highlights the need to study the interaction between ideas about childhood education and the nature of the social organization entrusted with that responsibility. Infant schools grew rapidly in the 1820s and early 1830s because most schools were highly decentralized and had to respond to the wishes of local parents. Similarly, even when educators and teachers thought that infant education was dangerous for the child's health, they did not have sufficient control over the admissions policies in most school districts to eliminate immediately very young children from the classroom. Finally, the infant school experience in the nineteenth century reminds us of the need for a broad, historical perspective. While our society congratulates itself for discovering the importance of early childhood education through the Headstart Program in the mid-1960s, our ancestors experimented with a similar program more than a hundred years ago.

One of the common findings in most analyses of the life course today is that much of our lives are age-graded. That is, cultural norms and the structuring of organizations on the principle of chronological age often dictates the kind of opportunities and expectations that are available to us. In the past society was much less age-graded. Society was more likely to be stratified along wealth or gender lines than on chronological age. Indeed, in the colonial period individuals sometimes did not even have an accurate idea of their own age since it was not a very important factor in their lives (Demos 1970). Yet today elementary and secondary public schools in the United States, for example, are highly age-graded.

The lack of attention to chronological age is evident in the education of children in colonial and early nineteenth-century America. Students usually attended a one-room schoolhouse that brought together children ranging from ages two or three to those in their early twenties. Scholars in these schools were not grouped by their age, but arranged according to their level of mastering the assigned texts. Since competence and achievement could vary from one subject to the next, individuals often found themselves working together with different groups of students depending upon which subject was being studied. Lacking any standard age for entering or leaving school and given the erratic pattern of seasonal or daily school attendance, it was common to find students of quite diverse ages studying the same texts.[15]

---

15. There are considerable variations in the experience of the development of school-

Many factors in the nineteenth century contributed to the eventual age-grading of education (Cohen 1982). The changing locus of education from home to school made it possible to gather more pupils in one setting. The increasing density of settlement and the growth of towns and cities greatly expanded the number of school-age children in a neighborhood. The shift from private to public schooling also increased the number of potential public school students and facilitated the division of one-room schoolhouses into graded schools. Graded schools were aided in the mid-nineteenth century by the increasing consolidation of local school districts into single centralized systems and by giving school committees the authority to assign students to graded schools (Katz 1971). In addition, the grading of schools by broad age-categories allowed for the employment of more female instructors since women were perceived as ideally suited for teaching the younger children and could be hired at less than half of the wages of male teachers (Vinovskis and Bernard 1978).

If the growing concentration of students in communities made graded schools possible, the creation of special classes or schools for the education of younger and older children reinforced that trend. Although most infant schools did not survive beyond the Civil War, they prepared parents and educators to accept the idea that young children should be grouped together in separate classrooms. The kindergarten movement in the second half of the nineteenth century also emphasized the importance of separate facilities and training for young children and even school systems that did not have kindergartens usually segregated their youngest pupils from older students. At the other end of the spectrum, the development of public high schools in the nineteenth century created distinct institutions for the oldest students. Although sometimes there was considerable controversy over the establishment of the relatively expensive and frequently under-utilized high schools, by the end of the nineteenth century they existed in many towns and cities throughout the United States (Katz 1968; Vinovskis 1985). Thus, during the second half of the nineteenth century many communities established separate primary schools, intermediate schools, grammar schools, and high schools and thereby created a graded school system that facilitated the eventual age-grading of education.

Age-grading was also made easier by the narrowing of the ages at which students were expected to attend school. As we have already men-

---

ing in nineteenth-century America (Kaestle 1983). Most of this discussion will continue to focus on developments in New England. Midwestern rural areas, for example, continued to use one-room schoolhouses well after they had been abandoned in most of the East (Fuller 1982). While the timing varies from region to region, the process was often very similar.

tioned, the growing hostility to infant schools in the antebellum period led to the elimination of very young children from Massachusetts schools in 1860. Simultaneously, Horace Mann and other reformers in that state were concerned about the large number of boys in their late teens and early twenties still attending school. These older students frequently disrupted the schools since their male teachers themselves were often only fifteen or sixteen years old. Mann estimated that one-tenth of all rural schools in Massachusetts in 1840 were forced to close prematurely because the older boys evicted the young male teacher (Kaestle and Vinovskis 1980). Therefore, the school reformers called for more regular school attendance so that everyone would complete their common school education by ages fifteen or sixteen. The result of all of these changes was that students entered school at later ages, attended more regularly during a longer school year, and left school at an earlier age. This meant that it was easier to group students together by age since they were more likely to enter at the same time, attend their classes on a more regular basis, and complete their education within a shorter overall timespan.

Educators in the nineteenth century also stressed the importance of having smaller and more homogeneous schools. Large, undifferentiated schools were seen as counterproductive to good teaching and effective learning by students. As Barnas Sears, secretary of the Massachusetts Board of Education, observed about the grading of public schools in the mid-nineteenth century:

> The most obvious advantage resulting from such an organization of the schools, would be the increased productiveness of the teacher's labors, without any increase of expense. Every good teacher attaches importance to a skilful arrangement of the pupils in classes according to age and proficiency. But in most of our district schools the diversity in these respects is so great that classes can be but imperfectly formed. The object of gradation is to classify the schools themselves, placing the young children in one, those of maturer age in another, and wherever practicable, those of an intermediate age in a third . . . . (Massachusetts Board of Education 1850–51, 30)

Nineteenth-century educators called for grading schools, but they expected that children would be advanced from one level to the next on the basis of achievement rather than chronological age. They explicitly did not want age to be used as a factor for promoting students from one grade to another (although sometimes in the initial classification of the student age might be a factor). Yet by developing an increasingly graded system of education, they provided a structure which in the twentieth century has become predominantly age-graded.

The simple fact of grading schools led to the assembling of younger and older students into different classrooms and schools. Once this occurred, older students in the lower grades felt increasingly uncomfortable in those surroundings and were more likely to drop out of school, thereby strengthening the apparent relationship between age and grade level. Psychologists and child development specialists in the early twentieth century began to link age with intellectual ability and reinforced the willingness of parents and educators to place children by age into an increasingly graded school system. In addition, there was a growing acceptance of the idea that it was more harmful for students to be left behind in a grade than to be advanced to one in which they were not fully prepared to do the work. All of this has led to the situation today where social promotion, particularly in the elementary grades, is widely accepted and practiced. As a result, our schools are now so age-graded that it is once again necessary for the teacher in the classroom to group students by ability and to assign them different tasks. Furthermore, the completion of a particular grade in school usually is a more reliable predictor of the age of the student than of their achievement level.[16]

Very little research exists on how the United States has evolved from a society in which age played a relatively small role in determining one's options and obligations to the situation now where many of our roles are age-graded. Even those historians who have analyzed the impact of age on life course transitions, for example, usually do not explain why age appears to be a better predictor of behavior in one historical period than another. Yet knowledge of the increase in age-grading in our society is essential in order to understand how the life course of Americans has been shaped by the development of age-graded norms and the changes in the organization and structure of the social institutions which guide and constrain our life experiences.

Conclusion

The analysis of family life in the past is now one of the central concerns of historians. Yet there is considerable disagreement over how one should study family life. Many of the initial strategies, such as the use of

---

16. Although the movement for age-grading in schools began in the second half of the nineteenth century, the close identification of age and grade in school in practice is a post–World War II phenomenon. David Angus, Jeffrey Mirel, and I are now investigating the emergence of age-grading in American education.

the concept of generations or the measurement of mean household size, have been abandoned. Others, such as the family cycle models, are being embraced by some historians despite the serious limitations of this approach.

Life course analysis appears to provide historians with a useful perspective for analyzing family life over time. It focuses on the development of individuals within the context of their families and takes into consideration cultural norms as well as the impact of social institutions such as schools and churches. Life course analysis investigates the historical experiences of individuals and is concerned with the timing, duration, and sequence of events in a person's life. While life course analysis is more difficult to define and to apply than a simple family cycle model, it reflects more realistically the complexity of our lives both in the past and today.

Life course analysis offers a useful perspective for investigating individuals over time, but it does not pretend to provide a framework for investigating how cultural norms or social institutions are organized or changed. Yet as we have seen in the increasing age-grading of our educational systems, the study of individuals needs to be combined with that of changes in values and social organizations. Indeed, one can even characterize the sets of rules and expectations that govern family life as part of a larger family system and then study the evolution of that system over time or variation from one culture to another (Harari and Vinovskis 1989). The challenge for scholars of the family will be to integrate their life course perspective within broader and more dynamic analyses of societal changes which then guide and constrain our individual behavior.

REFERENCES

Auwers, L. 1980. "Reading the Marks of the Past: Exploring Female Literacy in Colonial Windsor, Connecticut." *Historical Methods* 4:204–14.

Axtell, J. 1974. *The School upon a Hill: Education and Society in Colonial New England*. New Haven: Yale University Press.

Berkner, L. 1972. "The Stem Family and the Developmental Cycle of the Peasant Household: An Eighteenth-Century Austrian Example." *American Historical Review* 77:398–418.

Brigham, A. 1833. *Remarks on the Influence of Mental Cultivation and Mental Excitement upon Health*. 2d. ed. Boston.

Carr, L. G., and L. S. Walsh. 1977. "The Planter's Wife: The Experience of White Women in Seventeenth Century Maryland." *William and Mary Quarterly*, 3d ser. 34:542–71.

Censer, J. T. 1984. *North Carolina Planters and Their Children, 1800–1860.* Baton Rouge: Louisiana State University Press.

Chayanov, A. V. 1966. *The Theory of Peasant Economy*, ed. D. Thorner, B. Kerblay, and R. E. F. Smith. Homewood, Ill.: Dorsey Press.

Chudacoff, H. P. 1978a. "New Branches of the Tree: Household Structure in Early Stages of the Family Cycle in Worcester, Massachusetts, 1860–1880." In *Themes in the History of the Family*, ed. T. K. Hareven. Lunenburg, Vt.: Stinehour Press.

————. 1978b. "Newlyweds and Family Extension: The First Stage of the Family Cycle in Providence, Rhode Island, 1864–1865 and 1879–1880." In *Family and Population in Nineteenth-century America*, ed. T. K. Hareven and M. A. Vinovskis. Princeton: Princeton University Press.

Cohen, R. D. 1982. "Schooling and Age Grading in American Society since 1800: The Fragmenting of Experience." In *Prospects*, vol. 7, ed. J. Wall. New York: Burt Franklin.

Cott, N. F. 1977. *The Bonds of Womanhood: "Women's Sphere" in New England, 1780–1833*. New Haven: Yale University Press.

Cremin, L. A. 1970. *American Education: The Colonial Experience, 1607–1783*. New York: Harper and Row.

Czap, P., Jr. 1983. "A Large Family: The Peasant's Greatest Wealth: Serf Households in Mishino, Russia, 1814–1858." In *Family Forms in Historic Europe*, ed. R. Wall, J. Robin, and P. Laslett. Cambridge: Cambridge University Press.

Degler, C. N. 1980. "Women and the Family." In *The Past Before Us: Contemporary Historical Writing in the United States*, ed. M. Kammen. New York: Cornell University Press.

Demos, J. 1965. "Notes on Life in Plymouth Colony." *William and Mary Quarterly*, 3d ser. 22:264–86.

————. 1968. "Families in Colonial Bristol, Rhode Island: An Exercise in Historical Demography." *William and Mary Quarterly*, 3d ser. 25:40–57.

————. 1970. *A Little Commonwealth: Family Life in Plymouth Colony*. New York: Oxford University Press.

————. 1982. "The Changing Faces of Fatherhood: A New Exploration in American Family History." In *Father and Child: Developmental and Clinical Perspectives*, ed. S. H. Cath, A. R. Gurwitt, and J. M. Ross. Boston: Little, Brown.

Duvall, E. M. 1967. *Family Development*. Philadelphia: J. B. Lippincott.

Eisenstadt, S. N. 1956. *From Generation to Generation*. Glencoe, Ill.: Free Press.

Elder, G. H., Jr. 1978. "Family History and the Life Course." In *Transitions: The Family and the Life Course in Historical Perspective*, ed. T. K. Hareven. New York: Academic Press.

————. 1981a. "History and the Family: The Discovery of Complexity." *Journal of Marriage and the Family* 43:489–519.

————. 1981b. "History and the Life Course." In *Biography and Society: The*

Life Course Approach in the Social Sciences, ed. D. Bertaux. Beverly Hills, Calif.: Sage.

———. 1983. "The Life-Course Perspective." In *The American Family in Social-Historical Perspective*, ed. M. Gordon. 3d ed. New York: St. Martin's Press.

Fuller, W. E. 1982. *The Old Country School.* Chicago: University of Chicago Press.

Gordon, M. 1978. *The American Family: Past, Present, and Future.* New York: Random House.

Greven, P. J., Jr. 1966. "Family Structure in Seventeenth-century Andover, Massachusetts." *William and Mary Quarterly*, 3d ser. 23:234–56.

———. 1970. *Four Generations: Population, Land, and Family in Colonial Andover, Massachusetts.* Ithaca: Cornell University Press.

Haines, M. R. 1981. "Poverty, Economic Stress, and the Family in a Late Nineteenth-century American City: Whites in Philadelphia, 1880." In *Philadelphia: Work, Space, Family, and Group Experience in the Nineteenth Century: Essays toward an Interdisciplinary History of the City*, ed. T. Hershberg. New York: Oxford University Press.

Harari, S. E., and M. A. Vinovskis. 1989. "Rediscovering the Family in the Past." In *Family Systems and Life-Span Development*, ed. K. Kreppner and R. M. Lerner. Hillsdale, N.J.: Lawrence Erlbaum.

Hareven, T. K. 1974. "The Family Process: The Historical Study of the Family Cycle." *Journal of Social History* 7:322–29.

———. 1977. "Family Time and Historical Time." *Daedalus* 106:57–70.

———. 1978a. "Cycles, Courses and Cohorts: Reflections on the Theoretical and Methodological Approaches to the Historical Study of Family Development." *Journal of Social History* 12:97–109.

———. 1978b. "Introduction: The Historical Study of the Life Course." In *Transitions: The Family and the Life Course in Historical Perspective*, ed. T. K. Hareven. New York: Academic Press.

———. 1982a. "The Life Course and Aging in Historical Perspective." In *Aging and the Life Course Transitions: An Interdisciplinary Perspective*, ed. T. K. Hareven and K. Adams. New York: Guilford Press.

———. 1982b. *Family Time and Industrial Time: The Relationship between the Family and Work in a New England Industrial Community.* Cambridge: Cambridge University Press.

Hill, R. 1964. "Methodological Issues in Family Development Research." *Family Process* 3:186–206.

Hudson, W. W., and G. J. Murphy. 1980. "The Non-linear Relationship Between Marital Satisfaction and Stages of the Family Cycle: An Artifact of Type I Errors?" *Journal of Marriage and the Family* 42:263–67.

Juster, S. M., and M. A. Vinovskis. 1987. "Changing Perspectives on the American Family in the Past." *Annual Review of Sociology* 13:193–216.

Kaestle, C. F. 1983. *Pillars of the Republic: Common Schools and American Society, 1780–1860.* New York: Hill and Wang.

Kaestle, C. F., and M. A. Vinovskis. 1978. "From Fireside to Factory: School Entry and School Leaving in Nineteenth-Century Massachusetts." In *Transitions: The Family and the Life Course in Historical Perspective*, ed. T. K. Hareven. New York: Academic Press.

_____. 1980. *Education and Social Change in Nineteenth-Century Massachusetts*. Cambridge: Cambridge University Press.

Kagan, J. 1984. *The Nature of the Child*. New York: Basic Books.

Katz, M. B. 1968. *The Irony of Early School Reform: Educational Innovation in Mid-Nineteenth-Century Massachusetts*. Cambridge, Mass.: Harvard University Press.

_____. 1971. *Class, Bureaucracy, and Schools*. New York: Praeger.

Katz, M. B., M. J. Doucet, and M. J. Stern. 1982. *The Social Organization of Early Industrial Capitalism*. Cambridge, Mass.: Harvard University Press.

Kerber, L. K. 1980. *Women of the Republic: Intellect and Ideology in Revolutionary America*. Chapel Hill: University of North Carolina Press.

Kertzer, D. I. 1982. "Generation and Age in Cross-cultural Perspective." In *Aging from Birth to Death: Sociotemporal Perspectives*, vol. 2, ed. M. W. Riley, R. P. Abeles, and M. S. Teitelbaum. Boulder: Westview Press.

_____. 1984. *Family Life in Central Italy, 1880–1910: Sharecropping, Wage Labor, and Coresidence*. New Brunswick, N.J.: Rutgers University Press.

Kertzer, D. I., and A. Schiaffino. 1983. "Industrialization and Coresidence: A Life Course Approach." In *Life-Span Development and Human Behavior*, ed. P. B. Baltes and O. G. Brim, Jr. New York: Academic Press.

Ladies' Magazine. 1829. February.

Laslett, P., ed. 1972. *Household and Family in Past Time*. Cambridge: Cambridge University Press.

_____. 1977. *Family Life and Illicit Love in Earlier Generations: Essays in Historical Sociology*. Cambridge: Cambridge University Press.

Lebsock, S. 1984. *The Free Women of Petersburg: Status and Culture in a Southern Town, 1784–1860*. New York: Norton.

Lewis, J. 1983. *The Pursuit of Happiness: Family and Values in Jefferson's Virginia*. Cambridge: Cambridge University Press.

Lockridge, K. A. 1966. "The Population of Dedham, Massachusetts, 1636–1736." *Economic History Review*, 2d ser. 19:318–44.

_____. 1970. *A New England Town; The First Hundred Years: Dedham, Massachusetts, 1636–1736*. New York: Norton.

_____. 1974. *Literacy in Colonial New England: An Enquiry into the Social Context of Literacy in the Early Modern West*. New York: Norton.

Mannheim, K. 1952. *Essays on the Sociology of Knowledge*. New York: Oxford University Press.

Mason, K. O., M. A. Vinovskis, and T. K. Hareven. 1978. "Women's Work and the Life Course in Essex County, Massachusetts, 1880." In *Transitions: The Family and the Life Course in Historical Perspective*, ed. T. K. Hareven. New York: Academic Press.

Massachusetts Board of Education. 1850–51. *Annual Report*. Boston.

May, D., and M. A. Vinovskis. 1976. "'A Ray of Millenial Light': Early Education and Social Reform in the Infant School Movement in Massachusetts, 1826–1840." In *Family and Kin in American Urban Communities, 1800–1940*, ed. T. K. Hareven. New York: Watts.

Moran, G. F. 1979. "Religious Renewal, Puritan Tribalism, and the Family in Seventeenth-Century Milford, Connecticut." *William and Mary Quarterly*, 3d ser. 36:236–54.

Moran, G. F., and M. A. Vinovskis. 1982. "The Puritan Family and Religion: A Critical Reappraisal." *William and Mary Quarterly*, 3d ser. 39:761–86.

———. 1986. "The Great Care of Godly Parents: Early Childhood in Puritan New England." In *History and Research in Child Development*, ed. A. B. Smuts and J. W. Hagen. Monographs of the Society for Research in Child Development, vol. 50, nos. 4–5.

Morgan, M., and H. H. Golden. 1979. "Immigrant Families in an Industrial City: A Study of Households in Holyoke, 1880." *Journal of Family History* 4:59–68.

Murphy, J. G. 1960. "Massachusetts Bay Colony: The Role of Government in Education." Ph.D. diss. Radcliffe College.

Nock, S. L. 1979. "The Family Life Cycle: Empirical or Conceptual Tool?" *Journal of Marriage and the Family* 41:15–26.

———. 1981. "Family Life-Cycle Transitions: Longitudinal Effects on Family Members." *Journal of Marriage and the Family* 43:703–14.

Norton, M. B. 1980. *Liberty's Daughters: The Revolutionary Experience of American Women, 1750–1800*. Boston: Little, Brown.

———. 1984. "The Evolution of White Women's Experience in Early America." *American Historical Review* 89:593–619.

O'Day, R. 1982. *Education and Society, 1500–1800: The Social Foundations of Education in Early Modern Britain*. London: Longman.

Rodgers, R. H. 1962. *Improvement in the Construction and Analysis of Family Life Cycle Categories*. Kalamazoo, Mich.: Western Michigan University.

Ryan, M. P. 1981. *Cradle of the Middle Class: The Family in Oneida County, New York, 1790–1865*. Cambridge: Cambridge University Press.

———. 1982. "The Explosion of Family History." *Reviews in American History* 10:181–95.

Smith, D. B. 1980. *Inside the Great House: Planter Family Life in Eighteenth-Century Chesapeake Society*. Ithaca: Cornell University Press.

Smith, D. S. 1973. "Parental Power and Marriage Patterns: An Analysis of Historical Trends in Hingham, Massachusetts." *Journal of Marriage and the Family* 35:419–28.

Spanier, G. B., W. Sauer, and R. Larzelere. 1979. "A Empirical Evaluation of the Family Life Cycle." *Journal of Marriage and the Family* 41:27–38.

Stannard, D. E. 1977. *The Puritan Way of Death: A Study in Religion, Culture, and Social Change*. New York: Oxford University Press.

Stone, L. 1964. "The Educational Revolution in England, 1560–1640," *Past and Present* 28:41–80.

————. 1977. *The Family, Sex and Marriage in England, 1500–1800.* New York: Harper and Row.

Velsor, E. V., and A. M. O'Rand. 1984. "Family Life Cycle, Work Career Patterns and Women's Wages at Midlife." *Journal of Marriage and the Family* 46:365–73.

Vinovskis, M. A. 1977. "From Household Size to the Life Course: Some Observations on Recent Trends in Family History." *American Behavioral Scientist* 21:263–87.

————. 1983. "Home, Hearth, and History: American Families in the Past." In *Ordinary People and Everyday Life: Perspectives on the New Social History*, ed. J. B. Gardner and G. R. Adams. Nashville: American Association for State and Local History.

————. 1985. *The Origins of Public High Schools: A Reexamination of the Beverly High School Controversy.* Madison: University of Wisconsin Press.

————. 1986. "Young Fathers and Their Children: Some Historical and Policy Perspectives." In *Adolescent Fatherhood*, ed. A. B. Elster and M. E. Lamb. Hillsdale, N.J.: Lawrence Erlbaum.

————. 1988. "The Historian and the Life Course: Reflections on Recent Approaches to the Study of American Family Life in the Past." In *Life-Span Development and Behavior*, vol. 8, ed. D. Featherman and R. Lerner.

Vinovskis, M. A., and R. M. Bernard. 1978. "Beyond Catherine Beecher: Female Education in the Antebellum Period." *Signs* 3:856–69.

Wachter, K., E. Hammel, and P. Laslett. 1978. *Statistical Studies of Historical Social Structure.* New York: Academic Press.

Wall, R. 1983. "Does Owning Real Property Influence the Form of the Household? An Example from Rural West Flanders." In *Family Forms in Historic Europe*, ed. R. Wall, J. Robin, and P. Laslett. Cambridge: Cambridge University Press.

Wall, R., J. Robin, and P. Laslett, eds. 1983. *Family Forms in Historic Europe.* Cambridge: Cambridge University Press.

Wells, R. V. 1985. *Uncle Sam's Family: Issues in and Perspectives on American Demographic History.* Albany: State University of New York Press.

Wightman, J. M. 1860. *Annals of the Boston Primary School Committee from Its First Establishment in 1818 to Its Dissolution in 1855.* Boston.

Zuckerman, M. 1970. *Peaceable Kingdoms: New England Towns in the Eighteenth Century.* New York: Random House.

CHAPTER 4

History, Sociology, and Theories of Organization

Mayer N. Zald

Modern society is an organizational society. From birth in hospitals, to education in schools, to work in corporations, to burial, we exist in the shadow of complex organizations. At one time, the key organizational forms were family, community, and occupation; now complex organizations are a defining attribute of modern society, with a wide range and variety of organizations and organizational arrangements.

Academic disciplines have responded to this transformation of society. The study of organizations, their connection to society, their impact on individuals, and their internal structure and process have become important topics. Although the study of bureaucracies, administration, and management can be traced back to the end of the nineteenth century, one of the most exciting developments in the social sciences in the last thirty years has been the growth and mushrooming of theory and research on organizations. This growth is much more than just a quantitative expansion. New theoretical perspectives have generated large research programs; new journals have been started; exciting debate about and deepening insight into organizations have occurred. For instance, population-ecology models of organization (Hannan and Freeman 1977) have generated predictions and research on the survival of organizational forms under different environmental conditions. For another example, the "institutional" school of John Meyer and his collaborators (Meyer and Scott 1983) has broken from the instrumentalist base of much early organizational theory. In the process we have learned a great deal about how the structure, personnel, and norms of organizations are dependent upon societal processes that have little to do with economizing and production necessities.

The ferment in organizational theory and research extends well

I wish to thank John E. Jackson, W. W. Powell, Frank P. Stafford, and Charles Tilly for comments on earlier drafts of this essay.

beyond sociology proper. In economics, the theory of the firm has developed a structure and a body. Principal agent theory (Fama and Jensen 1983; Pratt and Zeckhauser 1985), transaction cost theory (Williamson 1975, 1985) and other approaches have allowed economists to tackle topics that were ignored or assumed away in earlier periods. The choice of organizational form, the tradeoffs among hierarchies, markets, and a variety of long term contractual arrangements are subject to analytic and empirical examination. Decision theory has been enriched by loosening the time horizon and seeing decisions as part of a stream of decisions, retrospective reconstructions, shifting coalitions, and the like. (See the various publications of J. G. March and his collaborators; for instance, Harrison and March 1986.)

Although this has been a period of real ferment and intensification in our understanding of organizations, most of the newer approaches do not explain the transformation of organizations in a historical context. The great transformation to an organizational society may be described by historians (see Chandler 1962, 1977) but sociological, psychological, and economic theories of organization and management proceed without reference to historical context and process. These newer approaches continue the nomothetic, ahistorical cast of organizational theory and, for that matter, most of social science. Models are developed and propositions are stated as if they apply to all organizations in all societies, over an indefinite time span. Even if some gross distinctions are employed, such as public sector organizations, firms, or nonprofit organizations, these categories are employed as if they have a timeless meaning. No historical characterization is given. The fact that the corporation as a legally bound institution is much different today than it was a century ago is ignored. Nor is there any attempt to place the analysis of organizations and their environmental dependencies in a historical and comparative socioeconomic framework. Although there has been a growth of comparative studies of organizations, these are usually done in a static, synchronic framework (see Lammers and Hickson 1979).

Now, if organizations were timeless entities whose structures and operations extended over long periods and across many societies, an exclusively nomothetic approach might be quite appropriate. Abstract models of organizational structure, coordination, and control, or of organization-environment relations could be developed and applied to organizations of various concatenations of variables. In fact, we know that most of the phenomena analyzed in organizational theory are very time dependent. On the historical record, they represent a blip.

The modern corporation, with its extreme separation of management and ownership and divisional decentralization, came into existence in the first third of this century, spread in the developed part of the capitalist world in the second third (especially after World War II), and may vanish by who knows when. It is a profoundly historical phenomenon. Yet our theoretical discussion of the corporation tends to downplay that historicity. How it developed is treated as a functionally necessary and efficient outcome of organizational complexity under competitive conditions (cf. Chandler 1962, 1977; Williamson 1985). I believe the explanation is more complicated than that and requires a more complex and historically contingent analysis.

If we ask how historical and comparative analysis might change our views, we would quickly note that at the end of the nineteenth and beginning of the twentieth century other nations legitimized cartels and bank linkages in a way that differed from the United States. Cartels were legally encouraged in Germany, and banks were part of trading groups in Japan. Thus, the forms of competition and cooperation and of investment linkages were different in these countries. Similarly, public agencies today differ greatly from public agencies of the nineteenth or eighteenth century; yet our synchronic approach to public administration has no account of the differences. It has no account of how we got from there to here, except a straight narrative account.

I believe—it is an article of faith—that nesting organizational theory in historical process and development will have many salutary effects. We will see organizational structures and processes as contingent on a more subtle set of societal processes that are often ignored in current theorizing. We will have a better sense of the extent to which organizational forms are embedded in legal and cultural systems and relationships. Our abstract models will be seen as applying within particular socioeconomic constraints, rather than as timeless universals. Our models will be more, not less, powerful, because we will be able to specify the conditions under which they hold.

Moreover, a historically nested, comparative approach to organizations should aid in policy application and formulation. Too often the public debate over organizational policy matters proceeds from abstract theory or ideology, with little attention to the experience of other nations or of historical options and choices—whether we are discussing tax policy, antitrust issues, or takeover policy. Although it is beyond the scope of this essay, historical and comparative analysis ought to be an aid to institutional choice.

It is one thing to assert the value of a historical nesting of organizational theory; it is quite another to demonstrate that value. This essay represents a programmatic effort rather than a demonstration of the power of historical nesting. I begin by being more precise about the

defining characteristics of organizations and how alternative classifications of organizations are tied to historical issues. The body of the essay
will discuss several historical trends and abstract characterizations that
can be examined profitably by interlacing history and sociology. By and
large the focus will be on societal determinants of corporate and business
structure and internal processes; that is, corporations and organizational
components are the dependent variable. I will have less to say about the
impact of organizations on individual lives or on society. The analysis
examines components of corporations such as management control
structure, the organization of labor on the shop floor, and the legal
status of corporations. My strategy is to historicize standard components
of organizations discussed in organizational theory.[1] Rather than treat
them as givens or as sole alternatives, the issue is what were the societal
and historical alternatives.

Organizational Types, Components, and History

What do we mean by the term *complex* or *formal organization*? How are
complex organizations different from other kinds of social organizations
(e.g., small groups, kin groups, societies, nations)? After presenting
alternative definitions, W. Richard Scott states:

> Organizations are collectivities oriented to the pursuit of relatively
> specific goals. They are "purposeful" in the sense that the activities
> and interactions of participants are centrally coordinated to achieve
> specified goals. Goals are specific to the extent that they are explicit,
> are clearly defined, and provide unambiguous criteria for selecting
> among alternative activities.
>
> Organizations are collectivities that exhibit a relatively high
> degree of formalization. The cooperation among participants is
> "conscious" and "deliberate;" the structure of relations is made
> explicit and can be "deliberately constructed and reconstructed." As
> previously defined, a structure is formalized to the extent that the
> rules governing behavior are precisely and explicitly formulated and
> to the extent that roles and role relations are prescribed indepen-
> dently of the personal attributes of individuals occupying positions
> in the structure. (1987, 21)

---

1. The methodological approach to combining history and theory used in this essay is
only one of many that might be adopted. See the appendix to this essay for a discussion of
several alternatives.

Organizations have relatively specific goals; they harness people together to accomplish those goals through incentives of various kinds; they develop authority structures, rules, and a division of labor that serve to coordinate and guide the actions of the members. Since organizations have relatively specific goals, they depend upon the larger society for the provision of resources and legitimation to function. They are more delimited than societies and exist, are constrained, and are shaped by the political demands of the larger political system.

It is possible to discuss the transformation of organizations over time as a kind of general process. Thus, one might argue that organizations have become larger over the last several centuries; at least there are more large organizations now than there were at the beginning of the nineteenth century. Similarly, more organizations employ wage labor for the production of goods, instead of contracting out or using family members or slaves (a change in the incentive and authority basis of organizations). Yet other kinds of organizations, for example, social movement organizations and traditional churches, are not necessarily that much larger than in earlier times. And although they may employ some wage labor and be more bureaucratized than in earlier times, they still attract members on the basis of solidary and purposive incentives (Clark and Wilson 1963; McCarthy and Zald 1973). Of course, social movement organizations and religious organizations change. For instance, the marriage of evangelical religion to the emerging technologies of satellite transmission and cable television has radically expanded the scope of some denominations and transformed the bases of religious participation for parts of the population (Hadden and Swann 1981). Still, they employ traditional rhetorics and incentive bases. Because different kinds of organizations have different historical and societal contexts, I think it is more useful to restrict our focus to particular types of organizations or to core aspects of organizations, rather than discussing the historical basis of the transformation of all organizations, combining historical context and general theory to arrive at overarching interpretations of organizations and society.

There is no agreement on a category or classification scheme for organizations comparable to those found in biology or zoology (on the problems of constructing classification systems of organizations see McKelvey 1982). Instead, scholars accept the common language terms, often generated out of enterprise form (defined in law by legal ownership), purpose (broad or narrowly conceived), and incentive basis. Organizations distinguished by enterprise form are sole proprietorships, partnerships, corporations, not-for-profit corporations, public corporations, and public agencies. Each type has a different standing in law, packages control and authority in different ways, has different relations to the state and to capital markets, and has different historical and societal incidence.

Organizations can be classified by broad purpose, such as social movement organizations (attempting to change society), businesses (aimed at making profits by selling products or services), religious organizations (concerned with human's relation to the ultimate grounds of being). More narrow categorizations of purpose may also be developed—e.g., manufacturing versus service businesses, or even more narrowly, steel manufacturing, personal services.

Finally, organizations can be classified by incentive system — coercive, material, purposive, or solidary (Clark and Wilson 1961; Etzioni 1975; Zald and Jacobs 1978). Coercive organizations achieve their ends through use of punishment and deprivation of liberty. Material organizations offer their members money and goods for participating in the organization. Purposive incentives offer the opportunity to achieve normative ends. Solidary organizations offer pleasing social relations and a sense of belonging.

Obviously, there are other bases for distinguishing among organizations, usually relating to some specific aspect of their functioning — technological development or kind of technological throughput, type of labor process, organizational structure (centralized or decentralized), and so on. Usually it makes more sense to discuss the transformation of structural aspects of organizations within a particular type (e.g., distinguished by enterprise form, purpose, or incentive system) than to discuss the transformation of structural arrangements in general. Some types of organizations will not face dilemmas of centralization or decentralization; some types of organizations do not have a transformation of wage labor.

While many kinds of organizations may share similar historical trajectories, it is more likely that they will have different historical and spatial careers. Phrased differently, there is no a priori reason to expect strong time and societal dependence for all types of organizations and their components. Different industries emerge at different points in time; societies encourage or discourage particular types of organizations and enterprises. Which aspect or type should be examined in detail is a function of investigator taste and the amount of leverage to be gained for a broader understanding of organizations and society. In this essay the focus will be upon a central organizational type of modern society—the business corporation—and the transformation of several of its key components.

The Making of the Capitalist Corporation

There are many ways in which the conjoining of history, sociology, and the study of particular processes or types of organizations could proceed. I will focus on the development of the modern corporation and its components. Clearly, the corporation is a central part of the modern economy, a power holder in its own right, and an important actor in the polity of all capitalistic nations. My purpose is to suggest some of the questions that are raised as the history of corporations is opened up to sociological analysis, and as we use history to challenge sociological formulations.

The issues raised range from micro (really meso) to macro. They also vary in their locus — problems internal to the firm, i.e., management control systems; the evolution of employee and labor relations; the transformation of interorganizational relations and networks; problems in the legal definition of organizations, and problems in the relation of the state to organizations. Each of these topics has received substantial treatment in the literature on organizations. The extent to which the topics have been given historical treatment varies, but all can benefit by nesting general propositions in historical and societal context. Although I will not treat each topic in equal detail, I will attempt to indicate the sociological and historical complexities of each of the routes chosen.

Management Control Systems

One of the great transformations of organizations over the last one hundred fifty years has been the development of management hierarchies and control systems. Size and complexity drove a wedge between owners and producing workers. As owners or their first-order delegates became more and more distant, as supervisors supervised supervisors supervising supervisors, problems of control loss became endemic to organizations. Control loss is accompanied by deflection from organizational aims and from economizing in the owners' interest, or so the theory goes (Williamson 1964). As organizations become larger and more differentiated (as measured by the number of occupations, products, and specialized functions) they become more bureaucratic, developing formal structures and standardized procedures. The general correlation between size, complexity, structure, and procedure holds in all modern societies, representing a well-established nomothetic proposition (see Hickson et al. 1979). Yet there are national and historical differences in how corporations met the challenge of control loss.

Alfred Dupont Chandler's (1977) *The Visible Hand* is devoted to a discussion of the growth of managerial hierarchies and control systems in the period of their great emergence in the United States around the turn of the century. (The multiple divisional form emerges later.) One major component of the control system that develops is the growth of managerial accounting systems. (As contrasted with public or financial accounting, managerial accounting is aimed at internal control and decision making.) Taken together, internal budgeting systems and cost accounting systems are powerful mechanisms for delegating responsibility, for reviewing the results of that delegation, and for developing standards for economizing judgments by management. Cost accounting information is especially critical for economizing decisions because it develops refined categories of unit costs and allows the manager to compare alternative mixes of fixed and variable direct costs and overhead costs in arriving at production decisions.

Accounting information and accounting systems are not costless themselves. They require specialized personnel and the devotion of time by both specialized and general personnel to data collection, recording, and analysis, and to report transmission. We have little sense of accounting costs for different organizations in different industries at different times (see the discussion in Johnson and Kaplan 1987). If accounting information was the sine qua non, the only route to effective internal control and decision making, one might just assume it as a prerequisite of organizational effectiveness. But, it is not the only route.

Both theoretically and empirically there is at least some reason to see cost-accounting techniques and cost-accounting personnel as socially nested developments. On the theoretical side, scholars have conceptualized alternative ways of minimizing control loss. Socialization, selection, and unobtrusive controls (Perrow 1972) and clanlike relations (Ouchi 1980) may create shared decision premises and solidary relations. And profit sharing and contract provisions may tie agents and principals, to some extent obviating the necessity of continual supervision and surveillance (Williamson 1985). Moreover, once the costs of information are taken into account, the decision-making value of standard operating procedures, derived from rules of thumb, as contrasted with more refined cost calculations, remains an alternative. Of course, cost-accounting systems do not emerge overnight but are historical accretions, in separate organizations, in industries, and in societal management systems.

On the empirical side, there is some evidence to indicate that managerial hierarchies vary in size and scope across national boundaries (see Lincoln, Hanada, and McBride 1986; Azumi et al. 1984). They may also employ detailed accounting systems to a lesser degree. John Meyer (1986) has argued that the processes of rationalization have taken different form in Germany, a more "corporatist" society, than in liberal Western societies. As a consequence, he argues that German managers have had less reliance on accounting and accounting information. Piore and Sabel (1984) argue that craft-based organization of the shop floor is an alternative to fragmented mass-production organization for many industries. Further, they argue that German industry retained a craft-based, plant community in many industries that had become mass-production based in the United States. They put forward the general supposition that both scientific management and cost accounting are more likely to be institutionalized in mass-production industries. Scientific management and rigid control systems are appropriate for long, standardized production runs. Sabel (1982) argues that faced with competition from low-cost overseas producers, many industries are moving toward more flexible production systems.

Taking both of these points together, several research questions are suggested:

— What was the size and distribution of accounting personnel and accounting effort internal to firms and industries over time? Marshall Meyer has described the correlates of growth of municipal finance offices (1985), but I am unaware of parallel studies in private firms. Typical business histories are more likely to report on the introduction of standardized accounting practice than they are on the costs or organization of accounting practice.
— How does accounting practice differ in the same industries in different countries? Industry is an important variable, since industries differ in size of firm, in the introduction of management, and in the ease of quantifiability.
— How does the growth of professional standards and governmental regulations effect internal accounting practices? The process of adopting new managerial practices results from a variety of forces including, but not restricted to, attempts to control costs and rationalize decision making (Zald 1986).

Fligstein (1987) provides evidence that over time personnel with a background in finance became more likely to head the largest corporations from the beginning to the end of the 1919–79 period. He shows that as a proportion of all of the chief executives, those with manufacturing backgrounds declined over the time span. To some extent, the switch is related to corporate strategy. At the beginning of the period the largest firms were often single product firms with a unitary functional structure. They were likely to be headed by entrepreneurs or managers with a manufacturing background.

Firms with a conglomerate and product-related strategy were more likely to have executives with a finance background, and those firms were more likely to be among the largest firms in the recent period. Again comparative studies of top personnel in industries in different countries would be well worth carrying out.

—Is there a constellation of management rationalization, including cost accounting, organization of the production process, and labor organization and labor relations that go together in the development of industries? Chandler (1977, 1962) does not devote much attention to labor relations and the actual management of production. For each of his exemplar companies, it would be fascinating to examine the status of their labor relations and the detailed nature of their internal management and organization of production processes. Piore and Sabel (1984; see also Sabel and Zeitlin 1985) argue that management practice is closely bundled with production technology and labor organization. But these differences may be revealed as much in national differences as in company to company variation, since management theories are part of national institutionalized ideologies and practices. Johnson and Kaplan (1987) argue that cost accounting developed more extensively in the United States than in Great Britain in the late nineteenth and early twentieth centuries because Britain had a more efficient competitive market system.

We have known for sometime (Bendix 1956) that national ideology and social structure shape managerial ideology. The historical and comparative thrust of this section suggests that even the most technically developed components of managerial practice, such as accounting rules, have a similar social embeddedness.

The Organization of Labor on the Shop Floor

Somewhat separately from mainstream organizational theory, there has been a torrent of studies of the organization of production as a labor process. Motivated by social history, by Marxist concerns about history from the bottom up, and by a desire to understand the actual social relations of production, many of these studies examine the interplay of technology, worker organization, capital and management, and the larger, state institutions surrounding production. The studies are both contemporaneous and historical. Some of these studies (Clawson 1980; Stone 1974) argue that the bureaucratization of the employment relation was as much a technique of management control as it was a mechanism for raising profits. Clawson actually goes further—he believes and pro-

vides some evidence that the substitution of direct employment for sub-
contracting, the earlier form of hiring labor, was done more for management control than for its contribution to profit making. Richard
Edwards (1979) examined the transformation and bureaucratization of
labor relations as we moved from personalism and personal domination,
to technical, and finally to bureaucratic and human relations models of
organizational control.

Harry Braverman's (1974) important work raised the deskilling
argument to center stage. Braverman argued that the long range trend in
American industry was for craft-based jobs to be replaced by semiskilled
and low-skilled job requirements, but the weight of the evidence is that
deskilling may occur in some industries, yet hardly occurs in all.
Granovetter and Tilly's (1988) careful evaluation suggests that, if anything, skill requirements, complexity, and the handling of nonroutine
tasks may have increased in the overall work force. Moreover, the
amount of deskilling is not a direct function of the amount of automation and technological substitution, as in Braverman's account, but a
complex outcome of bargaining power of workers and managers, the
state of the economy, rates of technical change that raise workers control
of tacit knowledge, and other factors.

Indeed, new studies might take into account the role of labor and
labor unions in creating deskilling at earlier times, as they contested with
management for the definition of jobs on the work floor. Unions wanted
precise job categories and inflexible assignment schedules as a defense
against management. Deskilling may have been the result. In the current
era, as international competition accelerates, management is pressuring
for job assignment flexiblity, increasing the number of tasks workers
must master (Sabel 1982). Zimbalist's (1979) important compilation of
case studies provides a good cross-section of the organization of production and labor relations in different industries.

Most of the literature attributes the transformation of the social
relations of production to the interaction of technological change, labor
solidarity or lack thereof (including the impact of unionization on both
unionized and nonunionized companies), and management rationalization. At least as important was the enactment of legislation governing
employment relations. Laws such as the wages and hours act, or more
recently, legislation on the requirements for vesting pensions, are major
forces for standardizing the terms of employment relations. Sanford
Jacoby (1985) examines the growth of professionalized personnel departments and the bureaucratization of labor relations as a long term contested process. Jacoby shows how the "demand drive" system, treating
labor as a pure commodity dominated by strong foremen, was trans-

formed. Reformers inside and outside of management argued that the demand drive system was inhuman and unproductive. Social workers, ex-socialists, and other labor missionaries came into management to transform the system; a professional social movement, if you will. Simultaneously, shifts in the economy promoted bureaucratization. As labor productivity declined in World War I — labor was scarce and quitting rates were high — the government pressured shipyards and other military equipment providers to adopt labor practices, rules, standard days, and so on, that would hold labor and generate higher productivity. The state played a major role in promoting the program of the emerging profession of personnel administrators again during the Great Depression. Baron et al. (1986) bring the story forward, showing how government agencies intervened in labor relations during World War II, pressing firms to stabilize and bureaucratize personnel relations.

It is possible to combine the historical evolution of management of labor force, in the manner of Edwards or Jacoby, with the more cross-sectional analysis represented in Zimbalist. That is, the organization of production in an industry is not only a function of the actual task-technology demands, but also a function of broader societal institutions of labor relations and management training. Moreover, we now have sophisticated notions of internal labor markets and personnel rating systems (Hay points) that help us understand how organizations structure careers within organizations, substituting for or complementing market exchange models.

This suggests both an empirical and a theoretical agenda. Historical studies of internal labor markets are in order. To the extent that personnel files can be retrieved or reconstructed, and to the extent that we have a knowledge of a firm's organizational structure, it becomes possible to reconstruct the evolution of a firm's internal labor market over time. Such research becomes part of a disaggregated approach to the study of social mobility and the transformation of stratification in emerging industrial society.

Two theoretical tasks are suggested. How do internal labor markets tie to the organization of production across industries? How do internal labor markets tie to social mobility and stratification? There are hints in the literature about how one would pursue such issues. With regard to the cross-industry generation of internal labor markets, they must be treated as a joint product of production process, labor-management systems, and state intervention. Internal labor markets tie to social mobility and stratification through the reification of job categories, career and job qualifications, and reward systems (see Stewman 1986; Rosenbaum 1984). These are extremely important topics for historical understanding and for the development of linkages between stratification theory and organizational theory.

These kinds of studies also tie to a number of policy and institutional choice issues. Internal labor markets and the organizational structuring of labor relations have deep implications for the productivity of firms and the career opportunities of minorities and women. Shop floor organization fascinates scholars and also has important policy implications.

Enterprise Form and Structural Options

A discussion of managerial control and of the organization of work as historically nested processes focuses on microprocesses even as it draws on larger cultural, political, and institutional processes. A consideration of enterprise form issues turns us to the law and the structured processes for mobilizing and allocating capital. Microissues do not disappear, but macroissues of legal change and political process come to center stage.

Enterprise form deals with the legal constitution of organizations and the assignment and disposal of property and property rights. As noted earlier, common language enterprise forms include sole proprietorships, partnerships, limited partnerships, private corporations, publicly owned or listed corporations, state owned corporations, public organizations (government agencies), associations, church organizations, and so on. Each enterprise form has a legal history, more or less complicated, that details how the terms of ownership, management, capital mobilization, and capital dispersal will take place. Moreover, each enterprise form actually constitutes a complex of rules and laws shaped by standard setting bodies, such as the Financial Accounting Standards Board, the Securities and Exchange Commission, and the Internal Revenue Service.

These terms of ownership may favor one group or another. To use an example much in the news in 1986 and 1987, if the incumbent board of directors of a corporation is legally allowed to stagger the terms of board members, new owners of the stock of the corporation are limited in their ability to dispose of and manage a corporation. Such rules are "poison pill" rules, legally enforceable and part of the enterprise rules of corporations. They are a defense against hostile takeovers.

Enterprise forms are different ways of packaging property rights to achieve individual and social ends. The adoption of enterprise forms in broad stroke (major form) and in fine grain (specific rule constellation) are subject to a historically nested political economy of choice. That is, the use of a particular enterprise form depends upon the perceived costs and benefits of its use in comparison with other available enterprise forms. Whether to structure a hospital as a for-profit corporation or as a not-for-profit, eleemosynary organization responds to changes in the availability of money in capital markets and changes in management and hospital technology. Transforming a publicly listed corporation into a private one is partly a function of capital availability and the possibility of shielding property control from takeover bids. Moving from corporate form to partnership form becomes desirable, if tax rates are much lower for partnerships.

Scholars writing about enterprise form in capitalist societies tend to write as if the modern American corporation was somehow inevitable. They write as if the general purpose (unrestricted charter) corporation, that limited the liability of owners and treated the corporation as a person, had an evolutionary dominance over other forms. Legal scholars, such as Lawrence Friedman (1985), noted how American states desiring to encourage economic development rushed to free capital of restrictive charters and personal liability. And Chandler (1962) treated the corporate form as part and parcel of the modern firm.

These interpretations ignore the historical alternatives. In particular, trusts and combinations as enterprise forms were outlawed, limiting the role of investment banks as controlling entities in the ongoing operation of goods producing and distributing firms. Cartels were actually encouraged by law in Germany until after World War II and Japanese trading companies had banks at their core. (For the contrast of European and American developments see Cornish, in Horn and Kocka 1979.) Stock markets became important earlier in the United States than in other countries, because alternative vehicles for capital investment had been narrowed. The absence of a national bank and limits on bank ownership of corporations forced corporations into the stock market as a source of investment. The success of the American corporate form and American political and economic hegemony following World War II suggested to other nations alternatives for the relation of banks to industry. The growth of the multiple division (M-form) firm, with corporate headquarters acting as an investment bank in relation to its decentralized divisions, was at least in part a function of American antitrust law, which limited banks in the direct control of corporations, and tax law, which levied lower rates on corporations than on individuals and which permitted retained earnings to be used in the business. Reich argues that the effect of M-form carries the separation of management from doing to an extreme, leading to "paper entrepreneurship," with disastrous effects.

The joint effects of tax law and antitrust policy are not well understood, but Neil Fligstein (n.d.) has shown how changing antitrust policy has reshaped the combinatorial possibilities for large corporations. First, the trusts were outlawed, which eliminated industry cartels dominated by banks and opened up the possibility of vertical and horizontal integration as a manufacturing strategy.

Later, the Cellar-Kefauver Act closed off the possibilities of these two forms of merger. The conglomerate form, combining divisions with unrelated products became the option for executives with extended credit lines and the ability to see the stock market potentials of large conglomerates. Fligstein also shows how regulatory policy limited entry and stabilized industries and firms that otherwise might have declined in size and profitability.

We do not have a well developed sociology of enterprise form, at this point, but one can begin to discern its outline. First, what are the stakes for political officeholders in creating and legitimating alternative enterprise forms? Andrew Creighton (1987) argues that in the Jacksonian period the corporation was feared as a monopoly holder. Created by the state for limited public ends, early corporations gave monopoly rights to businessmen to achieve public ends. Only later in the nineteenth century did legislators and judges in America rush to free capital. Both ideological and political economy motives were involved. To use a current example from the Soviet Union, Gorbachev hesitantly embraces limited private property forms — ideology clashes with political economy reality. Enterprise forms are legally embedded. State action is required and we must study the political process involved in creating and sustaining enterprise forms.

Second, the choice of enterprise form and which form comes to dominate has consequences for the rise and fall of class fragments, for the fine-grained texture of class cohesion and class action. William Roy (1986) demonstrates how the transformation of the mechanisms for accumulating capital, the growth of banks, and the emergence of different kinds of investment media, changed the structure of capital accumulation, investment, and the dominance of class fragments in America. Landed gentry and merchant capital gave way to the new corporate entrepreneurs. His tale, which is a historically contingent analysis of the interplay of the state, classes, and capitalism, gives a very different picture of the emergence of the modern corporation than Chandler (1962).

Current events make the general point vivid. The hostile takeover movement of the 1980s pits fragments of capital against each other; the outsiders using speculative money and new investment media (junk bonds) against established and entrenched management. The center of much of the action switches to law offices and investment banks. The white hats and the black hats are all within the capitalist class, though they vary in ethnicity, networks, and social legitimacy.

The hostile takeover movement also suggests another important issue: why is it that, although capitalism and corporations go hand in hand, in no other capitalist country does paper entrepreneurialism lead to such predatory transfers of ownership?

The Transformation of Organizational Environments

One of the staples of organizational analysis is the study of organizational environments and interorganizational relations. Interorganizational relations include conflictual, competitive, and cooperative relations. The analysis of organizational environments is more general than the study of interorganizational relations and often involves an attempt to characterize the overall stability, dynamics, and turbulence of the environment in which organizations exist (Emery and Trist 1965).

As a general proposition, students of organizations believe that the environments of organizations, and especially business organizations, are more turbulent today than during earlier times. Similarly, it is probably fair to say that there are a greater number and variety of interorganizational relations and forms for these relations than existed earlier. However, these broad propositions lack historical specificity. Giving them some historical specificity entails attaching them to the changing political economy and to the transformed possibilities made available through institutionalized repertoires of action. Both are large topics, but I can discuss the directions that analysis might take.

Emery and Trist characterized environments in terms of two dimensions, the degree of clustering (or power concentration) of environmental elements in contact with an organization (e.g., buyers, suppliers, government agencies, etc.) and the rate of change of relevant aspects of elements of the environment (e.g., technological and product characteristics, labor force supply, new elements coming and going). A turbulent environment is one in which there is a high rate of change in the elements and a great deal of clustering of the elements. An organization in a field with powerful unions, great governmental involvement, and rapid levels of technological and product change would be said to be in a turbulent field.

Although the general proposition of increasing turbulence may well hold, it is likely that different industries are on different trajectories. As Tushman and Romanelli (1985) argue, industries evolve at different rates and go through periods of stability and instability at different times, which reshape industry structure, the exit and entry rates of organizations, and the adaptive structure of firms. Indeed, it may well be that as the political economy changes, some industries become less turbulent;

there is a declustering of elements or a slowing down of rates of change. For instance, increased international competition has contributed in the United States (though not in Canada and other countries) to declining unionism and declining power of those unions that continue to represent workers, at least in those industries directly tied to international markets. If turbulence is related to concentration of elements, the decline of unions and union strength leads to a decline in turbulence.

Similarly, the conservative swing of many Western governments has led them to preach deregulation and lower intervention in industry affairs. (Of course, whether there has actually been a decline in intervention is an empirical matter.) On the other hand, even though the clustering of power elements may have declined in some industries, rates of change in elements may have increased. Both the auto industry and the airlines face higher rates of change at the same time that elements are less clustered. From a managerial point of view, I suspect that the environment looks more threatening and unstable, even while labor and government are "off their back."

Not only must organizational environments be analyzed in specific political economies, they must be connected to the changing repertoire of institutionalized forms. In an organizational and professional society, an engine exists to create new forms and possibilities for packaging organized action. As management schools have flourished, as the courts and government have permitted a wider range of interorganizational relations, and as managers and professionals have made choice of organizational form and attachment a rational act, rather than a traditional expectation, new repertoires of action are entertained.

There has been an explosion of governance forms. Franchise chains, long-term contracts, and arbitrational institutions have flourished. Theoretical work has begun to catch up with the empirical reality (Macaulay 1963; Stinchcombe 1985; Williamson 1985). But the history and description of the transformation has not been attempted. Stinchcombe titles his paper "Contracts as Hierarchical Documents." The image is apropos and begins to change our view of the structured relations of the economy. Long-term, complicated contracts are an alternative to joint ventures or vertical integration. As managers contemplate the choice of organizational structure, what is inside or outside of the organization becomes a matter of choice (see Powell n.d.). For instance, many hospitals now purchase custodial services from independent contractors, rather than employing custodial personnel directly. Although the automobile industry in America has long had long-term relationships with suppliers, international competition has led them to reconsider their out-sourcing of parts manufacture at the same time that it has created new joint ventures with a variety of competitors and suppliers, here and abroad. Similarly, strategic managerial services are sometimes hired on a part-time and even temporary basis, rather than provided by full-time permanent personnel (Pfeffer and Baron 1986). Of course, these new institutionalized forms are not used equally in all parts of the economy.

If, in fact, there have been increasing rates of change in many industries and if more aspects of interorganizational relations are more a matter of managerial choice than traditional givens, then we might expect to find a change in the job of top managers. More chief executives will find themselves dealing with interorganizational coalitions and alliances, and their role as internal managers will be handed over to others. Sooner or later we would expect to find a transformation in their training and selection, much as in earlier times we found a move to the selection of financial officers.

The Growth of the Positive State and the Organizational Society

Much of organizational theory is written as if the state does not exist, or the state is treated as part of the environmental context of organizations. We noted earlier that legislative and judicial enactments created the enterprise form of the general purpose, limited liability public corporation. The growth of the state and the transformation of its bases of taxation has been addressed. For instance, Ardant (1975) has described the limits of taxation forms in the early modern state. Recently, Roger Higgs (1987) has shown how the ratcheting of state expansion occurs as solutions are proposed to historical crises. What needs more attention is the history and sociology of the state as an administrative-organizational entity in its own right. How did the state change its administrative capacities? How did that transformation of the state impinge upon and create the conditions for an organizational society? One approach is to ask how the state creates the conditions for stable exchange relations over large populations. The rationalization of law and the creation of stable and universally accepted currency are state functions promoting larger markets. Even within this perspective, the state has further functions.

The role of Herbert Hoover in creating the conditions for an expanded, state facilitated economy through governmental standardization and cooperation is well known to students of the period (Arnold 1982). The modern state system works beyond national boundaries, of course. The globalization of industry is dependent on compacts and laws between nations that lead to enforceable contracts and the regular movement of goods and services.

The modern state, however, goes far beyond providing the context for large organizations. It provides infrastructural resources without which it is hardly possible to imagine organizations existing. Everything from public transportation systems to education systems that generate a pool of skilled and literate labor is dependent upon the state. Moreover, state policies regarding health, safety, welfare, capital exchange, and taxation deeply penetrate organizations. Although organizational theory often does not remark on this deep penetration, students of political economy, Marxist or otherwise, do (cf. O'Connor 1973; Shonfield 1969; see also Stafford and Robinson, this volume).

How might the historical development of state structures be linked to the study of organizations? There are several facets to the problem. Let me suggest three—the development of administrative capacity, national ideology and the legitimation of enterprise form, and jurisdictional geography.

Administrative capacity deals with the ability of state agencies to cope with the problems of delivering public goods in a systematic way. Consider an example: could a postal service made up of part-time political appointees be expected to fine-tune a mail service over a population of two hundred forty million people, coordinating the transportation of millions of pieces of mail? What kind of administrative apparatus is needed for securing public health? What is the administrative apparatus necessary for controlling government bureaucrats in a large democratic state?

Stephen Skowronek (1982) has begun to elaborate the administrative procedures, professional training grounds, and organizational capacities that went into the transformation of the American federal government as an administrative-effective organization. Skowronek argues that we were a nation of legislatures and courts, opposed to and without legitimation of executive and central administrative action. Martin Shefter (1977) has argued that the strength of administrative organizations interacts with the emergence of mass suffrage to shape the nature of political parties in Western democracies. Where administration was strong and could deliver services, political parties became more oriented toward policy and ideology. Where administration was weak, as in the United States, parties became vehicles for the delivery of patronage and pork barrel demands. Between nations, we expect that the relative strength and legitimation of state administrative action as a historical process would affect the ability of the state to effectively coordinate policy implementation, once the decisions to implement policy have been taken. France and Japan have encouraged a greater range and legitimacy of state action.

A second historical issue has to do with how state ideology has justified a variety of enterprise forms and how these have changed over time. Because we live in a state that allows and indeed encourages a variety of enterprise forms, we tend to forget how exceptional that state is. The size of the nonprofit sector, the encouragement of public corporations, the extent of voluntary associations, and the amount of government ownership of manufacturing and other organizations vary widely among modern nations. There are cycles of promotion or constraint of these forms, and the turning points in these cycles may be hotly contested and politicized. Frederick Pryor (1973) has discussed the variation among nations in the extent to which industries are likely to be in the public domain, to be regulated, or to be left relatively free of government ownership. For instance, even in socialist societies restaurants may be profit making; on the other hand, banking is either government owned or regulated in almost all societies. Ralph Kramer (1982) has documented national differences in the size of the not-for-profit sector. Garner and Zald (1985) have discussed the extent to which societies actively and passively encourage the social movement sector. Passive encouragement comes about through general tax laws, media access, and policy structures that do or do not hinder group mobilization. Active encouragement or discouragement occurs through the specific allocation of constraint or opportunities to specific social movements. The general trend, with many exceptions, is for western societies to loosen the reins on social movements.

Finally, the structure of state jurisdictions, the level of centralization or decentralization, and the parceling out of responsibilities among functional agencies shape the political matrix in which industries and organizations exist. These jurisdictions may change over time. For instance, as the federal government becomes a large element in the construction industry, federal policy affects the fate of labor and companies alike. As the federal government does or does not get involved in education at various levels, the extent to which educators and their professional associations turn to Washington or to state capitals will change (Zald, Jacobs, and Useem 1987).

Once we have a sense of how the positive state has grown and changed in its relations to organizations, we must return to the topic of how the state and organization interact, how they reach out toward each other. Phillipe Schmitter and his colleagues (Schmitter and Lehmbruch 1979; Streeck and Schmitter 1985) have discussed private interest intermediation and concepts such as corporatism as ways to get at these questions. Understanding the intersection of organizations and the state is facilitated by examining organizations as part of industries. Industry life cycles, industry structure, and the position of organizations within industries affect the ability of industries to mobilize and make demands upon the state and the issues that concern them. Often the state's interest in particular organizations is related to the industry in which it sits (Zald, Jacobs, and Useem 1987). These are large, difficult, and important issues.

Conclusions

This essay began from a large programmatic and metatheoretical premise — that the isolation of organizational theory from historical context and analysis impedes the progress of organizational studies. It leads to overgeneralization, ignoring historical alternatives, and misspecification of causation. Although I have argued that history and theory must be joined in the study of organizations, exactly how we are to do so is not perfectly clear. There are many alternatives, including the historical examination of particular types of organizations, the development of uniquely historical theories about specific features of organizations, and so on (see the appendix to this essay).

The strategy chosen here has been to identify a range of issues of concern to sociologists of organization, especially, but not exclusively, sociologists that deal with large corporations. These topics — management control systems, labor process, enterprise form and rules, environmental turbulence, and state action — are often treated synchronically with little attention to historical development, or they are treated as if there is one large master trend. My tack has been to ask how historical and comparative analyses might illuminate our understanding of the trend or of the processes underlying a given concept. Sources of variation are found in institutional history, political arrangements, social inventions, and historical conjunction. No singular organizational theory will do, and abstract concepts from economics, sociology, and political science will be invoked as they are needed.

I began this essay with a lament: from the point of view of the sociology of organizations, we are in danger of developing abstract theory unconnected to historical context. On the other hand, the chapter also offers an implicit challenge to historians of business and organizations; to the extent that they proceed without explicit theory or concepts, they stand in danger of getting trapped in the cultural understandings of the day, of assuming social forms and historical progression. If so, historians of organization and sociologists of organization need each other — badly. The approach I have taken is one among many that might be followed. But there are many other modes of breaching the wall. As one thinks about different solutions and different examples, one must try and avoid opposing pitfalls — the poverty of historicism and the emptiness of abstract generalizations.

My analysis also suggests an approach to institutional choice that blends historical, sociological, and rational choice models. Proposals for change at the microlevel of the firm or the macrolevel of the political economy presume goals and maximization of values. Inevitably any proposal for change, whether of enterprise form or of labor relations, addresses itself largely to the problem at hand, within the current frame of debate. However, institutional choice is constrained by the dominant hand of past choice as manifested in embedded practice and by ideological assumptions often unconsciously rendered. The historical and comparative approach suggested here might help to explore a wider range of alternatives at the same time that it weighed in against naive borrowing or grafting of those alternatives.

APPENDIX: AN EXCURSUS ON HISTORY AND ORGANIZATIONS

A large methodological issue is how one goes about combining history, theory, and the study of organizations. Since there are alternative approaches and meanings for each of these terms, a systematic discussion is well beyond the reach of this essay. A brief discussion will at least highlight the possibilities. History is the expression, discussion, and interpretation of events that occur in a time dependent sequence. Sometimes defined as a narrative of events over time, history usually deals with some change in the object under study over a time period. If the period is described in a synchronic or static fashion, it is usually assumed (at least implicitly) that the period studied differs from the period before or after in some significant regard.

A history-for-itself approach to organizations would treat organizational matters without reference to theoretical issues generated by the nomothetic social sciences. Historical studies would then be of value to the extent that scholars and others were interested in knowing the history of particular organizations, e.g., Ford Motor, or of particular components of organizations, e.g., the history of personnel departments in American corporations. Those histories might or might not fit into our larger understandings. Pure history-for-itself is important as it helps us to understand how a particular organization was transformed.

On the other hand, history-for-itself speaks to more generalizing concerns if the cases selected are believed to bear on more abstract concerns. For instance, as one of the first large mass production manufacturing organizations, Ford Motor Company "stands for" the emergence of mass production. The emergence and growth of personnel departments can be considered part of the bureaucratization of labor relations and, thus, histories of them help us understand that general process of bureaucratization (Jacoby 1985). To the extent that the historian studies a particular organization because it "stands for" or is "part of" a larger process, some implicit or explicit larger generalization is being invoked. The narrative for itself is no longer the goal.

A second use of the history of organizations would be as a testing ground for nomothetic propositions. Here the history of a single organization or of a sample of organizations is used to test hypotheses that predict differences in organizations as they experience different events and system states. Chandler's thesis (1962) that strategy causes structure was "proved" by examining the history of American corporations that were early adopters of divisional decentralization. Chandler argued that as company strategy led them into different product lines and manufacturing processes, it became more and more difficult for a functional departmental structure (with separate unitary marketing and manufacturing departments) to cope quickly and wisely with the complexity of operation. A structural change to a multiple divisional system was adopted. Similarly, Williamson (1975) used Chandler's data to argue for his own theory based on transaction cost advantages to explain which corporations would or would not adopt divisional decentralization.

A weaker version of this "testing grounds" approach is found in Zald's study (1970) of the Young Men's Christian Association. That study uses the history of the YMCA in the United States and in Chicago to illustrate the application of a political-economy approach to the analysis of organizations. Selznick's classic study of the Tennessee Valley Authority (1949) also uses history as illustrative ground for a theory. These are weaker approaches to the use of history because the possibility for disproof of specific propositions and predictions is hard to imagine. Instead, the theories or theoretical frames are found to be "useful" in explaining the historical events.

A third approach would be to develop historical theories of organizations. Historical theories make time dependent events or processes critical to explaining later states and events of organizations. They may be of several forms. Stinchcombe (1965), in a now classic paper, argued that the occupational mix and processes in an industry were very much dependent upon the knowledge of how to do things that was available when the industry was founded. This might be called the impact of foundations hypothesis. Another approach of historical theories would be to argue that if x occurs at t_1, y occurs at t_2. Although not dealing with organizations, Barrington Moore's (1966) argument about the relationship of class coalitions among landed aristocracy, peasants, urban workers, and bourgeoisie at the beginning of industrialization to the development of democracy, fascism, or communism is of this order.

Another historical theory would be one that postulated a conjunctural approach to organizational development. Here the occurrence of several events or processes together pushes organizations in one direction, while the occurrence of these same processes at different time points might lead in a different direction. Theda Skocpol's (1979) structural theory of revolutions, which postulates that successful revolutions require both exacerbated social conflict and a weak and discredited regime, is a conjunctural theory.

A final approach, and the one suggested here, is that of historical specification of core components. Historical process and societal differences are used to explain options that underlie the large transformations in particular kinds of organizations. Instead of assuming that the current shape of organizations has some kind of inevitability, historical data are used to understand the particular shape of the components of the organizational type being studied. It combines a soft kind of conjunctural analysis and explicit generalizations about the important transformations of organizations in society.

REFERENCES

Ardant, Gabriel. 1975. "Financial Policy and Economic Infrastructure of Modern States and Nations." In *The Formation of National States in Western Europe,* ed. Charles Tilly. Princeton: Princeton University Press.
Arnold, Peri E. 1982. "Ambivalent Leviathan: Herbert Hoover and the Positive State." In *Public Values and Private Power in American Politics,* ed. J. David Greenstone. Chicago: University of Chicago Press.
Azumi, Koya, David Hickson, Dezso Horvath, and Charles McMillan. 1984. "Structural Uniformity and Cultural Diversity in Organizations: A Comparative Study of Factories in Britain, Japan, and Sweden." In *The Anatomy of Japanese Business,* ed. Kazuo Sato and Yasuo Hoshino. Armonk, N.Y.: M. E. Sharpe.
Baron, James N., Alison Davis-Blake, and William T. Bielby. 1986. "The Structure of Opportunity: How Promotion Ladders Vary within and among Organizations." *Administrative Science Quarterly* 31(2): 248–73.
Baron, James N., Frank R. Dobbins, and P. Deveraux Jennings. 1986. "War and Peace: The Evolution of Modern Personnel Administration in U.S. Industry." *American Journal of Sociology* 92(2): 350–83.

Bendix, Reinhard. 1956. *Work and Authority in Industry.* New York: John Wiley.

Braverman, Harry. 1974. *Labor and Monopoly Capital: The Degradation of Work in the Twentieth Century.* New York: Monthly Review Press.

Burawoy, Michael. 1979. *Manufacturing Consent: Changes in the Labor Process under Monopoly and Capitalism.* Chicago: University of Chicago Press.

———. 1985. *The Politics of Production: Factory Regimes under Capitalism and Socialism.* London: Verso.

Chandler, Alfred Dupont. 1962. *Strategy and Structure: Chapters in the History of the American Industrial Enterprise.* Cambridge, Mass.: MIT Press.

———. 1977. *The Visible Hand: The Managerial Revolution in American Business.* Cambridge, Mass.: Harvard University Press.

Clark, Peter, and James Q. Wilson. 1961. "Incentive Systems: Theory of Organizations." *Administrative Science Quarterly* 6:129–66.

Clawson, Daniel. 1980. *Bureaucracy and the Labor Process: The Transformation of U.S. Industry, 1860–1920.* New York: Monthly Review Press.

Creighton, Andrew. 1987. "Some Aspects of the Emergence of Formal Organizations in the Early Nineteenth Century." Department of Sociology, Stanford University. Typescript.

Edwards, Richard. 1979. *Contested Terrain: The Transformation of the Workplace in the Twentieth Century.* New York: Basic Books.

Emery, Fred E., and E. L. Trist. 1965. "The Causal Texture of Organizational Environments." *Human Relations* 18:21–32.

Etzioni, Amitai. 1975. *A Comparative Analysis of Complex Organizations.* New York: Free Press.

Fama, Eugene, and Michael Jensen. 1983. "Separation of Ownership and Control." *Journal of Law and Economics* 26:301–25.

Fligstein, Neil. 1987. "The Intraorganizational Power Struggle: Rise of Finance Personnel to Top Leadership in Large Corporations, 1919–79." *American Sociological Review* 52(1): 44–58.

———. N.d. *States and Markets: The Transformation of the Large Corporation, 1880–1985.* Cambridge, Mass.: Harvard University Press. Forthcoming.

Friedman, Lawrence M. 1985. *A History of American Law.* New York: Simon and Schuster.

Garner, Roberta, and Mayer N. Zald. 1985. "The Political Economy of Social Movement Sectors." In *The Challenge of Social Control: Citizenship and Institution Building in Modern Society,* ed. Gerald Suttles and Mayer N. Zald. Norwood, N.J.: Ablex.

Granovetter, Mark, and Charles Tilly. 1988. "Inequality and Labor Processes." In *Handbook of Sociology,* ed. Neil J. Smelser. Beverly Hills, Calif.: Sage.

Hadden, Jeffrey K., and Charles E. Swann. 1981. *Prime Time Preachers: The Rising Power of Televangelism.* Reading, Mass.: Addison-Wesley.

Hannan, Michael, and John Freeman. 1977. "The Population Ecology of Organizations." *American Journal of Sociology* 82(5): 929–64.

Harrison, J. Richard, and James G. March. 1986. "Decision Making and Post-Decision Surprises." *Administrative Science Quarterly* 29(1): 26–42.

Hickson, David J., Charles J. McMillan, Koya Azumi, and Dezso Horvath. 1979. "Grounds for Comparative Organization Theory: Quicksands or Hard Core." In *Organizations Alike and Unlike: International and Interinstitutional Studies in the Sociology of Organizations,* ed. Cornelis J. Lammers and David Hickson. London: Routledge & Kegan Paul.

Higgs, Robert. 1987. *Crisis and Leviathan: Critical Episodes in the Growth of American Government.* New York: Oxford University Press.

Horn, Norbert, and Jurgen Kocka, eds. 1979. *Law and the Formation of Big Enterprises in the Nineteenth and Twentieth Centuries.* Gottingen, Germany: Vandenhoeck & Ruprecht.

Jacoby, Sanford M. 1985. *Employing Bureaucracy: Managers, Unions, and the Transformation of Work in American Industry, 1900–1945.* New York: Columbia University Press.

Johnson, H. Thomas, and Robert S. Kaplan. 1987. *Relevance Lost: The Rise and Fall of Management Accounting.* Boston: Harvard Business School Press.

Kramer, Ralph. 1982. *Voluntary Agencies in the Welfare State.* Berkeley, Calif.: University of California Press.

Lincoln, James R., Mitsuyo Hanada, and Kerry McBride. 1986. "Organizational Structures in Japanese and U.S. Manufacturing." *Administrative Science Quarterly* 31(3): 338–64.

Macaulay, Stewart. 1963. "Non-contractual Relations in Business." *American Sociological Review* 28(1): 55–70.

McCarthy, John D., and Mayer N. Zald. 1973. *The Trend of Social Movements in America: Professionalization and Resource Mobilization.* Morristown, N.J.: General Learning Press.

McKelvey, Bill. 1982. *Organizational Systematics: Taxonomy, Classification, and Evolution.* Berkeley, Calif.: University of California Press.

Marglin, Stephen. 1974. "What Do Bosses Do? The Origins and Function of Hierarchy in Capitalist Production." *Review of Radical Political Economics* 6:60–112.

Maurice, Marc. 1979. "For a Study of the 'Societal Effect': Universality and Specificity in Organization Research." In *Organizations Alike and Unlike: International and Interinstitutional Studies in the Sociology of Organizations,* ed. Cornelis J. Lammers and David Hickson. London: Routledge & Kegan Paul.

Meyer, John W., and W. Richard Scott, eds. 1983. *Organizational Environments: Ritual and Rationality.* Beverly Hills, Calif.: Sage Publications.

———. 1986. "Social Environments and Organizational Accounting." *Accounting, Organizations, and Society* 11(4–5): 345–56.

Meyer, Marshall W., with William Stevenson and Stephen Webster. 1985. *Limits to Bureaucratic Growth.* Berlin: de Gruyter.

Moore, Barrington. 1966. *Social Origins of Dictatorship and Democracy.* Boston: Beacon Press.

Nelson, Michael. 1982. "A Short Ironic History of American National Bureaucracy." *Journal of Politics* 44:747–78.

O'Connor, James. 1973. *The Fiscal Crisis of the State.* New York: St. Martin's.

Ouchi, William G. 1980. "Markets, Bureaucracies and Clans." *Administrative Science Quarterly* 25(1): 129–41.

Perrow, Charles. 1972. *Complex Organizations: A Critical Essay.* Glenview, Ill.: Scott, Foresman.

Pfeffer, Jeffrey, and James N. Baron. 1986. "Taking the Worker Back Out: Recent Trends in the Structuring of Employment." Research Paper no. 926, Graduate School of Business, Stanford University.

Piore, Michael, and Charles S. Sabel. 1984. *The Second Industrial Divide: Possibilities for Prosperity.* New York: Basic Books.

Powell, Walter W. N.d. In *Research in Organizational Behavior,* vol. 12, ed. Barry M. Stowo and Larry L. Cummings. Greenwich, Conn.: JAI Press.

Pratt, John W., and Richard J. Zeckhauser, eds. 1985. *Principals and Agents: The Structure of Business.* Boston: Harvard Business School Press.

Pryor, Frederick. 1973. *Property and Industrial Organization in Communist and Capitalist Nations.* Bloomington, Ind.: Indiana University Press.

Reich, Robert B. 1983. *The Next American Frontier.* New York: Times Books.

Rosenbaum, James E. 1984. *Career Mobility in a Corporate Hierarchy.* New York: Academic Press.

Roy, William G. 1986. "Functional and Historical Logics: Explaining the Relationship between the Capitalist Class and the Rise of the Industrial Corporation." Department of Sociology, University of California, Los Angeles. Typescript.

Sabel, Charles. 1982. *Work and Politics: The Division of Labor in Industry.* New York: Cambridge University Press.

Sabel, Charles, and Jonathan Zeitlin. 1985. "Historical Alternatives to Mass Production: Politics, Markets and Technology in Nineteenth-Century Industrialization." *Past and Present* 108:133–76.

Schmitter, Phillipe, and Gerhard Lehmbruch, eds. 1969. *Trends Toward Corporatist Intermediation.* Beverly Hills, Calif.: Sage.

Scott, W. Richard. 1987. *Organizations: Rational, Natural, and Open Systems.* 2d ed. Englewood Cliffs, N.J.: Prentice-Hall.

Scott, W. Richard, and John Meyer. 1983. *Organizational Environments: Ritual and Rationality.* Beverly Hills, Calif.: Sage.

Selznick, Philip. 1949. *TVA and the Grassroots.* Berkeley, Calif.: University of California Press.

Shefter, Martin. 1977. "Party and Patronage: Germany, England and Italy." *Politics and Society* 7(4): 403–51.

Shonfield, Andrew. 1969. *Modern Capitalism: The Changing Balance of Public and Private Power.* New York: Oxford University Press.

Skocpol, Theda. 1979. *States and Social Revolutions: A Comparative Analysis of France, Russia, and China.* New York: Cambridge University Press.

Skowronek, Stephen. 1982. *Building a New American State: The Expansion of National Administrative Capacities.* New York: Cambridge University Press.

Stewman, Shelby. 1986. "Demographic Models of Internal Labor Markets." *Administrative Science Quarterly* 31(3): 212–47.

Stinchcombe, Arthur L. 1965. "Social Structure and Organizations." In *Handbook of Organizations*, ed. James G. March. Chicago: Rand McNally.

_____. 1985. "Contracts as Hierarchical Documents." In *Organization Theory and Project Management*, ed. A. L. Stinchcombe and Carol A. Heimer. Oslo: Norwegian University Press.

Stone, Katherine. 1974. "The Origins of Job Structures in the Steel Industry." *Radical America* 7(6): 19–64.

Streeck, Wolfgang, and Philippe C. Schmitter. 1985. *Private Interest Government: Beyond Market and State*. Beverly Hills, Calif.: Sage.

Tushman, Michael L., and Elaine Romanelli. 1985. "Organizational Evolution: A Metamorphosis Model of Convergence and Reorientation." In *Research in Organizational Behavior*, vol. 7, ed. L. L. Cummings and Barry M. Staw. Greenwich, Conn.: JAI Press.

Williamson, Oliver E. 1964. *The Economics of Discretionary Behavior: Managerial Objectives in a Theory of the Firm*. Englewood Cliffs, N.J.: Prentice-Hall.

_____. 1975. *Markets and Hierarchies: Analysis and Anti-Trust Implications*. New York: Free Press.

_____. 1985. *The Economic Institutions of Capitalism*. New York: Free Press.

Zald, Mayer N. 1970. *Organizational Change: The Political Economy of the YMCA*. Chicago: University of Chicago Press.

_____. 1986. "The Sociology of Enterprise, Accounting, and Budget Rules: Implications for Organizational Theory." *Accounting, Organizations and Society* 11(4–5): 327–40.

Zald, Mayer N., and David Jacobs. 1978. "Compliance/Incentive Classifications of Organizations: Underlying Dimensions." *Administration and Society* 9(4): 403–24.

Zald, Mayer N., David Jacobs, and Michael Useem. 1987. "Organizations, Industry and the State." Department of Sociology, University of Michigan. Typescript.

Zimbalist, Andrew. 1979. *Case Studies on the Labor Process*. New York: Monthly Review Press.

CHAPTER 5

Industrial Growth and Social Institutions

Frank P. Stafford and Malcolm Robinson

Societies go through periods of dramatic transition and change. During these periods there is often public soul-searching on the capacity of existing social institutions to manage these changes efficaciously.[1] In the United States as in other mature industrial nations, the advent of widespread impacts of rapid internationalization of our financial and goods markets is seen to be testing the limits of our existing institutions to bring about the needed changes. The magnitude of increased internationalization is suggested by a few facts. The share of GNP originating in trade was about 5 percent in the early 1970s and has now risen to over 15 percent. One analysis claims that over 70 percent of our manufactured goods compete with those of other countries either in export markets or in our own markets. (President's Commission on Industrial Competitiveness 1985).

Absent our ability to succeed in the face of international competition arising in certain visible sectors, it is feared that there will be pressure for very shortsighted remedies characterized by expediency rather than choices that will provide longer term benefits. The shortsighted remedies could include protectionism, government ownership of "win-

---

This essay was developed from experience in teaching a course titled "Economic Analysis of Industrial Policy" in the Program in American Institutions at the University of Michigan. The course initially developed a critical review of a wide range of proposals and policies purporting to enhance industrial growth. From this initial conception it became clear that many of the proposals involve changes in existing social institutions. The essay represents an effort to develop a general statement of how social institutions and changes in them influence an economy's industrial structure in a world where there is international trade in goods and services and international capital markets.

1. By the term *social institution* we mean a combination of significant norms, rules, relationships, and organizations. This definition often applies to the word *institution*. More explicitly, following Matthews (1986), we can view institutions as sets of rights and obligations that affect and describe economic life. Thus, a system of institutions defines (1) what markets exist and the extent to which markets are used, and (2) how economic relations are regulated and the method of contract enforcement.

ning" or "losing" industries, and a host of political directives for the operation of what have been market sectors.

The role of social institutions in this period of change is perhaps unique: not only are social institutions essential in guiding changes, but the value of social institutions as they shape a country's economy relative to competitor economies is an essential part of the discussion. Many are now arguing that our ability to compete internationally in manufactured goods depends on the vitality of our social institutions as they affect different sectors of our economy. These influences are implicitly or explicitly compared to the effect of social institutions of other potential competitors on different sectors of their economies. Consider a specific illustration that is quite well-defined by economic variables. Recent studies have shown that the domestic tax laws across a set of countries are far more important in shaping trade flows than are current tariff and trade restrictions (Whalley 1980). It is suspected that the favorable tax treatment of residential housing may be having more impact on U.S. industrial investment than the recent repeal of special business investment incentives.[2]

Extending this tax illustration, different social institutions in the different countries are now presumed to be of far greater importance in shaping a country's international strengths than are raw materials or other exogenous endowments given by nature. More generally, we are urged to adopt the social institutions of other countries that appear to have aided particular success which they have had. For a country to entertain such proposals is not new, nor are such proposals restricted to specific social spheres. As an illustration, in the early 1900s, Yugoslavia adopted much of the legal code of Switzerland, and Japan adopted much of the legal code of Germany. The Chinese have recently decided to adopt market structures to encourage industrial growth and the Soviets have allowed limited private ownership of the means of production. It might, however, be a serious mistake simply to take a single institution from one society, transplant it to another culture, and expect that institution to "work." Ignoring the particular time frame in which the institution was successful or failing to consider the interconnection between a society's institutions could lead to unintended, negative consequences.

Another danger in the attribution of a country's successful economic performance to social institutions is that there may be numerous differ-

---

2. The favorable tax treatment of residential housing has deep support in the United States. For example, a former chair of the Council of Economic Advisers received critical remarks during his confirmation hearings; the blemish on his record was having once questioned the wisdom of deducting home mortgage interest.

ences between any two countries' social institutions. For example, when Japanese firms began to take large shares of the American markets for televisions, autos, and steel, there was a "which institution this month" flavor to the gropings of the American press to explain Japan's successes. Lifetime employment and its implications received a great deal of attention a while ago, as did the Japanese style of management. And there has been discussion of the role of the Ministry of International Trade and Industry (MITI) and the effects of its industrial policies. If there is a small number of performance or outcome differences, then the issue of causation can only be addressed by considering additional countries and additional performance differences or historical time series. This suggests a payoff to a more comprehensive and comparative approach that would statistically examine whether, for example, particular types of legal or commercial codes favored economic growth.

This essay contains three sections. In the first is developed a general conception of how social institutions shape the functioning of the economy. The second section illustrates areas in which the particular social institutions of the United States shape our competitive position in world markets. Here we examine macroeconomic policy making, labor market adjustments, management styles, and sponsorship of technology. The third section of the essay presents a sketch of differences across countries in key business and public institutions that are regarded as important for a vital manufacturing sector. It offers a possible research agenda for economists and others interested in studying the influence of social institutions on economic performance.

Social Institutions as They Shape the Economy

Basic Features

How does an economy respond to unanticipated or exogenous changes? For our discussion let us consider changes in the economy brought about by new technology, emerging international relationships, or such events as global climate changes as exogenous factors.[3] How can we conceptualize desirable ways of responding to such changes?

One way of responding to change is to enumerate future events as contingencies and formulate possible responses or new systems of control in advance. The main limitation on this approach is quite familiar to

---

3. To some extent each of these can be considered endogenous. Even climate may be shaped by incentives to burn fossil fuels. Further, we are often concerned about the unintended outcomes of endogenous changes and debate the wisdom of changing our social institutions as a response.

those who study the costs of contract: enumerating all the contingencies and compound contingencies and the ideal (or even a good) response is an overwhelming task. A second limitation is the normal impatience of people to contemplate events that could occur but have not yet occurred.

There are two other approaches. One is to respond to changes ex post facto. After the changed environment is observed, the response is to formulate a new system that is better able to deal with it. But this seems to contradict our understanding of what an institution is. Indeed, we might argue that a defining feature of an institution is its ability to persist. If we think of an institution as a social convention or a rule, then it would make little sense if it were constantly changing. Another drawback of this approach is that it creates its own set of uncertainties. Given that society has few anchor points around which people can formulate longer term plans, there will be costs imposed on some people as a consequence of the need to change society's policies, in unanticipated ways. This will be true even if the change makes people better off on average. Quarreling over the fairness of alternative ex post facto responses can create ill will and inhibit the implementation of new systems.

The second alternative is what might be called the constitutional approach. Here society formulates a small number of durable guidelines, expected to apply to a very wide range of contingencies. As part of the constitutional approach, society can assign wide scope for the operation of markets on the reasoning that under conditions which will hold broadly this form of organization will facilitate change without the need to reevaluate society's choice of control mechanisms.

It has been argued that markets and democratic voting systems are compatible (Halevy 1928). They both commit the society to general mechanisms for dealing with social change, and both mechanisms have a common structure of individual choice of consumers and voters as the method of exercising control and carrying out change. At another level it can be argued that the constitutional approach can provide an environment conducive to positive economic and social change. Proper constitutional choice will foster economic and other innovations that create long-term benefits for society.

Despite the arguments made for the use of a few durable social institutions, it seems inevitable that a good part of social change will consist of newly formulated control mechanisms or special adaptations of the constitutional elements to deal with changes that have not been foreseen and that cannot be handled well by existing social institutions. In a more positive vein there will be extraconstitutional mechanisms that have appeal as facilitators of change rather than mechanisms for coping with external shocks. An illustration might be the development of the industrial research consortium designed to provide support for research having public good properties for the company sponsors. Such an organization is in some ways outside the market paradigm, since it may conflict with the benefits of independent action of market competitors, and does not fit well into the political sphere, since it is not of general interest to the electorate or its representatives and is not funded by public taxes. It is illustrative of a new organizational form expected to provide benefits but which does not fit neatly into the simple constitutional categories of market or democratic voting mechanisms.

To put the preceding remarks in a more specific context, consider the rapid emergence of competition for U.S. manufacturing firms because of internationalization of our economy and the success of newly industrializing economies (the NICs) as well as peer economies of Europe and Japan. Of course, when we think about the U.S. experience of the early to mid 1980s we are really thinking about the massive inability of the U.S. economy to compete effectively. The deterioration of external competitiveness is captured by a few salient statistics. Looking at comparative industry prices one finds that the price of U.S. exports throughout manufacturing increased by large percentages over comparable import prices. Cumulative U.S. export growth for 1981–84 was actually negative, while imports rose by 75 percent. At the same time, the level of domestic manufactured production rose only 12 percent. As Dornbusch (1986a) has pointed out, trade sensitive sectors like manufacturing and agriculture justifiably felt left out of the U.S. domestic recovery.

One explanation of the U.S. position makes use of the Mundell-Fleming (M-F) model, one of the workhorse models of open economy macroeconomics (Fleming 1962, Mundell 1986). A key assumption of the M-F model is that international capital markets operate very efficiently, so that if a U.S. budget deficit drives up domestic interest rates above foreign rates, foreign asset holders will want to purchase U.S. assets. But to buy U.S. assets, foreigners must first buy U.S. dollars. This drives up the (real) value of the dollar which causes trouble for U.S. competitiveness and leads to U.S. balance of trade deficits (McCulloch 1986).[4]

Our traditional mechanisms for dealing with macroeconomic fluctuations, both in formal or legal terms or in macroeconomic policy practice, have not been fully appropriate for dealing with these economic

---

4. For an argument that expected future deficits matter along with actual deficits for the competitiveness of the U.S. economy, see Feldstein (1986) and the perceptive comments that follow by Dornbusch (1986b) and Stockman (1986).

issues. The M-F model tells us that under flexible exchange rates, the twin tools of macroeconomic policy-making will have different effects on an open as compared to a closed economy; the efficacy of fiscal policy is weakened by the internationalization of our economy, while the influence of monetary policy is strengthened.[5] This has no impact on the thrust of the argument that follows. The decisions for these two policies are made in separate organizations with perhaps separate agendas; much has been written about the unhappiness of the Reagan White House with the tight money policy of the Volker-led Federal Reserve. It is precisely to withstand such a motivation to create a political business cycle that the Federal Reserve was separated from the executive branch. Yet this creates another set of problems. How does the American government coordinate policy instruments or harmonize policy targets? Separateness may be beneficial in the Federal Reserve–White House conflicts and may lead to inadequate social institutions in the context of dealing with outside events arising from economic internationalization.[6]

Another way of thinking about the same problem is to reflect on how economic internationalization has affected the relative position of our industries. In international economics, a longstanding concept is that of comparative advantage. Textbooks often illustrate the relative strength of two economies with examples that suggest a natural durability to these strengths. The student is presented with tables in which the United States exports wheat to England and receives cloth in return. The comparative advantage for the two countries lies in nature-given endowment differences, and we can imagine larger (relative) agricultural land endowments for the United States.

Once we get past these pedagogic devices and consider research on trade patterns, we are told that the United States has a comparative advantage in highly skilled labor or human capital. Problems of interpretation arise since one could seriously doubt that a country's "human capital" is primarily an intrinsic given. Few would hold to the natural endowment view, but would in fact implicitly if not explicitly argue for the influence of various social institutions in shaping a country's human capital endowment. These institutions could include both market and extramarket institutions.

In the market category one could list specific factors such as pri-

5. Sachs (1980) has shown that, by altering the wage-price assumptions of the M-F model, the policy implications can be reversed.

6. Frankel (1988) studies the interaction of a fiscal authority and a monetary authority in a game theoretic framework. He argues that policy coordination need not be welfare enhancing if there is model uncertainty.

vately borne costs of parenting that create incentives for smaller families. Greater educational diversity, better response to career needs by schools, and sufficient private returns on human capital through moderate tax rates are part of a market-shaped skill acquisition system. In the nonmarket category one could list values parents have for their children's achievement or per capita success rather than numbers of children grants and other mechanisms to ensure access to education for qualified youth, and social influence redounding to those who work hard.

The point we want to emphasize here is that international competitiveness of a country's industries depends on not just some immutable or exogenous endowments as suggested by the textbook exposition of the comparative advantage concept. Rather, the international competitiveness of a country's industries depend on what we will call its competitive advantage. The simplistic "equation" we have in mind is competitive advantage equals comparative advantage plus the influences of social institutions and public policy choices.[7] The social institutions do, of course, include the scope of influence ascribed to the market as well as a variety of institutions that are extramarket, and some institutions that are neither obviously market or nonmarket. An example of the latter is the "macroeconomic policy framework" that could range from a highly market dependent approach to one with numerous interventions to stabilize a country's exchange rate relative to key trading partners (McKinnon 1987; Dornbusch 1986a). The macroeconomic policy framework could seek the development of transnational economic control mechanisms.

A Schematic Representation of the Social Institutions Approach to the Economy

It is assumed that there are basic or pure economic functions such as production, exchange, and investment that all societies must carry out. The way in which they are carried out is shaped by social institutions. These basic functions are the economic process or operation of the economy and can be thought of as having several levels of aggregation. The reason for aggregating is to achieve simplicity in characterizing system behavior, but at times this can obscure dispersion in outcomes at the microlevel and can lead to overlooking the individual choices that shape the overall outcomes.

A schematic representation is sketched out in fig. 1. The economic

---

7. An interesting case study on the shaping of competitive advantage is provided by Borrus, Tyson, and Zysman (1986) in their study of the Japanese and American semiconductor industries.

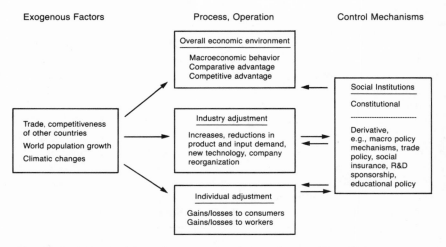

Fig. 1.   Social institutions and economic processes: An overview of linkages

process in the center has to operate in a changing environment. External or exogenous factors such as new trade patterns, competitiveness of other countries, or world population growth can influence what the economic system has to deal with. The way in which the system operates and responds depends on the control mechanisms in place. These control mechanisms are social institutions (represented on the right side of fig. 1).

Some social institutions are of the constitutional variety. For the United States, markets, the voting process, and bicameral legislature are seen as long-lasting institutions that provide continuity and are regarded as capable of implementing more specialized institutional structures suited to dealing with particular problems of economic organization. These are high-level institutions within which individuals or groups of individuals formulate specific control mechanisms. In response to occupational health hazards and to increased income risk arising from the transition to a manufacturing economy, specialized institutional structures using elements from the market and government control mechanisms were developed. In the second case, a quasi-market system of unemployment insurance was put in place in the United States.

A choice problem arises: which type of social institutions can best deal with a given type of problem? This is the paramount policy research question in the social sciences and it arises in a variety of different shapes in economics. A good deal of controversy centers on the efficiency of the market (M) versus the government (G). Is the market a sufficient institution to provide the optimal level of industrial R&D? When the government sponsors basic R&D to what extent should they rely on marketlike competition among the applicants?[8]

In contrast to the aforementioned examples of unemployment insurance and occupational health systems, it has been argued by Reich (1983) that a failing of the United States is to portray *G* and *M* as polar choices, as two separate cultures. In his particular version of the conflict, we in the United States are seen to believe that *M* is the control mechanism designed to create the most rapid and sustained economic growth, while *G* is largely regarded as a control mechanism to provide a fairer distribution of economic gains.[9] The failure of the United States in its shaping of social institutions is based on a blindness to the need of having *M* and *G* as complementary control mechanisms. In competition with societies not sharing the belief that *M* and *G* are substitutes, the United States is losing ground. Properly designed control mechanisms based on a blend of *M* and *G* are believed to provide these other countries with a competitive advantage, particularly for certain leading or strategic industries that are seen as heavily dependent on the choice of control mechanisms for their vitality.

Beyond the *M* or *G* controversy there is a host of more specialized questions of how to shape control mechanisms that will lead to better economic performance. It is claimed that in the area of entrepreneurship the United States has developed a type of social capital from the prior successful market operation of firms. This capital is now obsolete. Specifically, management "style" in the United States is said to be characterized by an excessive separation of strategic planning from industry-specific and process technology knowledge (Hayes and Wheelwright 1984). As a consequence, U.S. managers are seen as industrial dilettantes who are unable to compete internationally with their more knowledgeable counterparts abroad. Supposing this is true, the question arises as to the choice of the proper new set of control mechanisms. One answer is that the market itself will lead to appropriate changes in management; and since the evolution of institutions is being shaped by the pursuit of individual self-interest, the outcome will be efficient and optimal. All opportunities for mutually advantageous trades will have been

---

8. This question of *M* versus *G* is more than just a microeconomic concern. It is at the heart of the so-called Keynesian-monetarist controversy over the appropriateness of government macroeconomic stabilization policy.

9. Other versions of the conflict between "public action" and "private purpose" are developed by Hirschman (1981) and Schlesinger (1986). Brinkley (1986) provides a thoughtful essay on the "cycles" theory of American history.

exhausted. A striking and controversial example of this is the emergence of corporate raiders and merger specialists.

One interpretation is that evolving and specialized market-based institutions are forcing changes in U.S. management style. Previously, managers had their decisions insulated from the wishes of equity holders, but with an emergence of new financial markets, managerial discretion has been circumscribed through corporate takeover and reorganization. The threat of takeover forces firms to be run more effectively with closer attention to longer term profitability; it is argued that this will create U.S. firms more capable of dealing with international competition. Others have argued to the contrary, claiming that those institutions have evolved due to changes in the rules of the game made by the American government. In 1981, new owners of firms were allowed to take large accelerated depreciation write-offs based on the value of the firms' assets set by the buyers' own purchase price. Large subsidies were given to firms for takeovers employing borrowed money. The role of the state in creating the "playing field" thus complicates the argument that institutions necessarily evolve "optimally;" new institutional arrangements need not be Pareto efficient. Perhaps these evolving institutions encourage "paper entrepreneurs" and exactly those business dilettantes who are seeking short-term gain. It is the development of these institutions that will leave our industries further exposed to international competition. Longer-term banking relations, which play a larger role in Europe and Japan, will better support firms, it is argued, and will lead to a competitive advantage over U.S. firms.

The example of corporate takeovers again draws out important questions. How important are international differences in social institutions in shaping the relative competitive positions of industries? How do we know which social institutions are likely to have particular effects on industrial growth? What methods of implementation are best? Do our constitutional elements provide a framework for implementing desirable changes in social institutions of a more specialized variety?

U.S. Social Institutions and International Competition

General Issues

Macroeconomic institutions and policy choices are regarded by some as sufficient instruments of control to deal with the effects of the internationalization action of goods and financial markets. If resource allocation decisions are made through market processes, it is argued that "proper" macroeconomic policy will be sufficient to reveal the comparative advantage of the United States and no further detailed intervention is required to achieve our best growth path. The case for free trade is a simple one. It abstracts from macroeconomic issues like exchange rate swings and unemployment and runs something like this: international trade is a process by which goods that are relatively cheap in our country can be exchanged for goods that are relatively expensive for us to produce at home (or, put another way, goods that are relatively cheap for the foreign country to produce). We can determine which goods we should produce and which goods we should trade for (and thus not produce), thereby allocating our resources efficiently, by simply looking at the relative prices revealed by the marketplace. Hence, new and detailed intervention is seen as a barrier to effective uses of resources from a U.S. point of view because it will distort the signals sent to the marketplace for guiding the production process.[10] If macroeconomic policy decisions are made "properly" then the microeconomic trade mechanism should be relied upon to determine trade patterns. This argument has been advanced by both Robert Lawrence (1984) and Charles Schultze (1983) of the Brookings Institution.

In this perspective, our constitutional social institutions are seen as sufficiently robust and as enabling more detailed changes in control mechanisms to deal with exogenous factors influencing the overall economy, its specific industries, and individuals associated with these industries. What Lawrence and Schultze are further claiming is that existing, detailed social institutions shaped by the political process are, for the most part, adequate for the task at hand and that the market-based social institutions necessary to cope with change will evolve on their own, without resort to significant choices through political processes.

In more recent work (Lawrence and Litan 1986), there is an identification of some supplementary changes that are seen as necessary in conjunction with the operation of markets and macroeconomic policy. These include an expanded role for institutions that provide an insurance function, including subsidized retraining and financial compensation for income losses arising from trade. The argument is in fact about the efficacy of social institutions in shaping the economy. Lawrence (1984) is simply claiming that existing institutions are, for the most part, ade-

---

10. It is rarely pointed out that foreign distortions need not imply the need for retaliatory action by the domestic economy. Suppose that foreigners subsidize their computer chip industry and are capable of selling their chips below the price of the domestic industry. The "rational" action by the domestic economy is to accept the cheap chips as a gift from abroad due to inefficient resource allocation there. We should change our production plans given our knowledge of their gift. The case for free trade given imperfect competition requires a more subtle line of argument. See Grossman 1986 and Dixit 1986.

quate. Even his quarrel over the direction of macroeconomic events is one mostly over macroeconomic *policy choices* rather than the *choice of institutions* that control macroeconomic conditions. This is akin to saying the elements of an auto's design are adequate and integrated; if only the driver would head the right way there would be no problem! Lawrence and Litan (1986) propose some design changes, though quite circumscribed.

There are other assessments of needed institutional change that focus on a single area. Among business authors there are those who argue that management style is the primary source of U.S. weaknesses. Education and advancement of managers is claimed to have selected and reinforced decision makers who are unconcerned about and unaware of process technology and manufacturing techniques (Hayes and Wheelwright 1984). Changes in management style can take place within existing constitutional institutions but may require fairly major social change, involving changes in promotional and incentive structures within businesses, new forms of training of managers, and changes in the form of organizations.

One specific charge is that the corporate form identified as the M-form (Chandler 1962), which was well suited to the U.S. when our industries had a technological lead and could control world markets, may be dysfunctional as we compete globally for leadership in newly evolving technologies. The management style identified by Chandler involved profit centers of activity sponsored by a corporate financing and strategic core. While this structure provides some flexibility of operation within the profit center, it is seen as creating a gap between specific knowledge of product and industrial technology on one hand and planning and resource commitments on the other.

From a market perspective it is easy to argue that although changes to a new and more innovative management style could be important, these may be accomplished without involving the political process in a major way. Just as the M-form was copied by competitors when it appeared to be successful, alternative styles of organization better suited to the current environment can be identified and adopted. Market pressures can shape the transformation of management, and many argue that corporate raiding represents just such a market pressure.

The proponents of "industrial policy" are often those who see a need for more wide-ranging changes in our social institutions in order to achieve sustained economic growth. In terms of our schematic representation (fig. 1), they often see a need for changes at the constitutional level as well as at more detailed levels. As discussed above, one argument is that a high-level synthesis of market and governmental processes is necessary to create a competitive advantage for U.S. industry (Reich 1983). The belief is that the social institutions of Japan and Europe, lacking confrontation between the market and the government, are better able to coordinate interindustry relations than their U.S. counterparts. In particular, it can be argued that Japan uses not the blunt instruments of government directives, nationalization, or guaranteed subsidies, but rather organizations staffed by skilled people who formulate broader incentives aimed at accelerating the growth of industries that have a longer-term strategic position. Moreover, Japan has other, complementary social institutions and policy choices that, it is argued, create an overall environment far more favorable to industry than that in the United States.[11]

The agenda of others advocating industrial policy differs from that of Reich, but a common element is a belief that existing social institutions need to be changed significantly and that the necessary changes can be identified. From a business perspective, the changes sometimes involve a diminished scope for government or a simplification of legal structures and regulatory activity. The business perspective on industrial policy is often quite interventionist (President's Commission on Industrial Competitiveness 1985) and can be observed to embrace fairly major changes in diverse social institutions not immediately connected to the market.

Consonant with our argument in the first section of this essay, most changes in U.S. social institutions are seen as ex post facto ways to remedy problems. Little thinking is done in which anticipation of future possibilities is central and in which design of social institutions for coping with contingencies is the objective. In the United States our approach is to rely on a few durable constitutional elements and specify detailed extensions or changes on an ex post facto basis. Also consonant with our argument is the important role of explicit and implicit international comparison of social institutions in terms of market consequences. Those institutions believed better suited to improving our relative industrial strength are regarded as having value in this debate. A clear weakness is that nonmarket outcomes may also be shaped by social institutions, and

---

11. Saxonhouse (1983) has argued that little of the explanation of differences between Japan and the United States rests on differences in social institutions or deliberate industrial policy. Much of the difference in recent performances of U.S. and Japanese industry is argued to rest on endowment differences relating to natural resources and shipping costs. One area in which the two countries differ, namely savings rates, can be argued to be of less significance with the internationalization of credit markets. High savings rates in Japan can finance new ventures in the United States. For a contrary opinion emphasizing the value of Japanese industrial policy, see Yamamura 1986.

this makes the choices all the more difficult. For example, even if the American legal system is seen as an impediment to economic growth, it may still provide due process, which can be valued in its own right.

Specific Areas

Discussion of the impacts of international trade includes labor market adjustments. There are several mechanisms for dealing with job and income risk arising in an economy with a labor force specialized into different occupational and industrial categories. The basic idea is that through specialization and intracountry trade an economy can achieve a larger output. There is a cost to such specialization and this cost is the income risk arising from changes in technology and differential success of different firms and regional industries. International trade leads to greater specialization with added output gains but also to greater income risk, since it creates the possibility of exchange between economic regions with more diversity in natural endowments and greater diversity in social institutions.[12]

A diverse set of social institutions designed to deal with income risk includes education, social insurance, and geographic mobility. Education can provide people with general skills that can be utilized in many different labor market specialties. In the United States we have chosen to emphasize general skills and geographic mobility rather than employment stability in a given company or labor market specialty. We have also chosen to emphasize income recovery (such as unemployment insurance) rather than retraining.[13] To illustrate, at a peak in 1979 we spent 1

---

12. In an interesting paper, Eaton and Grossman (1985) model international trade as a process that risk averse individuals participate in. They demonstrate that free trade may not be optimal for an economy when the terms of trade are uncertain and when markets for contingent futures contracts are incomplete. See also Newbery and Stiglitz 1984 and Dixit 1987.

13. To have chosen income recovery over job retraining, policymakers must at least implicitly assume that their economy suffers the affliction of business cycles, that deviations from full employment are only temporary and not manifestations of some structural change. We think of this as the introductory-macroeconomics-textbook-vision-of-the-world where real GNP fluctuates over time along a trend line. Is the textbook vision of the world factually accurate? The statistical analog to this question is, "Does the time series representation of real GNP have a unit root?" Research by Nelson and Plosser (1982) and Campbell and Mankiw (1986) suggests that the textbook's worldview is inaccurate. But Evans (1986) finds results inconsistent with a unit root for real GNP after modifying Campbell and Mankiw's methodology.

percent of GNP on labor market policy in comparison to 3 percent of GNP for Sweden and 2 percent for Germany. The largest share of our resources was for income recovery rather than for retraining (Eliasson, Holmhund, and Stafford 1982).

As trade has expanded, have the dislocations of labor increased in frequency and in magnitude of earnings losses? This question is given various answers, but in general it appears that the magnitude of earnings losses have increased. Examining the earnings losses in Buffalo, New York, and Providence, Rhode Island, for 1960, it was found that earnings losses (Jacobson 1984) were a good deal smaller than those for autoworkers displaced from employment in 1980–82 (McAlinden 1986). Other studies have shown some erosion of the earnings of those in the middle range of the income distribution. Other research shows significant wage reductions for unskilled workers in manufacturing industries exposed to international competition (Heywood 1986). Although there is not ironclad evidence to indicate larger earnings losses, there is some, and it has motivated a number of policy changes.

Trade adjustment assistance can be seen as an extension of a well-established U.S. approach to labor market adjustment. Despite its numerous problems, including the question of whether the person's job loss was trade-related and why this should be different from a job loss for other reasons, it can be argued that the policy was put in place because it was part of a larger set of U.S. social institutions established to deal with job loss in this way. Namely, short-term income recovery is an appropriate government function, but location of a new skill or geographic location is seen as the individual's responsibility.

To tie this discussion into one of our main themes of international competitiveness, the efficacy of job loss systems can affect our competitive advantage. If persons contemplating a potentially fruitful but risky labor market specialization are not covered by quality insurance or retraining mechanisms, they will stay away from such endeavors even though this may be part of a rational international division of labor. On the other hand, social insurance mechanisms that subsidize unwarranted risks will lead to our country overspecializing in lines of business that are risky but simply do not provide an expected payoff justifying such risks. In short, well-designed social policy derived from parent social institutions is an essential ingredient in effecting an international division of labor. It is beyond the scope of this essay, but a detailed study of our social institutions and policies as they facilitate an optimal level of risk taking seems an important area of our international competitiveness. While a good theoretical perspective on this issue is available (Varian

1980), little has been done at the applied level addressing the issue in the context of international trade.[14]

Technology based industries are heavily shaped by social institutions. No one argues that the U.S. leadership in semiconductors is based on our natural endowment of silica! The global siting of the industry is seen to be heavily dependent on differences in countries' wage rates, but wages alone are certainly not sufficient to explain much of the international differences in scale of the industry. The main factors are seen to be the strength of certain basic sciences as embodied in geographically defined research centers, venture capital markets and entrepreneurial incentives, and strategic effects of industrial learning.

The basic research foundations of the industry started in the United States in an environment that was only weakly shaped by the market: Bell Labs (run from ample revenues prior to the deregulation of the telephone system) and the Department of Defense. Design was motivated by technical goals to be achieved rather than eventual market payoff. This aspect of the industry is similar to other U.S. export successes. Modern aircraft and computers were designed with technological objectives and were funded using nonmarket criteria. Later the private sector realized the payoff and developed these industries.[15] For those who argue that the market is a sufficient social institution for economic growth, there should be some embarrassment that the leading export sectors of the U.S. have nonmarket institutions shaping much of their embryonic development (Nelson 1984).

It seems clear, though, that the financial markets of the U.S. are pretty effective at getting resources to ventures that are risky but promise high returns. The kind of organizations being financed in this way have been extremely diverse, ranging from start-up firms in electronics to industrial giants like Boeing and Lockheed. Also, large traditional firms have established venture capital divisions for the purpose of entertaining proposals for highly speculative investments. Neither of these sources of funds became available to the failing or near-failing complex technology-based firms like Lockheed or Chrysler. Their financial straits raised more difficult questions than the immediate, "where will loan money come

---

14. There is some scattered research on international differences in wage and income insurance offered in the private sector. For example, Freeman and Weitzman (1986) have studied the influence of the Japanese bonus system and wage flexibility on unemployment.

15. Another example is the development of the machine vision industry. Here the basic research was sponsored as part of an effort to evaluate images of the earth's surface obtained from satellites. Later this technology was seen as an important link in flexible automation systems. At that point, the private sector sponsored a host of new firms that sprang up like mushrooms after a fall rain.

from?" or the prospective, "why will large firms rather than small firms receive government aid?"

In the case of large firms, there are complex systems of property rights that are only partly explicit. For example, when the government intervened on behalf of Chrysler in order to preserve a large number of American jobs, it was implicitly conferring upon certain workers a right to their jobs. This is not a right enumerated in any contract or law. Has the government then enacted a transfer of property rights from owners to workers? If Chrysler decides to close many of its American plants and move its operation to Korea, will these selfsame workers' property rights have been abrogated?

For large firms with venture-specific human and physical capital there can be problems which have the character of those in a longstanding marriage. Consider again the situation Chrysler found itself in during the late 1970s. When Chrysler's creditors demanded payments and Chrysler could not pay, some creditors—those legally first in line—planned to seize Chrysler's venture-specific physical capital and sell it at a loss for scrap. This action not only would have ruined Chrysler's productive future, but it also would have deprived Chrysler's other creditors of their chance of repayment. Here is where the government was capable of playing the role of marriage counselor.[16] An effective marriage counselor is one who achieves a compromise in the sacrifice by the partners to the "agreement," such that they are better off under the agreement than through separation and feel sufficient fairness in the solution to cooperate thenceforth. The question of social institutions here is about which ones can best provide these functions. Some argue that a relational contract that provides a few basic guidelines for resolution is superior to either a classical or neoclassical contract that attempts to enumerate the resolution of contingencies (Pollack 1985).[17] The reasoning is very similar to our distinction between constitutional and specialized social institutions and the strengths of the former.

From the perspective of sponsoring mature technology-based firms, do societies committed to the use of classical or neoclassical contracts and no third party interference have better industrial performance than those willing to use relational contracting and even ad hoc intervention

---

16. For a more detailed view of the Chrysler experience, see Stafford and Ehrbar 1985, which can profitably be read in conjunction with the present essay.

17. Here we can define a classical contract as one that specifies what will take place contingent on all possible events. A neoclassical contract specifies a particular resolution system (e.g., arbitrator) for disputes arising as the consequence of certain types of contingencies.

by government? The experience of Great Britain is emphasized by some as sufficient evidence of the weakness of relational contracting and government intervention. On the other hand, the industrial history of Japan shows instances of government intervention to support high technology firms which were subsequently successful. While British Leyland is offered as evidence of those supporting market-defined classical contracts, one could point to the role of relational contracting and government involvement in the case of Toyota and Mazda.

The limits of private, neoclassical contracts are at issue in three other elements of high technology firms: learning by doing, appropriability, and industry-wide scale economics. Learning by doing or the experience curve has been shown to be important in many technology-based industries (Hayes and Wheelwright 1984). In this case the firm with an initial lead on a new product can capture the returns necessary to motivate the investment and then some. In contrast to a situation where there is no learning by doing and where we have social institutions to protect innovators (such as patent laws), a situation of learning by doing may offer a country the opportunity to sponsor its infant industries to achieve a competitive position relative to incumbents.

Closely related to learning by doing is the question of technological appropriability. Instead of cumulative production experience as the barrier to new entrants, the case of technological appropriability is simply the case where the external firm cannot duplicate a product or process technology. The multinational corporation, based primarily in highly developed industrial economies, is seen as a market-based institution designed to capture the benefits of investment in such cases. In contrast to the infant industry case where subsidized production can be rationalized, here the government or other nonmarket entity is required to bargain for access to the technological secret. The United States has been argued to be backward on this score. On this assessment, we have lost out as a consequence of an asymmetry in which Japan insists on technology access in joint ventures of U.S. firms in Japan, but in which the United States uses market-based institutions that permit the choice of maintaining an appropriability barrier for joint ventures with Japanese firms in the United States (Reich and Mankin 1986).

Virtually all microeconomics textbooks show the possibility of long-run, downward-sloping supply curves and virtually all of these texts make some reference to industry-wide diversion of labor efficiencies in explaining the downward slope (Lipsey, Steiner, and Purvis 1986; Varian 1984).[18] Under these circumstances the actions of individual firms will not be

---

18. Ethier (1982) provides a theoretical justification for the claim that decreasing costs could be a rationale for protection policies.

sufficient to achieve cost reductions. If the relevant industry is defined within geographic boundaries or national borders, there would appear to be a role for nonmarket institutions that would coordinate the activities of the different firms. Some of this sort of activity is currently taking place in the U.S. auto industry where the largest firms realize the need for the restructuring of their supplier firms to be compatible with changes toward low-inventory, computer-controlled, flexible manufacturing.

Patterns of Business Practice and Policy Control Mechanisms in Selected Countries—What Works?

What institutional choices have the strong industrial nations made in the postwar period? What control mechanisms seem to have had a major impact on the success of the newly industrializing countries such as Taiwan and Brazil? In this section we present a stylized picture of what are believed to be the most salient institutional influences shaping the condition of selected postwar economies.

Both France and England have had a substantial influence of government ownership and control of industry. Although it has had its share of failures (most notably in the airframe and computer industries), most would judge France's performance to have been more successful. The French success appears to have been shaped by both a highly skilled bureaucracy and a targeting of industries that have substantial scale economies. Moreover these targeted industries are characterized by technologies that, while changing, have not had an abrupt or cataclysmic transformation; the industries that come to mind include automobiles, chemicals, nuclear power, and steel. The British experience has involved at least as great a role for the government, but unlike the French—and like the American—cultural tradition, the English question the legitimacy of their government's quite visible hand interfering in the marketplace. Perhaps this goes a long way toward explaining why, in place of a multitalented civil service, many of the high ranking positions in England are held by politicians with little engineering or other technical training. Concern about economic backwardness has occasionally led to halfhearted attempts at industrial policy. The failures of the automobile and nuclear power industries have forced the British government to scramble about after the fact searching for solutions. Apparently, the Band-Aid-like nature of these policies have led people who prefer nonintervention to almost continuous tinkering with these sectors as new problems arise. As Nelson (1984) aptly put it, "schizophrenic" describes British policies well.[19]

---

19. Other sources of weakness in the British economy have been identified by Hood and Young (1985).

There is a contrast between the French success in planning in more traditional manufacturing industries and their failure in some more recent ventures. The success in the auto industry can be contrasted with a succession of failures in electronics. According to Adams (1986), the difference can be explained by the difference in organizational structures required for the two kinds of industries. While large, stable bureaucracies can be compatible with success in heavy industry, smaller and more flexible structures are required for performance in what may be termed organizations of intangibles (Stafford 1987). In such firms, there is a strong connection between individual effort and success, but neither the product nor the process technology can bè unambiguously identified. Some of these organizations evolve into large, structured organizations but, it is difficult to identify the successes. The internal organizational structure is commonly beset with high costs of coordination that can be only partly offset by utilizing more resources for organizational design. When an industry's development is heavily dependent on firms with flexible structures, any use of centralized directions is likely to be ineffective.

Japan's postwar policy includes some of the successful outcomes of the French and some areas of achievement uniquely their own. During the 1950s and 1960s, Japan employed a substantial amount of planning to develop an infrastructure of basic industries such as shipping, steel, and chemicals (Tsurumi 1985). It is worth pointing out that this was essentially a period of catching up for Japan. During this time, the Japanese government searched the globe for useful technological innovations to feed its domestic industries. There were tight capital controls in place then; Japanese citizens, for instance, were unable to convert the yen into any foreign currency until 1964.[20] Again, up until 1964, tariff barriers were quite high, making the economy, for all intents and purposes, closed to most foreign competitors. It was in this environment that Japan nurtured its domestic firms until they were capable of competing internationally. As with France, a centralized planning bureaucracy (MITI) was used, and capital was channeled by centralized control to targeted industries via the Bank of Japan and a few other large banks. MITI also helped allocate foreign exchange to targeted industries so these industries could import raw materials and physical capital.

The first "winning" industry supported in this fashion was the shipbuilding industry. But when it became time for a different winner to be supported, the foreign exchange earned by the shipbuilders was funneled

---

20. Controls on external investment meant that the high Japanese savings rate made domestic physical capital accumulation easier.

to the auto industry. Most economists do not like the idea of picking "winning" industries. They argue that there is no reason a government should be able to pick the financial capital markets. Saxonhouse (1983) concluded that the funneling of capital through the Bank of Japan merely mimicked (albeit imperfectly) what a smoothly functioning equity market would have produced if such a market existed in Japan. It is easier to copy what the U.S. financial markets are up to than to pick winners blind and then aid them. But is a policy of aiding winners necessarily a bad thing? We have already pointed out that valid questions can be asked about whether the market can produce the optimal amount of R&D.[21]

A distinct difference between France and Japan appears to arise in the 1970s and 1980s.[22] In advanced electronics, Japan's instruments of control have included a striking variation on the French notion of indicative planning. Such planning is focused primarily on identifying the kinds of industries that could be successful and the needed set of supplier networks and technological resources. In some instances, favorable tax treatment and bargaining for access to foreign technology have been utilized.[23] These policies make sense for an industry dependent on organizations of intangibles. The policy is not to control firms directly, as in the French experience, but rather to provide financial incentives and technological access in industries where the future path of technology and organizational structure is highly uncertain. Another policy employed in Japan is the orderly scaling down of industries with contracting demand and labor displacement through improvements in process technology.

Newly industrialized countries such as Korea, Brazil, and Taiwan have utilized fairly significant doses of industrial planning similar to that employed by Japan in the 1950s and 1960s. Relatively few development

---

21. If one views the act of firms investing in R&D as the participation in a technology race replete with strategic interactions, then there is no longer an a priori case to be made for the market's solution. Indeed, it is well known that equilibria in such games may be inefficient and a government-aided market could be the best solution.

22. Certainly part of the change in Japanese policy is due to their tearing down of barriers to trade in both goods and financial assets. These actions have taken two powerful tools out of the Japanese arsenal. Another reason for change in Japan is the very success of their policies! Due to their success, many Japanese firms have accumulated sufficient retained earnings to break their dependence on the Bank of Japan.

23. According to Reich and Mankin 1985, joint ventures between Japan and the United States have been characterized by an asymmetry. Joint ventures in Japan have provided Japan with access to key technology while U.S. joint ventures have placed the United States in the position as the hinterland, with only assembly and marketing functions.

economists would attribute the success of these countries to a purely market-shaped environment, even though most would be willing to assign the use of markets a prominent role in their development. In terms of the approach set out earlier, the effectiveness of these countries' performance in international markets is heavily shaped by the choice of social institutions, which includes various extramarket institutions.

Perhaps the most significant policy choice has been an upgrading of educational levels, initiated by government policy. The educational upgrades are seen as more significant than access to international technology and the expertise of multinationals. Here the growth of the newly industrialized countries is seen to depend on bootstrap operations designed to create an infrastructure that complements the private sector's incentives rather than the consequence of importing technology or organizational structure from abroad. Korea, for example, has extended its educational program to include Ph.D. graduates as a method of access to high level technology. Currently the Ph.D. enrollment rate for Korea is the highest in the world.

This simplified picture illustrates how social institutions can influence economic performance. Much of it is drawn from studies that do not employ the usual methods of statistical evidence, so it is hard to know how to react to arguments that point out that since (1) Japan has an industrial policy and (2) is performing well economically, therefore (3) Japan's economic performance is due to its industrial policy and the United States should try to copy those policies. Clearly, (1) and (2) do not imply (3) under any system of logic. It is not even clear to some economists that Japan is better off than it would be otherwise due to MITI's policies. They argue that MITI tampers with comparative advantage, so life would be better in Japan if only MITI would cease and desist.

This seems to leave us in a position of being able to say nothing emphatic at all. Anecdotal evidence (look at Japan's economic performance) leads us in one direction while an article of faith (the marketplace works magic) leads us in another. Without an analytical framework for institutions, it is difficult to know how to evaluate these competing claims. We conjecture that a social insurance framework of intervention and institutions could be developed. Such a framework (parallel to Arrow's work on medical insurance [Arrow 1963]) would further our understanding of both what a government does and under what conditions a government should act. While this line of research develops, many hypotheses about institutions can be tested by gathering data on industrial performance at the level of industry for different countries and through time.

In some cases a wide range of established and newly industrialized countries have comparable definitions of the variables necessary to study the effects of wage rates or of such policy choices as tax laws. The effects of social institutions are difficult to assess at the constitutional level, but the more detailed or derivative policies and choices flowing from the constitutional mechanisms can be studied in more traditional ways, even though some of the questions seem very difficult to address. For example, do corporate mergers and raiding help or hinder the industries involved? Raiding may occur only in a few countries and may take place as a consequence of financial difficulties. If so, one has the problem of estimating a model in which raiding is endogenous (a function of both social institutions and industry conditions), and its influence must be identified in light of various other factors likely to influence the time path of the performance of the targeted firms.

In thinking about the influence of other social institutions, it appears that the required research is challenging, but not more difficult than attempting a study of the influence of macroeconomic policy on a country's business cycle. The study of social institutions as they influence economic performance needs to go beyond its current state, which uses casual comparisons, to the use of recognized methods of hypothesis testing. Only then can we have valid answers to the question of what works.

REFERENCES

Adams, James and Christian Stoffaes. 1986. *French Industrial Policy.* Washington, D.C.: Brookings Institution.
Arrow, Kenneth J. 1963. "Uncertainty and the Welfare Economics of Medical Care." *American Economic Review,* 53:941–70.
Borrus, Michael, Laura D'Andrea Tyson, and John Zysman. 1986. "Creating Advantage: How Government Policies Shape International Trade in the Semiconductor Industry." In *Strategic Trade Policy and the New International Economics*, ed. Paul R. Krugman. Cambridge, Mass.: MIT Press.
Brinkley, Alan. 1986. "Conflict and Consensus." *New Republic* 195(13): 28–31.
Campbell, John, and N. Gregory Mankiw. 1986. "Are Output Fluctuations Transitory?" Working Paper no. 1916. Washington, D.C.: National Bureau of Economic Research.
Chandler, Alfred Dupont. 1962. *Strategy and Structure: Chapters in the History of the American Industrial Enterprise.* Cambridge, Mass.: MIT Press.
Dixit, Avinash. 1986. "Trade Policy: An Agenda for Future Research." In *Strategic Trade Policy and the New International Economics*, ed. Paul R. Krugman. Cambridge, Mass.: MIT Press.
_____. 1987. "Trade and Insurance with Moral Hazard." *Journal of International Economics,* 23(3): 201–20.

Dornbusch, Rudiger. 1986a. *Dollars, Debts and Deficits.* Cambridge, Mass.: MIT Press.

———. 1986b. "Comment on Martin Feldstein." In *NBER Macroeconomics Annual 1986*, ed. Stanley Fischer. Cambridge, Mass.: MIT Press.

Eaton, Jonathan, and Gene Grossman. 1985. "Tariffs as Insurance: Optimal Commercial Policy When Domestic Markets Are Incomplete." *Canadian Journal of Economics* 18(2): 258–72.

Eliason, Gunnar, Bertil Holmlund, and Frank Stafford. 1982. *Studies in Labor Market Behavior: Sweden and the United States.* Stockholm: Industrial Institute for Social and Economic Research.

Ethier, Wilfred J. 1982. "Decreasing Costs in International Trade and Frank Graham's Argument for Protection." *Econometrica* 50(5): 1243–68.

Evans, George. 1986. "Output and Unemployment Dynamics in the United States: 1950–1985." Stanford University. Typescript.

Feldstein, Martin. 1986. "The Budget Deficit and the Dollar." In *NBER Macroeconomics Annual 1986,* ed. Stanley Fischer. Cambridge, Mass.: MIT Press.

Fleming, J. Marcus. 1962. "Domestic Financial Policies under Fixed and under Floating Exchange Rates." *IMF Staff Papers*, November.

Frankel, Jeffrey. 1988. "The Implications of Conflicting Models for Coordination between Monetary and Fiscal Policymakers." In *Empirical Macroeconomics for Interdependent Economies,* ed. Ralph C. Bryant et al. Washington, D.C.: Brookings Institution.

Freeman, Richard, and Martin Weitzman. 1986. "Bonuses and Employment in Japan." Working Paper no. 1878. Washington, D.C.: National Bureau of Economic Research

Grossman, Gene. 1986. "Strategic Export Promotion: A Critique." In *Strategic Trade Policy and the New International Economics,* ed. Paul R. Krugman. Cambridge, Mass.: MIT Press.

Halevy, Elie. 1928. *The Growth of Philosophic Radicalism.* New York: Macmillan Company.

Hayes, Robert, and Stephen Wheelwright. 1984. *Restoring Our Competitive Edge.* New York: John Wiley and Sons.

Heywood, John S. 1986. "Product Market Structure and the Labor Market." Ph.D diss. University of Michigan.

Hirschman, Albert. 1981. *Shifting Involvements.* Princeton, N.J.: Princeton University Press.

Hood, Neil, and Stephen Young. 1985. "The United Kingdom and the Changing Economic World Order." In *Revitalizing American Industry,* ed. Milton Hochmuth and William Davidson. Cambridge, Mass.: Ballinger.

Jacobson, Louis. 1984. "A Tale of Employment Decline in Two Cities: How Bad Was the Worst of Times?" *Industrial and Labor Relations Review* 37(4): 557–69.

Lawrence, Robert Z. 1984. *Can America Compete?* Washington, D.C.: Brookings Institution.

Lawrence, Robert Z., and Robert E. Litan. 1986. *Saving Free Trade.* Washington, D.C.: Brookings Institution.

Lipsey, Richard G., Peter O. Steiner, and Douglas D. Purvis. 1988. *Economics*, 8th ed. New York: Harper and Row.

McAlinden, Sean P. 1986. "Economic Losses of Laid-off Auto Workers." Ph.D. diss. University of Michigan.

McCulloch, Rachel. 1986. "Macroeconomic Policy and Trade Performance: International Implications of U.S. Budget Deficits." University of Wisconsin. Typescript.

McKinnon, Ronald J. 1987. "Monetary and Exchange Rate Policies for International Financial Stability: A Proposal." Stanford University. Typescript.

Matthews, R. C. O. 1986. "The Economics of Institutions and the Sources of Growth." *Economics Journal* 96:903-18.

Mundell, Robert A. 1968. *International Economics.* New York: Macmillan Publishing Company.

Nelson, Charles L., and Charles R. Plosser. 1982. "Trends and Random Walks in Macroeconomic Time Series: Some Evidence and Implications." *Journal of Monetary Economics* 10(2): 129-62.

Nelson, Richard R. 1984. *High Technology Policy.* Washington, D.C.: American Enterprise Institute.

Newbery, David, and Joseph Stiglitz. 1984. "Pareto Inferior Trade." *Review of Economic Studies* 51(1): 1-12.

Pollack, Robert. 1986. "A Transaction Cost Approach to Families and Households." *Journal of Economic Literature* 23(2): 581-608.

President's Commission on Industrial Competitiveness. 1985. "Global Competition: The New Reality: The Report of the President's Commission on Industrial Competitiveness." Document no. PR40.8:C73/G51/vol. 1-2. Washington, D.C.: January.

Reich, Robert B. 1983. *The Next American Frontier.* New York: Times Books.

Reich, Robert B. and Ed Mankin. 1986. "Joint Ventures with Japan Give Away Our Future." *Harvard Business Review* 65(2): 78-86.

Robinson, Malcolm. 1986. "International Monetary Policy Games: Some Approaches and Applications." University of Michigan. Typescript.

Sachs, Jeffrey. 1980. "Wages, Flexible Exchange Rates and Macro-Economic Policy." *Quarterly Journal of Economics* 94(4): 731-47.

Saxonhouse, Gary. 1983. "What Is All This about Industrial Targeting in Japan?" *World Economy,* September.

Schlesinger, Arthur M., Jr. 1986. *The Cycles of American History.* Boston: Houghton Mifflin.

Schultze, Charles. 1983. "Industrial Policy: A Dissent." *Brookings Review,* Fall.

Stafford, Frank. 1987. "Organizational Theory and the Nature of Jobs." *Journal of Institutional and Theoretical Economics* 143(4): 519-36.

Stafford, Frank, and Hans Ehrbar. 1985. "What Can Be Learned from the

Chrysler Experience?" Institute of Science and Technology, University of Michigan. Working paper.

Stockman, Alan. 1986. "Comment on Martin Feldstein." In *NBER Macroeconomics Annual 1986,* ed. Stanley Fischer. Cambridge, Mass.: MIT Press.

Tsurumi, Yoshi. 1985. "Japan's Challenge to the United States." In *Revitalizing American Industry,* ed. Milton Hochmuth and William Davidson. Cambridge, Mass.: Ballinger.

Whalley, John. 1980. "Discriminating Features of Domestic Factor Taxes in a Goods Mobile-Factors Immobile Trade Model: An Empirical General Equilibrium Approach." *Journal of Political Economy,* 88(6): 1177–1202.

Varian, Hal. 1980. "Redistributive Taxation as Social Insurance." *Journal of Public Economics,* 14(1): 49–68.

Varian, Hal. 1984. *Micro Economic Analysis.* 2d ed. New York: W. W. Norton.

Yamamura, Kozo. 1986. "Caveat Emptor: The Industrial Policy of Japan." In *Strategic Trade Policy and the New International Economics,* ed. Paul R. Krugman. Cambridge, Mass.: MIT Press.

CHAPTER 6

Relations between Organizations: Institutions, Self-interest, and Congressional Oversight Behavior in the United States

Joel D. Aberbach

Institutional Design, Individual Motives, and Congressional Oversight Behavior: An Overview

The prevention of tyranny was a major goal of those who designed U.S. governmental institutions. Based on the assumption that human beings naturally act in their own self-interest, the Founders devised a system where ambition would be made to counteract ambition. Through a system of different constituency bases and overlapping functions, office-holders would check one another in what was to be "a harmonious system of mutual frustration."[1]

The bureaucracy was not an overt part of this system because the Founders did not foresee a substantial administrative component for the new government. However, a large administrative state developed in the twentieth century, with special impetus from the New Deal, World War II, and the postwar period of world power and a maturing welfare state. As the administrative state grew in size and importance, the question of its control also loomed larger and larger.

Initially, the president was given major new responsibilities for coordinating and controlling the growing bureaucracies of the government, and his influence increased accordingly. However, this led to concern that Congress was losing its influence, especially vis-à-vis policy and its administration (increasingly seen as intertwined). Part of this concern

This essay is drawn from a draft of the concluding chapter of my Brookings Institution book entitled *Keeping A Watchful Eye: The Politics of Congressional Oversight* (1989). I would like to acknowledge financial support from the National Science Foundation (Grant Nos. SES 78–16812 and SES 80–23315) and the Academic Senate of the University of California. Special thanks to Sylvia Goodwin who typed the manuscript.

1. Richard Hofstadter as quoted in Burns 1963, 22.

was registered in the complaint that oversight of the large bureaucracy is "Congress' neglected function," i.e., that it is not done or, when done, it is uncoordinated, unsystematic, sporadic, and usually informal, with members of Congress (or groups of members on narrowly based committee units) seeking particularistic influence or publicity for purposes of reelection. Members of Congress neglect oversight, say such scholars as John Bibby, Seymour Scher, and Morris Ogul, because they have few incentives to do it (Bibby 1968; Scher 1963; Ogul 1976). There are more payoffs from other activities. And when they do oversee, they do it sporadically, for the quick payoff, usually with little long-term significance.

In this incentives-based view, any stirrings of more intensive oversight behavior will be transitory. As Ogul said in describing the surge of oversight activity in the early 1970s during the Nixon administration: "These stirrings . . . should be viewed more as a transitory phenomenon than as the first step toward an enduring pattern of vigorous legislative oversight" (1976, 199).

A closely related, recently elaborated perspective on congressional oversight behavior, although portraying Congress in a much stronger position vis-à-vis the executive, sees Congress as mainly responding to "fires" (complaints or scandals) (see McCubbins and Schwartz 1984). Rather than actively seeking evidence of how programs are working, let alone evidence about program effectiveness or about the role of programs in the broader context of government, Congress sits back and waits for information to come to it. Proponents of this "fire alarm" strategy say that it is rational and effective, using easy and efficient means of gathering information and checking on the bureaucracy. Congress receives information on administration and policy from the environment and acts on it in a manner that serves the interest of relevant members (committee members or individuals doing casework for their constituents). Hence its emphasis on solving constituents' problems, reacting to scandal, and seeking publicity; its preference for informal contact with administrators; and its very limited use of formal oversight mechanisms; such as hearings, except in unusual cases such as scandals where substantial publicity can be secured.

The explanations put forth for the dominance of these types of behaviors, like those put forth by Bibby, Scher, and Ogul, stress congressional incentives in the American system — representatives are cast as entrepreneurs seeking reelection and influence, while operating in a weak party, independent institution. Time is better, more effectively, and more efficiently spent in responding to complaints brought to the attention of Congress by constituents and interest groups rather than in formal oversight procedures such as hearings or in an active search for information about programs and policies. This accounts for both the sporadic formal oversight activity and the intensive, usually informal, and overwhelmingly reactive particularistic oversight activity.

In essence, both those who feel that oversight has been a sadly neglected function of the Congress in the era of the administrative state and those who argue that oversight, if properly understood and recognized, is common and effective both seem to agree on certain basic facts. (1) Formal oversight activities are uncommon. (2) Informal activities that play some role in tracking administrative behavior are more common (although I should note that Ogul firmly believes that even adding what he calls "latent" oversight to the "manifest" oversight considered by most scholars still leaves unaltered the intermittent and noncomprehensive character of the performance of the function) (Ogul 1976, 180). (3) Congressional behavior in the oversight area (as in others) is best explained by the incentives experienced by members of Congress. Reelection-seeking political entrepreneurs spend their time and resources on activities yielding the most payoff, and the cost-benefit ratio of much of what we think of as oversight behavior is low relative to the alternatives. Therefore, formal activities (such as oversight hearings) that involve an active orientation to review of administration and policy have a low priority, and much of what is learned about administration and policy is a function of passive (reactive) information gathering by Congress or is a byproduct of endeavors undertaken for other purposes (oversight that is "latent" in other activities, to use Ogul's term) (Ogul 1976, 153–180).

There is disagreement among these scholars about the effectiveness of the congressional oversight behavior observed. And even those who believe that the oversight done is effective in monitoring (and influencing) administration and policy disagree about whether it is rational for the system as a whole.[2] There is agreement, however, that the pattern of oversight behavior observed is individually rational. Most legislators are purposive; they respond to the incentives presented to them by their environment. No amount of wishing or pontificating about what ought to be done can significantly change this.[3] From this basic notion comes

---

2. For example, contrast Morris Fiorina (1979, 124–42) with McCubbins and Schwartz (1984). Fiorina is much more skeptical.

3. See the interchange between Richard Fenno and Representative John Culver in U.S. Congress 1973, 15–16. Culver was distressed by the fact that academics stuck to the realpolitik notion that oversight was infrequent because of the lack of political incentives to do it, no matter how much some in Congress might wish otherwise.

Ogul's conclusion that the oversight stirrings of the early 1970s would surely be "a transitory phenomenon" (Ogul 1976, 199).

When we look at the available data, however, we see strong evidence of behavioral change (Aberbach 1989). In the early 1970s, the incidence of formal oversight activity (hearings) started to increase. Contrary to expectations in the reigning literature, that increase has been sustained in both absolute and relative terms (that is, as a percentage of total hearing activity). Furthermore, there is significant evidence to suggest that Congress became much more active than previously in seeking out information about the executive branch. Given what we thought we knew about oversight behavior, why has this change taken place? And what is its significance for the general consensus view on the causes of oversight behavior?

In increasing its oversight activity, Congress was acting in response to the demands of a citizenry frustrated by government growth and complexity, to heightened institutional rivalry with the president, to conditions of relative resource scarcity that changed the balance between available resources and program costs and made it harder to create new programs, as well as in response to internal changes (such as increased decentralization within the Congress). All of these factors gave members greater cause to oversee the bureaucracy actively. As a consequence, it appears that formal oversight activity such as the conduct of oversight hearings is now a very common activity; aggressive information search also appears to be more common.

The stirring of oversight behavior at both the formal and informal levels, and especially its apparent maintenance for at least a decade, should give us pause. The literature in the field does not lead us to expect this. Perhaps the incentive-based, self-interest dominated view of congressional behavior is in need of fundamental modification.

I believe the incentive-based, self-interest perspective needs to be refined, not discarded. Institutional design features and related elements of the U.S. political culture provide the environment in which self-interest is defined for Congress as well as for others in the political system. These design features interact with other environmental conditions in defining what members of Congress will see as in their interest. Even though incentives are very important in determining behavior, incentives are not static. What tends to be most neglected in the literature is the fact that behavior offering little payoff in one period may well be much more attractive in another.

The Madisonian system of separate institutions sharing powers gives Congress great influence and independence. Because of such features as different constituency bases, terms of office based on fixed time periods, and overlapping functions protected by constitutional mandate, the interests of members of Congress and of the president can be, and often are, different. And Congress has the means to act on those differences. This does not mean that Congress and the president always disagree, but the Constitution provides for a system where the "tone," "terms," and "balance between the combatants [may] change constantly," but "the conflict is unending" (Sundquist 1981, 482). Since the roles of the president and Congress vis-à-vis the administrative agencies is one of the most ambiguous areas in an already ambiguous system, there is always the possibility that those in the Congress will choose to assert themselves in this area. Indeed, the Madisonian system means to set ambition against ambition and permanent quiescence would be a warning sign of failure.

The possibility that Congress will assert itself is strengthened by features of the party system. Not only is it possible for Congress (or one chamber of Congress) and the presidency to be dominated by different parties, it has become commonplace. Add to that the strong local basis of the parties, a nominating system dominated by primaries, weak discipline in the chambers, and all the familiar trappings of a committee system in which members often secure positions on the basis of their constituency interests, and one has many more reasons for Congress to differ with the president about matters of administration and policy and to keep a watchful eye in these areas in order to protect its own interests.

By constitutional design, then, supplemented by related features of the party system, Congress is in a position to protect and pursue its own interests. Members have the means as well as strong incentives to guard institutional and individual prerogatives. This system does not guarantee a high level of congressional hearing activity or informal assertiveness in oversight or in any other area. But it does mean that Congress has the potential to behave in this manner and, if the system works as described, that is, if it harnesses and directs self-interest, Congress should do so when conditions are favorable.

As noted, in increasing formal oversight activity, such as hearings, and in becoming much more active in seeking out information about the executive branch, Congress was acting in response to the citizenry, to conditions of relative resource scarcity, to heightened rivalry with the president, and to internal change (i.e., to increasing decentralization and increased staff resources within the Congress itself). These changes, and changes connected to them, worked together to increase the payoff of oversight relative to other activities in the following ways.

1. When congressional elites believed that the public was highly receptive to government solutions to problems and to a larger and

larger government role, they quite naturally saw a much bigger pay-off in creating new programs than in overseeing those already in existence. For the obvious reasons, creating new programs would have the greater appeal: the accomplishment would almost always look more substantial (perhaps it would actually be more substan-tial); the chances to increase one's constituency base or help one's established constituency would be greater; and the benefits of the new programs could be advertised more easily and the costs fairly easily masked. When those in Congress began to believe that the citizenry was increasingly burdened by government size and com-plexity, or even disenchanted with government per se, then there was a shift in the relative payoffs of creating new programs as compared to overseeing those already established. Oversight, especially visible manifestations such as oversight hearings, now looked more attrac-tive than before. And though the new level of attractiveness was not so great that it made oversight a dominant activity, oversight was now attractive enough to be pursued more often. The citizenry cer-tainly seemed more receptive to it, and the complexity of govern-ment provided a wealth of topics.

2. Supplementing this logic of a new balance in the relative payoffs of congressional activities, now shifted more than before toward oversight, was the related pressure caused by a growing resource scarcity. I refer to the situation as one of relative resource scarcity because the problem in this instance is not one of declining societal resources, but one where the demand for resources is high relative both to the current supply and to the willingness of decision makers to increase supply. In such a situation, there are fewer opportunities to create new programs. This gives those in Congress a greater incentive than before to oversee programs already in exis-tence. Their aims in these oversight endeavors are usually one or more of the following: (1) to protect favored programs against pres-sure to limit their scope, to decrease their budget shares, or even eliminate them; (2) to maintain a full agenda of committee unit activities; and even (3) to get more output for the dollars spent in a tight budget situation, i.e., to actually increase program efficiency.

3. Part of the Congress' struggle with President Nixon centered on spending control, but of course the struggle went well beyond that. The Vietnam War had already exacerbated executive-legislative tensions in the Johnson administration. However, Nixon's gradual development of an "administrative presidency" strategy brought struggle with the Congress over policy and administration to a fever pitch (Nathan 1975, 1983). Nixon's aim was to bypass the Congress

and seize effective control of the government. With its institutional position as well as many of its favored programs threatened, Congress fought back vigorously, using oversight as one of its tools. Restrictive legislation was a favored means, but oversight was a mechanism totally under Congress' control and therefore easy to employ.

What Nixon did was to push the normal tensions of legislative-executive relations in the American system of separate institutions sharing powers to a high point. He chose an administrative strategy to push his agenda, and Congress reacted in kind. Congress was motivated by institutional and policy reasons of substantial import to behave as it did, but narrower desires to protect individual power were also consonant with the actions taken. After all, the value of a seat in a greatly subordinated Congress is of much reduced value to a reelection-seeking entrepreneur. Assertiveness against presidential abuses helped to establish a more active and aggressive oversight posture by Congress, and, once in place, institutional routine combined with lingering suspicion helped carry it forward.

4. In the early 1970s, Congress altered the locus of actual committee decision making, making subcommittees much more autonomous than they had been previously. This increased the relative attractiveness of oversight. With many more decision makers effectively in place, fortified by greatly increased staff resources (personal, committee, and support agency staff), and confronted with the environmental changes outlined above, the incentives to undertake oversight increased. Even without the changed environmental factors, decentralization of decision making encourages oversight (that is, holding other factors constant, true decentralization is associated with greater levels of oversight). Subcommittee chairs and staff have greater time, opportunity, and incentive to build expertise — and, therefore, to seek out information aggressively — in their narrow areas of jurisdiction than full committee personnel do. And since subcommittees are almost always more limited than full committees in what they can do legislatively, their personnel are more likely to want to spend time on oversight in order to gain maximum visibility from their positions.[4]

In short, the factors just elaborated gave members greater incentives than they had previously to oversee policy and administration more

---

4. See Aberbach 1989, pt. 1, for a discussion of the value of visibility beyond pure publicity payoffs to Members.

actively. As a consequence, formal oversight proceedings (such as oversight hearings) are now very common, and it appears that aggressive information search is also more common. The institutional design features of American government actually encourage the growth of oversight under the circumstances outlined.

Congress is a peculiarly independent entity in the American system of government. It yields great power over policy and administration to the President from time to time as it did, on balance, in initial reaction to the growth of the administrative state, but it is jealous of the power given. When there is pressing institutional interest or narrow political advantage to members of Congress in interjecting themselves into the administrative side of government, they do so with relative ease. The system that the Founders designed works well in this regard. In fact, to keep the logic of the incentive theorists in place, but turn the outcome they so comfortably explain on its head, Congress has great incentive to pursue a more vigorous and variegated oversight strategy under the conditions outlined, and it does. As the political situation shifts, Congress responds — not necessarily immediately or even well, but noticeably and apparently with significant effect.

The Nature and Effects of Congressional Oversight

The contemporary Congress pursues very active and rather aggressive oversight of policy and administration (see Aberbach 1989, pt. 1; Aberbach 1987). It has a well developed information network. It is a significantly more aggressive seeker of information than would be suggested by "fire alarm" conceptions that rationalize (and describe as fact) more passive strategies. Its committee oversight agendas are, to be sure, strongly influenced by jarring stimuli like scandals or policy crises when they occur, but other (nonscandal, noncrisis) causes are also important sources of agenda setting. Most committee units are sensitive to constituency and interest group concerns about policy or administration, alert to agency decisions during the course of policy implementation, interested in assisting programs they favor, and even moved at times by a sense of duty to review programs and agencies with an ongoing life. Committee units have active staffs that seem not to be running amok, but rather doing what their employers want. And committees use an impressive array of oversight techniques, use many of them quite frequently, and employ them in a quite logical pattern related to the reasons they choose for placing items on the oversight agenda.

Top staffers report that Congress employs a wide variety of techniques for oversight, with the frequency of their use closely related to their perceived effectiveness (Aberbach 1989, pt. 2). Very briefly, staff contacts with the agencies and various types of hearings (primary-purpose oversight hearings, hearings on the reauthorization of programs, and hearings on the amendment of existing statutes) represent four of the seven most frequently used oversight techniques. Of the nonhearings approaches to oversight, staff reviews (investigations and program analyses done by committee staffers) are also used quite frequently. Piecemeal review techniques (piece by piece, generally unsystematic, and superficial checking or scanning of information about the agencies) as well as comprehensive review techniques (mainly program evaluations prepared by noncommittee personnel) are used occasionally by the committee units studied. While the use of the latter is not at a stunningly high level (except for program analyses done by the congressional support agencies, which are special cases), it is about as frequent as the use of the stereotypical piecemeal techniques. The fact that piecemeal approaches are used less than staff reviews buttresses the notions about the contemporary Congress's often active information search mode. And the relative parity of piecemeal and comprehensive approaches is another indicator that Congress does not confine itself to one easily categorized approach.

The factors of importance in motivating units to undertake oversight mesh well with the approaches they take. Piecemeal approaches to oversight are used most commonly when there are pressing problems to which committee members want a rapid response. The frequent use of comprehensive approaches is associated with units whose staffers report a strong commitment to the review of ongoing programs and agencies. And committee units tend to specialize in quite sensible ways in the types of hearings they use for oversight. Units with heavy concentrations of programs authorized for only a few years tend to use reauthorization hearings for oversight. Those with numerous redistributive programs in their jurisdictions more frequently use amendment hearings for oversight (most likely because redistributive programs tend to be permanently authorized). Specialized oversight units tend to concentrate on primary purpose oversight hearings. Again, this represents a basically sensible and efficient pattern, a good matching of motivations, structural factors, and environmental factors to oversight techniques used.

Congressional oversight has a significant effect on agency behavior. While I cannot assess these effects with any precision, the existing literature and indications in my interview study and in the roundtable held with federal executives at Brookings suggest that this is so.[5] Herbert Kaufman's study shows the emphasis federal bureau chiefs place on their relationships with Congress, including great concern about their performance in congressional hearings (Kaufman 1981). Classics such as Richard Fenno's *The Power of the Purse* and Aaron Wildavsky's *The Politics of the Budgetary Process* confirm these same facts in the appropriations area (Fenno 1966; Wildavsky 1964). And small wonder. Congress plays an active role both in writing the laws that establish the skeleton and muscle and in setting the budgets that give the life blood to administrative agencies. When Congress shows an interest, agencies ignore such signs at their peril.

Clearly, oversight activity must be taken as a sign of interest, although agency personnel obviously try to judge in each case just how serious the interest is. Where the oversight is done in connection with a legislative undertaking, the potential effects on the agency are often obvious enough so that the agency must react as if the committee's interest is serious. Even threats of action only implicit in legislative hearings are probably quickly perceived and frequently acted on by relevant agency personnel.

The place where the seriousness of the Congress may be hardest for administrators to gauge is in what are called primary-purpose oversight hearings, where oversight and not legislation is the focus of congressional activity. However, data I collected from top staff personnel indicate that committees do a variety of things to signal the agencies in this regard, with sizable proportions doing things to signal that they are concerned.[6] Seventy-seven percent "usually" follow up primary purpose oversight hearings by communicating with the agency involved (only 4 percent report that they "never" or "usually do not" do this). Fifty percent "usually" issue reports, and almost 48 percent "usually" followup oversight hearings with legislation (this figure goes above 50 percent if oversight units are not included in the calculations).[7] Even assuming

---

5. As part of my research project, a roundtable discussion with a group of federal executives was held at the Brookings Institution in June of 1979. Remarks at the conference were transcribed verbatim.

6. Top staffers ($N = 95$) from a sample of congressional committee units were interviewed for the study (Aberbach 1989).

7. These figures exclude appropriations committee units because the question was not asked of their staffers. The exact wording of the question was as follows: "Do you usually followup oversight hearings with: a) reports; b) communications with the agency; c) legislation." Answers were coded on the following scale: "1) Yes, usually do; 3) Depends; 5) No, usually do not; 6) Never."

some overreporting of activity here, the results indicate the extent to which oversight hearings are followed up and the effects they may have.

Moreover, federal executives are alive with indications of the effects of oversight. Executives, for example, often focus their complaints about oversight on what is often called micromanagement, the intrusion of Congress into the details of administrative decision making. To quote one very experienced hand: "For whatever reason, the oversight, in my view at least, tends to get distorted into an arena in which [the Congress] becomes really a participant in the carrying out of policy, which I think is potentially a pretty serious problem . . . . I think it really weakens [the true mission of] congressional oversight. I think it compromises their objectivity. I think it tends to divert attention to details which perhaps seem fairly significant individually but at least seem to me . . . not nearly as significant as some of the overall policies and issues" ("Round Table Discussion on Congressional Oversight," 9).

Whatever its faults, however, this attention to details by Congress often yields results from administrators. For instance, an executive told a story about a senator who took a deep interest in an agency's delinquent accounts. In fact, he had them listed each year in the Congressional Record. The agency responded to the senator, who although in the minority party was a member of a committee of import to the agency, by working each year to give a better "report card" to the senator. The belief of the executive was that this response took the agency's attention away from more important things and thereby "distorted and biased the efforts of the executive branch" ("Round Table Discussion on Congressional Oversight," 15), but the agency responded all the same because "the political realities of the bureaucracy are that they respond to that sort of thing" ("Round Table Discussion on Congressional Oversight," 16). For the moment, that is the key point.

The bureaucracy does respond. And not just on "micro" issues, although one can argue that they are the real stuff of policy. A recent report on the *Management of Rulemaking in Regulation Agencies*, for example, talks about "the incentives for agency officials to respond at *every stage* [emphasis mine] to the concerns of their congressional overseers" (21). Administrators, naturally enough, do not often find it one of the pleasures of the job to respond to those who intrude too deeply into what they regard as their space, but they do respond. The source of their disquiet is worth consideration, especially as it reflects a lack of coherent policy direction, but the disquiet is part of the evidence that oversight has telling effects.

So far, then, my portrait of oversight can be interpreted quite positively. At the macrolevel, Congress responds to environmental changes in seemingly appropriate ways. While oversight may well not be Congress's top priority in terms of what its members would prefer to do in the best of all worlds, Congress operates in a real world where calculations based on individual interest, policy needs, opportunities within institutional structures, and institutional interests are made in a dynamic environment. And the nature of its oversight is rather impressive. Oversight is not only more frequent than it was before, it is based on a widespread and often aggressively operated intelligence system. It involves a variety of motivations and techniques, sensibly joined. It seems to have an effect on administrators, so much so that it often makes them uncomfortable. It appears fair to say that it addresses problems and checks, and even corrects, many errors affecting at least the more organized and articulate members of the polity. As a result, it probably improves policy at the margins. Not bad for a maligned system. In fact, not bad for any system.

Criticisms and Shortcomings of Oversight

Yet all of this activity will probably not satisfy many critics of congressional oversight, because part of the reason for their dissatisfaction is qualitative, not quantitative. The nature of the advocacy context in which Congress oversees is the basis for one criticism (Aberbach 1989, pt. 2). Congress may indeed now keep a more watchful eye on policy and administration, but it looks at them through a narrow myopic lens. Another, related, criticism concerns the uncoordinated nature of much congressional oversight activity. This lack of coordination inhibits continuity in oversight and reinforces what critics see as the inadequate accountability resulting from it.

The first criticism — that Congress's oversight is neither comprehensive nor systematic enough, that it takes neither a broad nor objective enough view — has two closely related components. One component concerns the approaches Congress uses to gather information and the other how information is interpreted.

Congress, like any organization or person, does not operate the way a textbook scientist (or even a textbook social scientist) would want (March and Simon 1959; Cyert and March 1963). While it uses a large number of information sources and casts its net more widely and aggressively than many believe, it does not gather information from all possible sources or even from a random sample of sources. Some people and groups (interest groups and professional groups especially) are clearly advantaged in the process. Their views receive greater attention. Congress learns much, but more from some than others.

And what Congress learns, it learns in a value-laden context. Those on congressional committees represent constituencies with interests, have frequent contacts with administrators with interests, and themselves often have strong interests, even if for some in Congress the interest is mainly in reelection. Oversight most often takes place in an advocacy environment, an environment of support for the basic goals of programs and agencies. Once programs are established, there are built-in biases in favor of program maintenance. Further, the current committee system, particularly the system for selecting members and the lack of party discipline, significantly reinforces this bias. This is most emphatically not to say that congressional committees are uncritical of programs or agencies, or that they are unaffected by events or by the related tides of public opinion, but that oversight does take place in an advocacy context that shapes how criticisms and events are interpreted.

Even those most likely to use comprehensive approaches to oversight generally share the advocacy posture common in the Congress. This helps to explain the otherwise surprising finding that while comprehensive approaches to oversight are quite widely used, critics nevertheless typically do not regard Congress as a comprehensive overseer. For in their view, no matter what techniques Congress might be using, it still does not take a broad or objective enough view of the typical program or policy.

So, what we have is a clash between the rather impressive real and the often yearned for ideal in congressional oversight of policy and administration. The contemporary Congress learns a lot and from many sources, but does not learn enough or with the proper balance to satisfy some critics. It does use, on average, the results of studies employing what pass for scientific techniques in the world of program analysts, but it tends to consume (and, by implication interpret) the results of those studies in an advocacy context. Congress, in other words, is a political body filled with people who have preferences and who are given license to pursue those preferences through their committee assignments. The political nature of the body and its members' preferences do not inhibit, or even much limit, the occurrence of oversight in its many manifestations, but they do tend to shape what occurs. Members of Congress, it appears, want to know and do know more than we might naively suspect, but naturally enough they want to know more about some things than about others. And the information they do get is viewed through their politically ground lenses and used for their own purposes.

All in all, then, to reiterate a point, this is a pretty good system — flexible, responsive to large environmental changes and to many policy problems, open to a variety of approaches and sources, and evidently with impact on administrators — one that can probably be improved, but one whose good points are readily apparent.

However, some of the unease about oversight and the broader issue of control of bureaucracy in the United States will also be apparent when one tries to answer the following question: How effective is congressional oversight and control of the bureaucracy in the United States? There are at least two quick answers to the question: (1) at the level of checking and even correcting errors directly affecting the (most organized or articulate) citizenry and of improving policy at the margins, quite effective; (2) but at the level of coordinated review and control of policy and administration, relatively ineffective. And there is an irony here: the very weaknesses of the American system in regard to coordinated, centrally directed policy making and administrative control make it highly responsive to groups and vociferous individuals in the society. As a result, many irritants are responded to, but in an uncoordinated manner, and the system can career along without coordinated direction, a situation that is in tune with the institutional design features of a governmental system that was not set up with a large state role and, therefore, with a large administrative apparatus in mind. The administrative system is at once highly responsive and accountable in the narrow sense, and not well coordinated or centrally controlled in the broad sense. The system has many virtues, but an easily identified set of central political authorities cannot reasonably be held accountable for its operation.

Reforming the System

The evidence indicates that, in its oversight behavior (as presumably in other areas), Congress responds to changes in its environment. When there are changes in the relative payoffs of different types of behavior, and when resources change, Congress reacts. Our system brings together the self-interest of congressional politicians and the performance of oversight. And if one accepts the basic assumptions of a sloppy governmental system like our own, a system designed with the prevention of tyranny as its foremost goal rather than the promotion of efficiency or centralized accountability, then one can say that it works remarkably well when it comes to oversight. It is open; information flows freely (certainly in the domestic policy area); elected politicians have a staff system that gives them access to information; and Congress has the means to express itself relatively free from executive dominance. Evaluations of programs and policies are produced not only by executive branch agencies, but by committee staff and by support agencies linked directly to the Congress. There are obvious problems of coordination, inconsistent messages to the bureaucracy (and the possibilities for manipulation inherent in such a situation), and errors that go uncorrected in this system, but the benefits may well outweigh the costs.

The fact that the system may have a positive balance is no reason to ignore possible improvements, although one should always be aware that reforms of highly complex systems can unintendedly make things worse rather than better. In this section I want to look at some issues that have been raised about oversight and at some reforms meant to address these issues. The discussion will be at a general level, with an emphasis on the overall effects of reforms, not on the details. I will start with mere tinkering, with reforms that are unlikely to change things fundamentally because they leave intact basic structures and relationships, and work my way to reforms that would clearly make fundamental changes.

In a leading work published in 1976, but based on case studies done a decade before, Morris Ogul summarized the current critiques of congressional oversight behavior and evaluated some suggested reforms. Ogul was very skeptical that either the quantity or the quality of oversight could be sharply increased, primarily because reelection incentives pushed congressmen to give priority to other things, but also because congressional structures inhibited substantial change (Ogul mentioned bicameralism and the system of relatively autonomous standing committees specifically). The quantity of oversight has increased sharply since and I have, I hope, provided a good basis for assessing the reasons for the increase. The qualitative issues are more difficult because conceptually they are more elusive. I will turn to them shortly, but first let me say a word about a way to influence the quantitative level of oversight.

If one's goal is simply to put a floor under the level of oversight in times less favorable than those existing now, then the establishment of committees and subcommittees whose main function is oversight (i.e., specialized oversight units) is clearly a good way to go.[8] Oversight units do significant amounts of oversight in years when the overall level of oversight behavior by other units is low. Other units adjust their behavior to meet changing conditions, but oversight units are quite steadfast in doing oversight. As circumstances change, it is likely that nonoversight units will once again shift away from oversight (although one would expect lags due to habit, built-up expertise, etc.). But oversight units are limited in what they can do. Therefore, on the assumption that the chairs of specialized oversight units will in the future continue to prefer over-

---

8. Along this same line of keeping the level of oversight up when conditions are less favorable to oversight than they are now, continued decentralization of committee decision making also will contribute to this end. See Aberbach 1989, pt. 1.

sight activity to the alternative, which is mainly inactivity, the maintenance of existing oversight units and the establishment of new ones is a
simple and straightforward course to recommend.

In terms of the qualitative side of oversight, the issues are more
complex. In his concluding chapter, which covers qualitative issues as
well as reform, Ogul talks about congressional failure to do comprehensive and systematic oversight, about continuous rather than sporadic and
intermittent oversight, and about problems in coordinating oversight
activity (Ogul 1976, 181–202). Precisely what *comprehensive* and *systematic* mean is not entirely clear — these are, for all of us, attractive but very
elusive terms — but for the sake of this essay, let us assume that what
Ogul (and others) have in mind when it comes to the qualitative side is
oversight that has the following characteristics: (1) It is more objective
than what we seem to have now (that is, it uses what passes for scientific
approaches to gathering and interpreting evidence, and is therefore relatively unbiased). (2) It is done on a scheduled basis and not merely in
response to signals that a problem of some sort exists or on whims of
decision makers. (3) It is coordinated within the Congress and perhaps
even with the executive branch. Reforms to produce quality oversight
defined in these ways are quite a tall order, especially if one limits oneself
to reforms that do not change the system too fundamentally, my self-
imposed mandate for the early part of this section.

The goal of producing greater objectivity in oversight as defined
above is particularly challenging. The best predictor of frequent use of
program evaluations is the motivation labeled "duty" — a commitment to
review ongoing programs (Aberbach 1989, pt. 2). The simple injunction
to recruit staff and members to congressional committees who are so
motivated is easy, but obviously futile.

However, it is not futile to maintain and even expand the current
analytic capacities of congressional staff agencies and of other sources of
program evaluations. The data show that the overall level of use of
program evaluation is modest, not low, and that evaluations are also
used more frequently when there is concern in a member's district about
an agency or program. A reasonable interpretation of these data is that
the mere existence of available program evaluations probably has an
impact on use, particularly in the "member's needs" situation where anything readily available that might possibly help is frequently consulted.

The latter point should give us the proper caution in interpreting
what use may often mean. Even making the heroic assumption that
program evaluations are always objective, there is probably a fair
amount of both selective use and selective interpretation by congressional personnel. One would expect little else in the real world of politics; in

fact, most of us would be less than happy with politicians who were devoted too much to judging evidence rather than to representing interests.[9]

Still, there are some ways suggested by the data or by logic to increase the likelihood that the objective will receive greater emphasis. One is to encourage more specialized oversight units which tend to be self-professed neutrals on the advocacy/opposition measure. That should help, but may not be an especially strong means for achieving the end. When oversight units get down to actual cases, they tend to show quite a bit of support for the basic charter or purpose of the agencies or programs they are overseeing (Aberbach 1989, pt. 2). Even they, after all, often have set jurisdictions and the leeway to select topics for oversight, factors that encourage basically supportive relationships between committees and agencies.

However, the reasons why basic advocacy tends to predominate in Congress gives us the guide we need to suggest a second, and likely more effective, approach. The method used in Congress to select (better, self-select) the membership of committees promotes an advocacy posture. Once on committees, members are drawn to support at least the basic aims of programs and agencies over which their committees have jurisdiction. Basically, they need the program to give their committee assignments value. Even shifts in party control do not appear to shake this tendency.

What might affect it substantially would be rotating committee assignments. If committee members served limited terms on committees, they would not form the same political and emotional attachments to programs and constituent groups, they could not easily link their committee assignments and their constituency interests in the manner the current system not only permits but encourages, they would develop a broader perspective, and so on (Fiorina 1979). The obvious question is why members would voluntarily choose to alter the committee system in the manner suggested. The brief answer is that there is no obvious reason for them to do so other than to redirect their own behavior in ways that will not benefit them politically or even institutionally.

It is important to note that the institutional benefits of such a change would be mixed. In exchange for a better balancing of the inter-

---

9. Note that members and staffers, as well as bureaucrats themselves, are probably quite open to studies accepting the basic premises of their programs, but suggesting ways to improve them. It is when the programs themselves are threatened or important clienteles are likely to be severely disadvantaged by the implementation of study evaluations that resistance sets in.

ests represented on committees, a diminishing of the tendency toward an advocacy posture by members, and consequently a greater willingness to take an objective look at programs, one would expect a decided diminution in the level of member expertise and interest. With the prospect that tomorrow's assignment would not be today's, members would have less incentive (and time) to develop expertise. This would lessen their interest in the future of programs (and in oversight). It would increase the power of committee staff and of the congressional support agencies. These outcomes are good neither for oversight nor for democratic influence over policy and administration (at least as expressed through Congress). So, on balance, the costs of this reform probably outweigh the benefits if congressional oversight is a major concern.

A proposed reform that has been much more prominent on the congressional agenda and that aims to produce systematic, comprehensive, and continuous oversight of the type Ogul and others seem to hope for is commonly labeled "Sunset" (for a case study on Sunset, see Malbin 1980, chap. 4). This was actually a live issue in Congress — a version of it actually passed the Senate in 1978 (*Congress and the Nation* 1981, 842, 851) — although late enough in the session so that its passage was primarily symbolic. The heavily symbolic nature and failure of Sunset, in fact, tells us much about the problems inherent in much oversight reform.

There are enough versions of Sunset so that no brief synopsis could do it full justice, but the basic idea is to place a termination date on statutes so that Congress is forced to review them on a periodic basis, thereby ensuring continuous oversight of programs. The most prominent version of Sunset, sponsored by Senator Edwin Muskie, is the one I will focus on here, after a brief discussion of the general issues. I chose the Muskie version because it not only aimed to produce systematic, and comprehensive oversight, but because the threat it represented to committee autonomy reveals much about Congress's reactions to centralizing reforms.[10]

Periodic review by itself would mainly affect the workload of Congress. Numerous programs are actually already on a limited term authorization/reauthorization cycle.[11] From that narrow perspective (workload), therefore, the problem is difficult, but not insurmountable.

---

10. The analysis in the text is based on interviews done by the author focusing on Sunset in general and the Muskie proposal in particular.

11. For example, according to a Congressional Budget Office memo on the subject in late 1979, "The House Budget Committee (HBC) groups all federal activities into 279 major programs. Of the 279, 133 have no expiring legislation, and 146 at least in part expire." (November 9, 1979; mimeograph)

Reviews would surely be superficial in most cases, but all items would at least make a nominal appearance on the agenda for review. At this primitive level, Sunset is another scheme that would increase — or at least put a floor under — the quantity of oversight, and it would ensure more continuous albeit often rather nominal reviews.[12]

On the quality side, some Sunset proposals would require that each committee target a subset of its programs for thorough evaluation (U.S. Congress 1979, 150–52). Such targeting would almost surely increase the use of systematic studies, at least to the extent that more studies would be produced in certain areas and there would be a greater likelihood that studies would at least be considered, although not necessarily consulted more carefully or with a more neutral perspective than now prevails. As with cases where systematic studies are now used by Congress, the basic advocacy context would still prevail.

What might produce a much more significant change would be an element of the original Muskie proposal that went well beyond Sunset in the narrow sense of a forced review of some sort for each program brought on by a fixed termination date. It even went beyond proposals requiring committees to target a subset of programs for systematic evaluation. Indeed, it addressed an issue often latent in the call for continuous, systematic, and comprehensive oversight, namely, centralized control.

What Muskie proposed was quite radical in its political implications. In addition to the relatively straightforward goal of forcing reconsideration of programs and tax expenditures via limited-term authorizations of five years (certain entitlements and payments of interest on the public debt would have been excepted), Muskie proposed to

> establish a schedule for the reauthorizations of program and activities on the basis of groupings by budget functions and subfunctions. Programs within the same function would terminate simultaneously. [The effect] would be to give Congress an opportunity to examine and compare programs in an entire functional area rather than to do so in bits and pieces. The schedule would be set up so that all of the functional areas would be dealt with within one five-year cycle. (Davidson 1977, 160)[13]

---

12. Note that most Sunset proposals exempt entitlements and revenue provisions of federal statutes, facts understandable in light of the way their threatened expiration would affect large constituencies or basic government finances. However, exemptions of important programs clearly undermine the basic purpose of Sunset.

13. Note that Davidson was the Staff Counsel for the Muskie subcommittee that had jurisdiction over Sunset.

What this meant is that Muskie, and the Budget Committee he chaired, would have gained significant additional power because all programs in a budget function or subfunction would have been vulnerable in the same year. Programs in a given area would have been subject to comparative examination. Sunset reviews for an entire functional area would have provided input to the Budget Committees, which could then have acted more effectively as central arms to coordinate programs and policy.

Congressional personnel were also uneasy about Sunset for a variety of other reasons. They were, for example, concerned about workload problems and problems with inflexible scheduling provisions in many of the proposals. They were troubled about the exemption of some programs (entitlements) and the inclusion of others (controversial programs in the labor and civil rights areas that might be severely threatened if an automatic termination mechanism was in place).

Sunset eventually faded away due to a lack of enthusiasm for imposing a cumbersome set of requirements that offered little benefit to most committees while threatening their autonomy. Many of the objections were arguably well founded, but I want to stress an underlying point here: the more a reform opens the possibility of centralized control of the oversight agenda and the more comprehensive the reviews it encourages — reviews cutting across committee jurisdictions and increasing the vulnerability of programs to actions by those outside the committees — the more resistance it is likely to meet in Congress. Members of Congress want the institution to be powerful, especially when Congress faces threats to its power from outside, but members want to surrender as few of their own power opportunities as possible. The more comprehensive reviews of policy and administration are in scope, and the better they fit into a centralized system of control, the less attractive they are likely to be to most in Congress. This is not surprising in a separation of powers system with an independent legislature, especially one lacking a strong, disciplined party system and organized around relatively autonomous committee and subcommittee units.

Before turning to some of the implications for oversight of systems where the legislature is not independent or where party systems are strong, I want to look briefly at congressional experience with a modest reform designed to foster greater coordination in oversight. The House of Representatives adopted a set of committee reforms in 1974. The version they adopted was watered down from reforms originally proposed by a Select Committee on Committees commonly known as the Bolling Committee (Davidson and Oleszek 1977). The Bolling Committee proposed that the Government Operations Committee, after consul-

tation with the leadership and representatives of the standing committees, issue a report within sixty days of the convening of a new Congress.
The report was to outline the review plans of each committee, recommend steps to coordinate oversight activities among authorizing, appro-
priating, and Government Operations committees, and suggest oversight
priorities (Committee Reform Amendments of 1974, 66–68). Most of
this proposal, a pale version of the Bolling Committee's more aggressive
earlier ideas for a leadership coordinated oversight agenda, eventually
found its way into the reforms the House actually adopted (known as the
Hansen substitute) (see U.S. Congress 1974b, 58–59).

Even this attempt at coordination was a failure. The Government
Operations Committee was clearly reluctant to risk the ire of other committees by actively carrying out its new mandate, contained in clause
25(c) of House rule X, "to assist in coordinating all of the oversight
activities of the House" during each Congress. It noted in its very first
report that it was compiling plans from the various committees, but no
more (U.S. Congress 1975, 7–9). In the last report it issued, before what
was to it the welcome abolition of the requirement, the Government
Operations Committee continued to express in strong terms its reluctance
to supervise other committees' oversight activities (U.S. Congress 1985,
2). The remnants of that chore now rest with the Committee on House
Administration, which reviews committee budget requests. It likely will
tread lightly. When it gets down to it, the House clearly prefers not to
have its oversight activities coordinated.

Much more could be said on the subject, but it should be clear that
Congress is reluctant to accept or to carry out large (and even small)
changes that might help to coordinate oversight and to provide the kind
of continuous, systematic, and comprehensive overview that many
reform advocates call for. The simple reason is that while most members
like the concepts involved in principle, they are very uneasy about important aspects of them in practice. This is especially true of any change that
involves coordinating oversight behavior with an eye to helping centralized decision makers — including those in Congress itself — make decisions that might impact negatively on programs or policies in the jurisdictions of substantive committees.

Congress (or, better, its committees) is quite willing to oversee programs and policies frequently, and even to use the products of systematic
studies. What its committees have not shown is a willingness to be bound
by requirements that they oversee on a schedule fixed by others, or
oversee in a manner designed to increase the possibility of central control. They want to make their own decisions, based when possible on the
preferences of their members, the needs of their constituencies, and on

what they see as the underlying needs of "their" agencies. This, I reiterate, does not preclude frequent oversight, attention to error correction, or even the use of systematic studies, but oversight is done in a decentralized system that gives great weight to the often overlapping needs and preferences of committee members, agencies, and the constituencies of both. The disadvantages of such a system are apparent, even allowing for the positive features. There is favoritism toward established programs and groups, and there are problems that flow from lack of coordination. Programs are usually considered in isolation from one another. Administrative accountability often focuses on narrowly based congressional committees and can be blurred by conflicts between the executive and legislative branches or even within the Congress itself. Responsiveness, accountability, and error correction may well exist, but are insulated from broader forces.

The solutions suggested for these problems usually involve efforts to strengthen the party system or even to institute a parliamentary system such as Britain's, thereby coordinating control of the bureaucracy and enhancing accountability (Fiorina 1979, 124–42). A recent, detailed consideration of the basic issues in U.S. constitutional reform can be found in Sundquist (1986). Numerous essays on the subject are collected in Robinson (1985). Whatever the potential benefits of such reforms in terms of coordinated control, coherent policy, and clearer accountability to the public of elected officials, they are very likely to decrease oversight of policy and administration by the legislative branch. To put it in propositional form, the more centralized and coordinated authority in a government becomes, the less likely it is that the legislative body will be an active overseer of policy and administration. Those in control, be they the leaders of a disciplined governing party in both the legislative and executive branches or the major ministers of a cabinet government (although probably even more so in the latter case), will have a strong interest in maintaining as much control as possible over evaluation of policy and administration.

The case of Great Britain, admittedly a polar case, is instructive here. Ordinary members of Parliament, chafing under government control, have struggled to increase their influence over the executive via the establishment of a system of specialized parliamentary Select Committees. British reformers, in fact, have looked to the United States for guidance (Smith 1979). However, the efforts to allow Parliament a more effective role have been only a limited success. Clive Ponting, a civil servant who achieved some notoriety in Britain when he was tried by the government for passing documents to a Labor MP about the sinking of the Belgrano during the Falklands War, says the following:

How effective have the new Select Committees been? They have certainly not caused any tremor of fear to run through Whitehall. They bear little resemblance to the powerful Congressional Committees in the United States. They are still composed of politicians who in the last resort will give their loyalty to the party . . . . When dealing with relatively uncontroversial areas, the committees have produced some good reports but when they investigate highly political issues, the system breaks down and the members retreat into their respective party positions. (Ponting 1986, 155)

Michael Rush, in his book on parliamentary government in Britain, identifies three interrelated

obstacles to allowing Parliament a greater involvement in the scrutiny of the executive and the formulation of policy. First, governments simply find it easier that way. Governments do not want to lay themselves open to wider and possibly more effective scrutiny, thus making life potentially more difficult; . . . Second, governments do not wish to share power any more widely than absolutely necessary. . . . Third, and arising in part out of the second point, parties in power (and those who aspire to power) do not wish to see their ability to implement their policies diminished. (Rush 1986, 100–101)

There is a dilemma here: the very discipline and electoral accountability of a democratic system with effectively centralized and coordinated authority over policy and administration is more than compatible with a restricted legislative role in oversight and with a situation in which an experienced civil servant can conclude that "Whitehall is not, in any real sense, accountable for the way in which it works" (Ponting 1986, 158). In fact, an astute minister in this system wrote the following:

How effectively does Parliament control [a minister]? How careful must he be in his dealings with Parliament? The answer quite simply is that there is no effective parliamentary control. All this time I have never felt in any way alarmed by a parliamentary threat . . . . I can't remember a single moment in the course of legislation when I felt the faintest degree of alarm or embarrassment and I can't remember a Question Time, either, when I had any anxiety.[14]

---

14. Crossman 1976, 628; as quoted in Ponting 1986, 153.

The larger issues of accountability are beyond the scope of this essay, and a brief look at one case can only whet our appetites for more analysis, not prove a point. But it would be well worthwhile to look at legislative oversight and the broad questions of administrative accountability comparatively, choosing systems where the roles of parliament and the nature of party systems vary (for a similar point, see Rockman 1984, 434). That way we can better evaluate what has been suggested above, namely that the very system feature (disciplined, centralized decision making) that seems to enhance the accountability of decision makers to the public may actually do more than restrict the role of legislative bodies in oversight, it may also limit bureaucratic and political accountability by increasing the ability of central decision makers (and civil servants) to restrict the flow of information. Whatever the nature of the tradeoffs involved, it is clear that the committees of the U.S. Congress will not easily surrender their prerogatives vis-à-vis policy and administration, either to the president or to central decision makers in the Congress itself. While dooming serious steps toward central control of policy and administration, that may not be altogether such a bad thing.

Some Concluding Notes

To understand the motivations and behavior of political actors, we must understand both institutional context and the broader political environment. This is as true for congressional oversight as for other aspects of political life. Members of Congress (like all of us) usually pursue self-interest as they see it, but their self-interest is defined in a changing environment.

Congress may cede much influence over administration to the executive during periods of program expansion, but it adjusts its behavior when circumstances change, and the system of separate institutions sharing powers gives it both the means and the incentives to make the adjustments. The lack of formal oversight activity and the passivity in information seeking noticed by many earlier observers made sense in light of the greater returns (both individual and institutional) then available from other activities and modes of search. The same logic can explain the more active stance now evident in these areas.

The built-in prospects in the Madisonian system for tension between the legislative and executive branches, and the loose nature of our party system, with its consequent reinforcement of the entrepreneurial tendencies of members, mean that Congress can indeed be an active overseer. And that oversight, while usually done in an advocacy context, is often vigorous and even systematic.

However, the same institutional features and motivational forces that make active oversight likely also inhibit coordinated review of policy and administration. Crisis may temporarily bridge the gaps enough to produce coordinated review, or Congress may defer to the president for a time, but the situation is inherently unstable. This lowers democratic control of policy and administration of an idealized sort — coherent, coordinated, programmatic in the responsible parties sense — but in a real and imperfect world much can be said for it. While it does push bureaucrats to play a complex part in the policy process — a part unimagined by our founders who did not consider the problems of a state with a large administrative apparatus — it also subjects the bureaucracy to much scrutiny in a flexible and adaptable system.

In essence, there are costs and benefits in any system. The one we have now has certain distinct advantages, and it may well fit our pluralistic culture better than others. Given that the U.S. governmental system was not designed with a large administrative sector in mind, its ability to expose bureaucratic behavior to public scrutiny and to promote administrative responsiveness is impressive. The somewhat chaotic nature of congressional oversight of policy and administration, as of political control of policy and administration generally, is of a piece with the chaotic nature of American politics and the competition inherent in the design of our institutions. A society as skeptical about authority as this one may well bear the costs of lack of coordinated direction better than the costs of coordination. We might well like the results of substantial change far less than what we have now, a comforting statement since we are unlikely to see substantial system changes anyway.

The knowledgeable pushing, hauling, poking, and advocacy of the Congress as it keeps a watchful eye on policy and administration can be criticized, but it is consistent with Congress's role in a system of separate institutions sharing powers. What we have is far from perfect, not even pretty or neat, but we could do far worse. At least two cheers for Madison.

REFERENCES

Aberbach, Joel D. 1987. "The Congressional Committee Intelligence System: Information, Oversight, and Change." *Congress and the Presidency* 14:51–76.
Aberbach, Joel D. 1989. *Keeping a Watchful Eye: The Politics of Congressional Oversight.* Washington, D.C.: Brookings Institution.
Bibby, John. 1968. "Congress' Neglected Function." In *The Republican Papers,* ed. Melvin Laird. Garden City, N.Y.: Anchor.

Burns, James MacGregor. 1963. *The Deadlock of Democracy.* Englewood Cliffs, N.J.: Prentice-Hall.

Congress and the Nation, 1977–80, vol. 5. 1981. Washington, D.C.: Congressional Quarterly.

Crossman, Richard. 1976. *Diaries of a Cabinet Minister.* Vol. 1. New York: Holt, Rinehart and Winston.

Cyert, Richard M., and James G. March. 1963. *A Behavioral Theory of the Firm.* Englewood Cliffs, N.J.: Prentice-Hall.

Davidson, James. 1977. "Sunset — A New Challenge." *Bureaucrat,* 6:159–64.

Davidson, Roger H., and Walter J. Oleszek. 1977. *Congress Against Itself.* Bloomington: Indiana University Press.

Fenno, Richard F., Jr. 1966. *The Power of the Purse.* Boston: Little, Brown.

Fiorina, Morris. 1979. "Control of the Bureaucracy: A Mismatch of Incentives and Capabilities." In *The Presidency and The Congress,* ed. William S. Livingston et al. Austin: LBJ School/LBJ Library.

Kaufman, Herbert. 1981. *The Administrative Behavior of Federal Bureau Chiefs.* Washington, D.C.: Brookings Institution.

Malbin, Michael. 1980. *Unelected Representatives.* New York: Basic Books.

Management of Rulemaking in Regulatory Agencies, A Report by a Panel of the National Academy of Public Administration. 1987. Washington, D.C.: National Academy of Public Administration.

McCubbins, Mathew, and Thomas Schwartz. 1984. "Congressional Oversight Overlooked: Police Patrols and Fire Alarms." *American Journal of Political Science* 28:165–79.

March, James G., and Herbert A. Simon. 1959. *Organizations.* New York: John Wiley.

Nathan, Richard P. 1983a. *The Plot That Failed.* New York: John Wiley.

———. 1983b. *The Administrative Presidency.* New York: John Wiley.

Ogul, Morris S. 1976. *Congress Oversees the Executive.* Pittsburgh: University of Pittsburgh Press.

Ponting, Clive. 1986. *Whitehall: Tragedy and Farce.* London: Sphere Books.

Robinson, Donald L., ed. 1985. *Reforming American Government: The Bicentennial Papers of the Committee on the Constitutional System.* Boulder, Colo.: Westview Press.

Rockman, Bert A. 1984. "Legislative-Executive Relations and Legislative Oversight." *Legislative Studies Quarterly* 9:387–440.

"Round Table Discussion on Congressional Oversight." 1979. Brookings Institution, Washington, D.C. Transcript.

Rush, Michael. 1986. *Parliament and the Public.* London: Longman.

Scher, Seymour. 1963. "Conditions for Legislative Control." *Journal of Politics* 28:526–51.

Smith, Geoffrey. 1979. *Westminster Reform: Learning From Congress.* London: Trade Policy Research Centre.

Sundquist, James L. 1981. *The Decline and Resurgence of Congress.* Washington, D.C.: Brookings Institution.

_____. 1986. *Constitutional Reform and Effective Government.* Washington, D.C.: Brookings Institution.

U.S. Congress. 1973. U.S. Congress House Select Committee on Committee Organization in the House. 93d Cong. 1st sess. Vol. 2, pt. 1.

_____. 1974a. Committee Reform Amendments of 1974. H. Rept. 93–916, pt. 2.

_____. 1974b. Committee Reform Amendments of 1974: Explanations of H. Res. 988 as Adopted by the House of Representatives, October 8, 1974. Staff Report of the House Select Committee on Committees. 93d Cong. 2d sess.

_____. 1975. House Government Operations Committee, Oversight Plans of the Committees of the U.S. House of Representatives. H. Rept. 94–61. 94th Cong. 1st sess.

_____. 1979. "Conduct of Sunset Reviews by Legislative Committees," Section 7 of H. R. 5858, "Sunset Review Act of 1979," Hearings before the Committee on Rules of the House of Representatives, Sunset, Sunrise, and Related Measures, Part 2, 150–52.

_____. 1985. House Government Operations Committee, Oversight Plans of the Committees of the U.S. House of Representatives. H. Rept. 99–25. 99th Cong. 1st sess.

Wildavsky, Aaron. 1964. *The Politics of the Budgetary Process.* Boston: Little, Brown.

CHAPTER 7

Political Mobilization in America

Jack L. Walker

The American political system is one of the most permeable in the world. Not only are there hundreds of pathways through which influence can be exerted, but there seem to be literally thousands of people who are determined to exploit these opportunities in order to get their point across. There are as many as five thousand lobbyists active in Washington at any time — at least ten for every elected official. Despite the profusion of organizations and advocates, however, not all social groups have equal representation before Congress, the bureaucracy, or the courts. One obvious example of inactivity that is especially puzzling is the lack of political organization among the unemployed — a large group that obviously is suffering distress. Members of Congress often call for action to end unemployment, and several pieces of legislation meant to deal with the problem have been passed during recent sessions of the Congress, yet no organization is operating in Washington claiming to directly represent those who are out of work. Trade union leaders attempt to speak for them, but usually oppose measures like the graduated minimum wage, subsidized employment of teenagers, or any other proposal that might possibly impose costs upon their membership, or diminish their control over entry into the skilled trades.

No democratic system could ever insure equal representation for all conceivable social or political groups, but all systems must face the ques-

This essay grows out of research on interest groups funded by grants from the Earhart Foundation and the National Science Foundation. Thanks are also due to the Program in American Studies at the Woodrow Wilson International Center for Scholars, where I spent a stimulating year of research, and to the Guggenheim Foundation for a fellowship that helped to pay for it all. Special thanks go to Thomas L. Gais and Mark Peterson, who have assisted in this research and also taught me a great deal about this subject. The Institute of Public Policy Studies, my home base at the University of Michigan, paid certain costs of reproducing this essay, and important editorial assistance was given by Mark Peterson and Jackie Brendle. The essay was produced on the University of Michigan's word processing system through the wizardry of John Hankins and Judy Jackson.

tion of who will be represented, and who will not. Why is it that some kinds of people are organized into associations dedicated to advancing their interests, while others — like the unemployed — are either given partial representation through sympathetic third parties, or are ignored altogether? This is one of the central questions of democratic political theory. The National Association for the Advancement of Colored People is actively seeking to preserve the civil rights of blacks, the National Organization for Women advances the cause of females, several groups exist dedicated to the well-being of homosexuals, others represent the manufacturers of motorcycles, or those who plant and cultivate mushrooms, but no group is dedicated solely to furthering the rights of the unemployed.

Psychological Explanations of Political Mobilization

We cannot automatically assume that the unemployed want to be part of an organization that advocates their needs but are somehow prevented by established forces in the system from having their wish. It is at least possible that they are satisfied with their status, or more likely, not concerned enough to take part in efforts to influence the policy process in their own behalf. The simplest answer to our question, therefore, might be that people will organize if they feel intensely enough about their grievances — when people are not organized it is because they feel no need to organize.

Underlying this explanation is the rather unlikely assumption that the interest groups we see in operation at any time are a perfect reflection of the desires and discontents alive in the society. Recent studies of unemployment conducted by Schlozman and Verba, however, clearly show that the unemployed are suffering an extraordinary amount of personal distress, and that most of them believe that the government should take measures either to create new jobs or help them find work (Schlozman and Verba 1979). Almost all of those surveyed felt that the government was not doing enough to alleviate their distress. The unemployed are not as politically aware as employed workers; they are dispersed, typically uneducated, and not well equipped for political activity; but they believe that their government should intervene in the economy in their behalf, and that they have a right to such aid. These same surveys also uncovered virtually no evidence of any organizational activity on behalf of the unemployed. Most of those who lost their jobs immediately dropped out of their unions, leaving them isolated and politically impotent.

There is no way to prove that the unemployed in America *ought* to be better organized for political advocacy than they are, but research has shown that their feelings, attitudes, and beliefs make them ripe for political action. Since so many new political organizations representing other distressed groups (blacks, Hispanics, native Americans, the handicapped, children, the mentally ill) have been organized during the past twenty years, the question arises once again. Why is there no organization that directly represents the unemployed? To state the problem broadly, why within the same political system do levels of organization differ for what would seem to be analogous social groups?

An Institutional Explanation of Political Mobilization

Without entirely discounting the importance of the great differences in the capacity of citizens to understand questions of public policy, or in the skill with which they utilize the political resources at their disposal, I believe that the differential rates of political mobilization among social groups within any population are mainly a product of the structure of opportunities presented to each citizen by the legal, political, and organizational environment. Members of different social groups face entirely different sets of opportunities and obstacles to political activity. The actions they engage in depend not so much upon their level of education or their annual income, their values, or the intensity of their feelings, as upon the organizational, legal, financial, and institutional environment in which they find themselves.

Political action is seldom a spontaneous outburst of frustration, anxiety, or personal strain. In predicting whether the unemployed will organize for political action, it is useful to know whether they feel exploited or whether they believe that they have a right to relief from the government; but it is much more important to understand the political scope allowed by the tax code to not-for-profit agencies working in their behalf, whether foundations exist that will take an interest in their cause, how willing government agencies are to sponsor political advocacy in their favor, or even more important, the likely political or financial sanctions that would be applied against any individual or organization that took up their cause.

To put my central point more precisely, the amount of political action engaged in as a result of individual distress in the American political system at any time is determined mainly by political and administrative policies toward political activity, the presence and accessibility of willing patrons of political action, and the patterns of conflict and social cleavage in the society. If groups do not materialize representing the unemployed, this does not automatically mean that people who are out of work are essentially satisfied with the prevailing distribution of goods or status. Nor is it necessarily an indication that they are too cynical or alienated to take part in the democratic process. Although citizens are not likely to become involved in politics if they feel no distress at all, or have no desires that could be fulfilled through public policy, institutional and organizational variables are more important as determinants of political mobilization than the attitudes, feelings of political efficacy, or the political beliefs of individual citizens. Political action is largely the result of the differential impact on citizens of the rules of the political game.

The Pluralists and Political Mobilization

I know of no fully developed theory that relies entirely upon the characteristics of individual citizens to explain the levels of mobilization in a society. I do not want to create an imaginary theory and then proceed to demolish it. Most writers who attempt to analyze the roots of political behavior employ several types of variables in their explanation, but even so, most contemporary theories of political mobilization are founded upon a set of assumptions and hypotheses about the behavior of individual citizens. Robert Dahl, for example, begins his analysis of political mobilization in the book *Who Governs?* by dividing the population into two ideal types: *homo civicus* and *homo politicus*. The civic man is in search of direct gratifications, and politics typically appears to be a much less attractive source of pleasure

> than a host of other activities; and, as a strategy to achieve his gratifications indirectly, political action will seem considerably less efficient than working at his job, earning more money, taking out insurance, joining a club, planning a vacation, moving to another neighborhood or city, or coping with an uncertain future in manifold other ways. (Dahl 1961, 224)

The vast majority of the citizenry can be classified as members of the genus *homo civicus*. They sometimes become involved in politics, but only if the actions or inactions of governments threaten their primary goals. Since there are few such instances, most people usually pay almost no attention to public affairs. If an immediate and tangible threat arises, such as an increase in taxes, the construction of a highway through the neighborhood, or a proposal for drafting young people into the armed forces, *homo civicus* may become involved in public affairs, sometimes intensely, but members of this class can be counted on to lapse into inactivity as soon as the stimulus disappears, and to resume their search for gratification through more direct, nonpolitical means. In Dahl's words: "*Homo civicus* is not, by nature, a political animal." (Dahl 1961, 225)

Homo politicus is the opposite of the civic man. A tiny minority of the population derives both direct and indirect gratification from political activity and the exercise of influence over others. Dahl provides no reasons for this fundamental difference among citizens. He simply begins his argument with the assertion that although most people avoid politics because it is too costly and boring, there remain a few who plunge into public affairs as if it were a calling. These differences are matters of taste and personal preference, but they also are the keys to the successful operation of a democratic political order. All political systems operate largely by habit and inertia and are vulnerable to changes in their economic or social environment. The energy needed to overcome inertia and engineer the changes in policy that are required to meet the challenges facing the system are supplied by gifted leaders from the political class. As in Schumpeter's classic analysis of the capitalist economy, *homo politicus* acts as an entrepreneur, working constantly to gain influence over other citizens in order to assemble the political resources necessary to renew the system. In Dahl's words

> Political man can use his resources to gain influence, and he can then use his influence to gain more resources. Political resources can be pyramided in much the same way that a man who starts out in business sometimes pyramids a small investment into a large corporate empire. To the political entrepreneur who has skill and drive, the political system offers unusual opportunities for pyramiding a small amount of initial resources into a sizable political holding. (Dahl 1961, 227)

In such a fluid system, an obvious danger arises that some member of the political class will pyramid enough political resources to become a threat to the democratic order. Dahl has become increasingly concerned over the past decade with the power of great private corporations that control vast amounts of political influence and "loom like mountain principalities ruled by princes whose decisions lie beyond reach of the democratic process" (Dahl 1983, 117). He is concerned that these huge entities will be able to gain control of the civic agenda, resist the efforts of government agencies to control them, and even shape the preferences and ideologies of the citizenry through clever exploitation of the media of mass communication.

Dahl recognizes these dangers to democracy and speculates that they may soon rise to the top of the political agenda, but he also believes that the democratic order has many built-in safeguards against tyranny.[1] One important constraint on potential tyrants is the system of "dispersed inequalities." In any open system there are many different kinds of resources available to different citizens, and these resources are almost always unequally distributed. People with social standing, for example, usually do not control large numbers of votes, or cannot dominate all important organizations in the community, or control all of its wealth. Dahl does not rely entirely upon fundamental cultural differences between citizens to explain why some people participate more actively in public affairs than others. Differences in education, occupation, levels of income, access to certain organizations, and other economic or social factors play a role in determining the extent to which any individual will seek to gain influence in the political system. In Dahl's opinion, however, almost everyone in the society, with rare exception, has access to some kind of political resource. The increasingly aggressive political actions of the business community are a threat, but a political order that maintains many competing political entrepreneurs within a system of "dispersed inequalities" will be able to offer strong resistance to centers of concentrated power.

The success of entrepreneurs from the political class in countering undemocratic tactics from their competitors depends, in the end, upon more than their skill in marshaling political resources and employing them decisively. The most important defense against tyranny in Dahl's theory is the consensus among all citizens on the essential importance of maintaining democratic procedures in the conduct of public affairs. If the system is to be protected and constitutional protections against tyranny are to be enforced, the citizenry must be willing to answer the call from members of the political class for counteraction against potential tyrants. Even *homo civicus*, according to Dahl, can be counted on to become active in the defense of the fundamental principles of democracy, and since potential offenders are aware of the possibility of such uprisings, they are not likely to challenge these procedural norms. If they are foolish enough to do so, however, other members of the political class can usually be counted upon to react to the danger by rallying the citizens against the offender.

Dahl's theory relies upon a broad consensus on the underlying val-

---

1. Dahl not only forecasts that these issues will become controversial in Dahl 1983, 184–85, but also recently made an effort to further the debate by offering a bold argument in favor of governing private corporations through democratic means in Dahl 1985.

ues of democracy as the last line of defense against tyranny. He not only argues that such a consensus exists, but also asserts that when average citizens become convinced that these values are being challenged they will be willing to take action to defend them. The members of the genus *homo civicus*, who normally pay almost no attention to the conduct of public affairs, nevertheless exercise a powerful indirect influence over the political leadership, because they control the latent power to destroy the political career of any leader who violates the fundamental political consensus. Leaders are constrained by the fear of awakening this sleeping giant, and thus the seemingly passive citizens of a democracy are much more powerful than they look.

Critics of Pluralism

Dahl's theory of indirect influence rests on the assumption that citizens can be mobilized for sustained political action when they perceive a threat to the democratic consensus. Murray Edelman was one of the first to challenge this view by showing how easy it was for political leaders to dissipate the energy and commitment of broadly based social movements by using symbolic gestures of reassurance rather than concrete changes in public policy (Edelman 1964). Edelman's demonstration of the ease with which public perceptions and attitudes could be manipulated in order to induce quiescence underlined the inherent advantages of intense minorities over majorities in democratic systems of government.

Edelman questioned whether large social groupings without information or any basis for a sustained commitment could be expected to insure the democratic system against domination from centralized power. A more direct challenge to Dahl's theory, however, was made by Mancur Olson (1965). Olson dealt mainly with economic interest groups in his work and never speculated on the problems of protecting the guarantee of free speech or some other aspect of civil liberties, but in his treatment of economic issues he has shown why most citizens cannot normally be counted upon to take action in the defense of collective goods like those that underlie the democratic consensus. Olson's analysis makes it doubtful that citizens would take action to protect democratic values even if they were aware that these values were being threatened and also were convinced that they would be better off if these values were protected.

It is the nature of collective goods that they are provided to everyone in the group if they are provided at all, so Olson argues that rational individuals would take advantage of this dilemma by refraining from making contributions to the common effort, knowing full well that they would receive as much benefit as everyone else once the good was secured. Small groups might be able to induce their members to contribute to common objectives through peer pressure, but Olson argued that large groups could not be expected to act in their collective self-interest in most cases. Olson argued that this crucial "free rider" problem could be solved only if groups were able to make selective benefits available to contributing members that were unavailable to others, or unless sanctions were employed that forced members to contribute to the common effort, whether they wanted to or not. Olson's analysis shows how difficult it would be for political entrepreneurs, no matter how skillful, to rally citizens against most threats to the society's fundamental political consensus.

Olson's theory is based upon narrow assumptions about human motivations that political scientists have found confining and unrealistic (Wilson 1973; Moe 1980), but his work highlights the great obstacles facing those who wish to organize deprived elements of American society. His theory suggests that a balanced representation of group interests cannot be achieved from entirely voluntary political action by individuals when the marginal costs of participation differ so greatly among social groups and individual incentives to engage in politics are generally so weak.

A few groups with large memberships pursuing collective benefits are able to flourish in the American system without providing any selective material benefits or employing any form of coercion to retain their members, but these groups attract mainly those with good educations and ample incomes, for whom the annual dues represent a painless way of amplifying their ideological views and gaining a sense of involvement in the national political process. More than 90 percent of the members of Common Cause have attended college, 43 percent hold graduate or professional degrees, and their average family income is almost twice the national average (McFarland 1984). But associations representing socially disadvantaged elements of American society that attract individuals of moderate means and depend entirely on support from their members in response to mainly purposive incentives, have typically been short-lived (Gaventa 1980; Jenkins 1985).

The Role of Institutions in Political Mobilization

Both the pluralists and their critics, although providing many important insights into the process of political mobilization, have paid insufficient attention to the crucial role of institutions, and the public policies that control them, in determining who is mobilized for political action in

America. To begin with, most citizens are represented indirectly in the pressure system, whether they realize it or not, by the institutions that employ them. In almost any political setting beyond the neighborhood or immediate community, many of the organizations engaged in advocacy are made up of business firms, hospitals, churches, or other large organizations, not individuals. In a survey of all the interest groups listed in the *Congressional Quarterly's Guide to Washington* that I conducted in 1980, only 36 percent of those who responded had only individuals as members. The memberships of the remaining 64 percent were made up of organizations, or were mixtures of organizations and individuals (Walker 1983).

Academics, for example, are represented in Washington by the American Council on Education (ACE) and dozens of other organizations whose members are colleges and universities, rather than individual faculty members. No one would argue that all faculty members would endorse all the positions taken by the ACE, or even that all faculty members working in the fields of public administration and public policy analysis would endorse all the positions taken by the National Association of Schools of Public Affairs and Administration (NASPAA), a small organization made up of universities with graduate programs in public administration and public policy. Yet dozens of associations of this kind — some broadly based and others narrowly focused — claim to speak for the interests of all academics within their limited jurisdictions.

Almost certainly, there are instances in which associations composed of organizations take positions that a large minority of the workers within their jurisdictions would strenuously oppose, but most of the time the associations probably take positions that almost all those working in the area would support. I know of no study that compares the amount of indirect representation in different segments of the society, although I suspect that it is quite uneven. Organizations providing indirect representation have been growing in importance in recent years and also have begun making efforts to mobilize workers from within their jurisdictions to take direct political action. The largest campaigns of grass roots lobbying mounted in Washington during recent sessions of Congress, for example, were organized by trade associations representing the country's banks and savings and loan associations, and by the American Telephone and Telegraph Company. In both cases, thousands of employees and clients of these businesses got in touch with their elected representatives and contributed to political campaigns in carefully orchestrated efforts to influence the shape of public policy, and in both cases these organizations were able to persuade Congress to give them what they wanted (Wines 1984).

When plant managers or regional sales executives within large business firms are asked by their superiors to make efforts to influence members of Congress, they may sometimes regard the request as an imposition upon their rights as citizens, but most of the time such requests are carried out without protest. The increasingly open political activity of large businesses — many of which maintain several political action committees (AT&T maintains 16 PACs) and elaborate lobbying operations in Washington — warrants much more attention from political scientists, as does the somewhat less visible activity of large not-for-profit institutions, such as hospitals or universities. In many cases, these organizations have shown that they can outperform trade unions, interest groups, or political parties, the institutions traditionally regarded as the principal instruments of political mobilization. Their actions in this realm raise many important questions about the representation of individual citizens in a democracy and point up the crucial role of the society's established institutions as agents of political action and indirect representation.

The Institutional Basis for Political Mobilization

If any political organization is to endure over an extended period of time, no matter what its objectives or the nature of its membership, its leaders must find the money and other material resources needed for its maintenance. If the group emerges from a well-defined professional or commercial community and concentrates exclusively upon advancing that community's welfare — as most successful groups do — it should be possible to maintain a collective effort and support the full-time staff of the organization with resources that are collected primarily from the membership itself.

The maintenance of a political organization is made even easier if its members are institutions, like business firms, hospitals, or government agencies, rather than individuals. Although little research on this subject has been done, it seems likely that most institutions can afford to wait longer than most individuals for the political results they seek. Stability, autonomy, and reasonably secure sources of income allow institutions to be more consistent supporters of interest groups, and leads them to expect more than most individuals would in terms of advocacy and political action and less in specific material benefits in return for their support. As Salisbury has pointed out, when individual citizens are compared with institutions as political actors,

Institutions have greater latitude — more discretionary resources and more autonomous leadership authority — to enter the political arena. Institutions have less need to justify their political efforts by reference to membership approval or demand. Institutions may also have a wider range of specific policy concerns . . . [and] possess more resources which, combined with a greater sense of efficacy in political action, lead to a considerably increased probability of participation at any given level of intensity of interest or concern. (Salisbury 1984, 69)

Institutions play the crucial role of patron in the maintenance of political organizations of all kinds, including voluntary associations that have members and the profusion of think tanks and independent advocates that rely entirely upon grants and contracts to stay alive. Furthermore, among the institutions that are inclined to act as patrons of political action, business firms clearly predominate. As a result of the character of the available patrons, groups that represent business interests currently outnumber those of any other type — a situation that has prevailed for many years (Schlozman 1984). Organizations such as the American Enterprise Institute, the Heritage Foundation, or public interest law firms working to reduce the scope and effectiveness of government regulation all receive financial support from a large number of corporate patrons.

In recent years the business community has mounted a major counterattack against the legislative centerpieces of the Great Society. Trade associations have increased their lobbying staffs, many companies have opened offices of their own in Washington, thousands of political action committees have been formed by companies, and many firms have engaged Washington law firms to represent their interests. Given the size and wealth of the business sector in the United States, it is easy to assume that they will predominate in any struggle where money and organization count. But while the business community obviously is a powerful element in the American political universe, it is not without competitors. Just as business firms have been engaging more openly in political activity in recent years, so have churches, foundations, and government agencies. In the years since the New Deal, a great many new professional roles have evolved that are carried out within not-for-profit agencies of many kinds. Social workers who work with the elderly or who are employed in one of the programs that service the needs of handicapped children or the mentally ill have come to believe that political advocacy in behalf of their clients is a kind of professional obligation. The institutions employing these public sector professionals are not as large or as rich as the country's major banks or manufacturing firms, but they provide an organizational foundation and source of funds that can be drawn upon by political entrepreneurs who wish to defend or expand the welfare state (Zald and McCarthy 1980; Zald and Ash 1966).

In order to avoid the creation of a vast federal social service bureaucracy, Congress in building the welfare state has consistently mandated that state and local government agencies and private not-for-profit contractors be used whenever possible to actually deliver social services that are being largely paid for by the federal government (Mosher 1980). This policy has led to the rapid growth of many quasi-private, not-for-profit, social service agencies supported by a mixture of charitable gifts and governmental appropriations. It has also laid the organizational foundation for efforts to mobilize the professionals who provide these services, and eventually their clients. E. E. Schattschneider sensed the development of these two opposing centers of organizational strength and patronage a quarter of a century ago when he argued that "the relations of government and business largely determine the character of the regime" and that "the struggle for power [in America] is largely a confrontation of two major power systems, government and business" (Schattschneider 1960, 115).

In an institutional theory of political mobilization, the steady expansion of the power and responsibility of the federal government figures as one of the major causes of the recent growth of new organizational devices for linking citizens and their government. Elaborate networks of policy professionals have grown up around policy areas like housing, environmental protection, and national security, or around constituencies such as the elderly, children, the mentally ill, the handicapped, and Hispanic-Americans. These policy communities bring together public officials and policy specialists from Congress, the bureaucracy, the presidency, university research centers, private consulting firms, think tanks, interest groups, law firms, and state and local governments (Heclo 1978; Walker 1981; Laumann, Knoke, and Kim 1985).

An informal division of labor grows up within these policy communities, allowing political entrepreneurs to employ several different formulas for organizational maintenance. Some groups specialize in collecting data, while others offer midcareer training for professionals in the field, engage in campaigns of public education or propaganda, or serve as technical advisors or consultants for public bureaucracies, leaving a small number of groups to take the lead in the more conventional tasks of legislative lobbying. As the representational system in each policy area matures, political entrepreneurs and their patrons are able to create highly specialized membership and nonmembership groups that are only viable because they fill a niche in a larger policy community (Hannan and Freeman 1978; Knoke and Laumann 1982; Laumann, Knoke, and Kim 1985).

The elaboration of sources of patronage outside of the profit-making, corporate realm is one of the most important reasons for the rapid increase during the past twenty years in the number of groups dedicated to the protection or enhancement of broad public goods like world peace, civil rights, environmental quality, or consumer protection. The steady expansion of the educated middle class, many of whom are pursuing careers in the not-for-profit realm — the much discussed "New Class" (Bruce-Briggs 1981; Brint 1984) — has provided a ready audience for associations built around ideas or causes, and in a few cases it has been possible to sustain large groups of this kind mainly through direct mail solicitation (McFarland 1984). Most citizen groups, however, are not able to sustain their activities through the support of their immediate membership. My research has clearly shown that groups dedicated to the advancement of a cause that have no intimate connection to a commercial or professional community are the most reliant of all upon support from wealthy individuals, activist foundations, government agencies, and other institutional patrons of political action (Walker 1983).

Three Classic Modes of Political Mobilization

There are essentially three main formulas for success in organizing political groups that have been used in our political system. These three schemes form the basis for the three central methods of political mobilization in America.

The first and most familiar organizational formula is to base an association upon a tightly knit commercial or occupational community in the profit-making sector whose members share a concern for protecting or advancing their economic interests. Such a group usually can be supported with membership dues and patronage in various forms from business firms operating in the area. The most familiar and numerous political organizations in American politics are classic economic interest groups of this type, such as the American Petroleum Institute, the National Association of Automobile Manufacturers, or the Mortgage Bankers Association.

The second formula for organizational maintenance is also rooted in occupational communities and capitalizes upon the possibilities for strong institutional support, but entrepreneurs following this strategy operate in the not-for-profit or governmental realm and often make strong appeals to the professional needs and obligations of their potential members. Groups of this kind, such as the National Association of State Alcohol and Drug Abuse Directors or the Association of American Medical Colleges, are often instigated, supported, and encouraged by permanent agencies of government. These groups began appearing in Washington in the latter part of the nineteenth century and have grown in numbers in recent years, stimulated by the rapid growth of government since the late 1960s.

The third type of successful organizational formula taps the enthusiasm and energy of social movements. Groups like the Wilderness Society, Common Cause, Citizens for Clean Air, and the Women's International League for Peace and Freedom are based upon the commitment of individuals attracted by a cause, along with a package of financial contributions and other forms of patronage from foundations, wealthy individuals, churches, and other institutions that operate mostly in the not-for-profit realm.

In order to illustrate how these three organizational formulas are used in the real world of interest groups as the basis for the mobilization of large segments of the population, three sets of interest groups operating at the national level in 1980 are examined in table 1. First, there are the groups that claimed to represent farmers, a classic economic policy community; second are groups representing the handicapped, a policy community dominated by public sector professionals who acted as advocates for their disadvantaged clients, with support and encouragement from many institutional patrons including the government; and third are groups making up the women's movement, a community of interest groups that emerged from one of the most important social movements of recent years.[2]

The data in table 1 show that each of the three policy communities was dominated by a different kind of group. The table shows that most groups with an interest in agricultural issues in 1980, not surprisingly, had members who came from occupations in the profit sector. Most of the groups in this field actually were built around the cultivation of specific crops or were restricted to certain areas of the country. A small number of groups were built around public sector professions, such as feed grain inspectors or agricultural educators, and in recent years a few

---

2. Most of the groups included in these three subsamples were collected from the 1980 issue of the Congressional Quarterly's *Washington Information Directory*. Separate efforts were made through interviews with group leaders to obtain data from all groups representing these three constituencies even if they were too small to appear in the directory.

citizen groups were organized in this area, usually attempting to represent consumers or seeking to raise environmental issues. The citizen groups increased in number during the 1970s and interjected new issues and an unfamiliar source of conflict into this once settled, predictable policy community.

Presenting a sharp contrast to those in agriculture, most organizations that expressed an interest in the problems of the handicapped in 1980 were made up of public sector professionals working in not-for-profit agencies engaged in delivering services to handicapped people. There were a few trade associations made up of firms that manufactured products or equipment used by the handicapped, and there were a number of citizen groups operating in this field, often begun by the parents of handicapped children or by social service professionals concerned in general about the social status of handicapped persons.

Among the groups engaged in the debate in 1980 over women's issues, citizen groups predominated. There was a small number of women's groups at the time made up of professionals in the profit-making sector, but even these groups were principally concerned with the general status of women in the society. Since there were few social service programs targeted specifically for women in 1980, there were not many social service specialties that could serve as the foundation for interest groups in this area.

As we can see in table 2, the funding patterns for the groups in these three policy communities fit neatly with the types of groups that predominated in each area. Patronage for political activities in the agricultural area was available from large firms that manufacture farm implements, chemicals, and feeds, and in dues from the individual farmers who could expect to receive important individual benefits if their advocates were successful in the legislative process. Financial support was available to

TABLE 1. Types of Interest Groups Representing Three Policy Communities, by Percentage

	Policy Communities		
Group Types	Farmers (N = 52)	Handicapped (N = 35)	Women (N = 50)
Profit	83	3	8
Mixed	10	3	8
Nonprofit	4	57	14
Citizens	4	37	70

Note: The typology is based upon the occupational character of group numbers. The theoretical justification for the typology and the operation used in constructing it are discussed in Walker 1983, 2392–94. Column 1 totals more than 100 percent due to rounding.

women's groups from wealthy individuals who believed in the cause, from dues and small contributions collected through direct mail solicitation—a form of fund raising that thrives on controversy—and from a small circle of activist foundations who were willing to risk involvement in a good cause even if it was controversial. The groups representing farmers were the most dependent upon dues from their membership, while the handicapped groups had the most diversified sources of income, including foundations, wealthy individuals, and government agencies, and received less than half of their support from membership dues. The women's groups depended least upon membership dues and most heavily upon patrons outside of government, such as private foundations and wealthy individuals.

Since many of the members of the occupationally based groups in the agricultural and handicapped areas were business firms or social agencies rather than individuals, table 2 does not accurately portray the amount of patronage received from institutions. Even where a group is made up entirely of individuals, their participation often has been encouraged and subsidized by employers who believe that these activities add to the knowledge and professional standing of their employees.

These data illustrate the importance of financial support from institutions and other patrons of political action, but patrons cannot operate in the political realm with impunity. They must be careful not to put their own operations in jeopardy by supporting causes or taking actions that might invite some form of political retaliation. The extent to which patrons support political causes depends to a large degree on the amount of conflict existing in the area and upon the likelihood that important political leaders would come to their defense if they came under attack for becoming involved in controversial questions of public policy. Patrons do not automatically withdraw once conflict begins, but they are

TABLE 2.   Sources of Financial Support for Interest Groups in Three Policy Communities, by Percentage

	Policy Communities		
Sources of Support	Farmers (N = 40)	Handicapped (N = 33)	Women (N = 40)
Dues-publications[a]	75	44	39
Government patronage[b]	7	11	9
Private patronage[c]	3	18	26
Other miscellaneous sources[d]	15	27	26

[a]Membership dues, publication sales, and conference fees
[b]Grants or contracts from government agencies
[c]Gifts and grants from individuals, private foundations, and other associations
[d]Fees or commissions for services, royalties, interest, and loans

likely to continue their activities only so long as they feel that they can muster the necessary political support to protect their interests.

This sensitivity to conflict is illustrated in table 3 where I summarize the answers of groups in the three communities to questions about whether there were any organized opponents to their political activities in 1980. The entries in table 3 show the number of standard deviations between the mean for the groups in the cells of the table and the mean for the entire sample of national interest groups in the 1980 survey. A positive number in the table indicates that groups report more organized conflict in the area than average, and a negative number means that less conflict is reported than average.

This table reveals an uneven pattern of conflict that helps to explain the types of patronage these groups depended upon. Both the women's groups and the agricultural groups were more likely than average to report the existence of organized opponents working against their interests. Both areas stand in sharp contrast to the handicapped groups, who seldom reported the existence of any organized opposition. Many political leaders strenuously opposed the Equal Rights Amendment or called for an end to agricultural subsidies. Some also complained about the size and cost of the welfare state and called for a general reduction in government spending, but no prudent politician in 1980 would have openly attacked programs for the handicapped. In highly consensual policy areas dealing with the handicapped, the aged, children, or other obviously vulnerable groups, government agencies could risk providing financial aid for their constituents, but they were bound to be much more cautious in the conflictual atmosphere surrounding policies toward women or agriculture (Nelson 1984).

The varying configurations of conflict and the demands of organizational maintenance determine the relationships between government agencies and interest groups. Advocates for the handicapped were able to make strong financial and political alliances with normally cautious administrative agencies of government in 1980 because they were almost never directly confronted by interests intent on reducing benefits or terminating programs designed for their clients. The Department of Agriculture had a close, supportive relationship with most of the largest

TABLE 3.   Amount of Political Conflict within Three Policy Communities

Policy Communities	Level of Reported Conflict
Farmers ($N = 45$)	.31
Handicapped ($N = 26$)	−.69
Women ($N = 28$)	.31

Note: Entries in the table represent standard deviations from the sample mean.

interest groups that represented its constituency because these groups are closely allied with the committees and subcommittees in Congress that exercised control over the department's affairs. Women's groups, on the other hand, were not closely allied with any large bureau or agency because there were few programs in place at the time that delivered social services directly to women. Lacking close ties with government, most of the women's groups engaged in highly controversial efforts to change established social customs and public policies.

The situation facing the women's movement might have been entirely different if Richard Nixon had not vetoed the Comprehensive Child Development Act in 1972 that was designed to create a national system of day-care centers. Such a large national program, employing many social service professionals, would have been an important source of leadership and patronage for political action — important enough, perhaps, to have produced a different type of women's movement in the 1980s with much closer ties to government. It was organizational and strategic considerations of this kind, shaped by history and the development of public policy, that determined for each of the three policy communities the characteristic relationships with agencies of government that they experienced in 1980. These relationships are illustrated by the data presented in table 4.

In order to produce an index of cooperation between government agencies and interest groups, answers to three questions concerning relations with government agencies were combined. A group receiving the very highest score on this index reported that a member of its staff served on an advisory committee for a government agency, that the group had a high level of interaction with government agencies, and that agencies

TABLE 4. Degree of Conflict with Bureaucratic Agencies within Three Policy Communities, by Percentage

	Policy Communities		
Index of Bureaucratic Cooperationa	Farmers (N = 52)	Handicapped (N = 35)	Women (N = 50)
High	84	90	42
Low	16	10	58

aThis index is an additive combination of answers to the following questions:

"Does the Executive Director or any member of the permanent staff currently hold a position on an official government advisory committee or commission?"

"How frequent is the interaction of this association's staff and officers with agencies of the national government? Frequent, infrequent, no interaction."

"Is this association regularly consulted by government agencies when they are considering new legislation or changes in policy?"

consulted with the group prior to making policy decisions. Groups with the lowest possible score had no advisory committee memberships, little interaction, and were not consulted prior to policy making. Scores were combined to produce only two categories of high and low cooperation. The results of this index reported in table 3 reveal that groups representing the handicapped, which were predominantly composed of public sector professionals and not-for-profit social service agencies, reported the closest relationships with government agencies, followed closely by the groups representing farmers. Women's groups, not surprisingly, were clearly the least well-connected on average, with only 42 percent reporting high scores on government interaction. In fact, almost one-third of the women's groups reported no contact of any kind with agencies of the federal government.

Groups that experience little conflict and enjoy close, cooperative relationships with government agencies are unlikely to spend much time trying to influence public opinion. Programs are usually in place designed to serve them, and their access to government policy makers is one of their most important sources of strength. These advantages lead them to work within the established legislative process in order to exploit their favored role in the system. The opposite might be expected of groups that are not readily accepted within the inner circles of government and whose financial support comes largely from sponsors who expect strenuous advocacy for controversial causes in exchange for their patronage. Such groups might be expected to adopt an "outside" strategy, one directed toward changing the fundamental political environment as a first step toward achieving their goals. The choice of tactics engaged in by any interest group, in other words, is a reflection of the financial, organizational, and political realities it faces.

In order to illustrate the sharp differences in the tactics employed in 1980 by the groups representing farmers, the handicapped, and women, an index of "inside" strategies was created based on the degree to which groups engaged in lobbying Congress or administrative agencies, and a contrasting index of "outside" strategies was created based upon whether groups made appeals to the public through the mass media, staged large informational conferences open to the public, and engaged in protest demonstrations. The dramatic differences between these three policy communities is illustrated in figure 1, where the balance between inside and outside strategies is portrayed.

If groups emphasized inside over outside strategies, their score is below the line in the graph, but if outside strategies were emphasized, scores appear above the line. The graph shows clearly that the agricultural groups were trying to exploit their connections to policy makers in

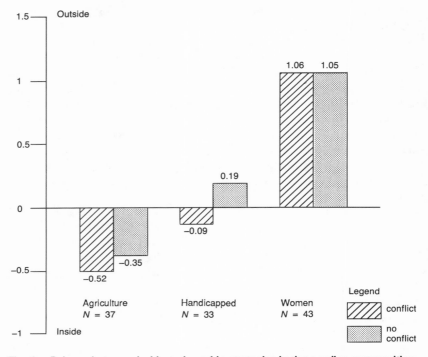

Fig. 1. Balance between inside and outside strategies in three policy communities

1980 by heavy reliance on lobbying and almost no efforts to mold public opinion, while the women's groups were mainly trying to expand the scope of the conflict through appeals to the public and acts of protest rather than concentrating on conventional means of policy making through the established procedures of the legislative process. The groups representing the handicapped enjoyed close relationships with policy makers, but also engaged in efforts to educate the public about the special problems of their members, thus employing an almost even balance of tactics, with those experiencing conflict tending slightly toward an outside strategy and those not perceiving conflict relying more upon inside strategies.

Summary and Conclusion

Political mobilization is seldom spontaneous. Before any large element of the population can become a part of the American political process, organizations must be formed and advocates must be trained who have the knowledge and the material resources needed to gain the attention of national policy makers. The key to successful political mobilization is seldom an upsurge of intense feelings of discontent within the disadvantaged group—many important political movements in America were underway long before there was any indication of widespread discontent among those in whose behalf the efforts were being made. The essential prerequisites for successful political mobilization are mainly organizational, and many are subject to manipulation through public policy.

The Reagan administration, for example, in its campaign to "defund the left," proposed a change in the rules covering government contractors that would prevent any group receiving federal funds from using the space or equipment paid for with these funds in any form of political advocacy. This would have required many organizations in Washington to rent separate facilities and equip them with separate telephones, furniture, and office machines if they wanted to make presentations to Congress or the bureaucracy on behalf of their members or clients (Barringer 1983). Even though this rule was not enacted in such an extreme form, it illustrates how dependent the modern advocacy system has become on the rules governing contracting and consulting with the federal government, on the tax laws that govern the political behavior of business firms and not-for-profit corporations, and on a series of other rules and common practices that regulate the interactions among advocates, their patrons, elected policy makers and their staffs, the court system, the federal bureaucracy, and the electoral system.

Most citizen groups that emerged from social movements in the past have simply faded away once the intense enthusiasms of their followers began to cool or when a string of policy defeats or compromises caused marginal supporters to lose hope. In the 1980s, however, many of the citizen groups born during the 1960s and 1970s are still in business, with help from their individual and institutional patrons, even though public interest in their causes has declined. These groups promote concern for their issues and stand ready to exercise leadership whenever there is a new burst of public enthusiasm.

Political mobilization led by social service professionals, government agencies, private foundations, and other patrons from the not-for-profit sector has been successful mainly in areas of low controversy. It cannot be used whenever the level of controversy rises, because the policy professionals and bureaucrats who take the lead in this process cannot count on support from the political leadership to protect their agencies against hostile critics. If a single majority party with a clearly articulated ideology were firmly in control of the entire governmental system for a prolonged period—as the Social Democratic Party of Sweden was for more than four decades after the 1930s — bureaucratic leaders might enter more willingly into potentially explosive policy areas. In the decentralized American political system, however, where control of the presidency and each house of Congress is often not in the hands of the same political party, public officials must exercise caution. The Administration on Aging may work openly to organize the elderly — sometimes going so far as paying to transport their clients to state legislatures in order to lobby their elected representatives in favor of programs for the aged — but government agencies working in less consensual areas must be careful not to make themselves vulnerable to attacks from antagonists who do not approve of their programs or missions (Pratt 1976; Nelson 1984; Hayes 1981; Chubb 1983).

My analysis takes us full circle back to the problem of representation for the unemployed. One of the principal reasons there is no organization dedicated exclusively to advancing the welfare of the unemployed is that their cause is inherently controversial and there are no readily accessible patrons prepared to subsidize political entrepreneurs who might wish to organize them. There are no agencies of the government or private foundations that feel politically capable of organizing bus loads of the unemployed for marches on their state capitols — much less Washington. Marches on Washington by Coxey's Army of the unemployed in 1894 or the Bonus Army of unemployed veterans in 1932 were met with hostility, and eventually the marchers were dispersed by force. Without the appropriate political, organizational, and financial prerequisites, a group called the National Association of the Unemployed is unlikely ever to appear.

The reason why some of the most deprived elements of American society are either ignored or are represented in the legislative process only by small nonmember organizations is not that they are essentially satisfied with their status and have no interest in political activity: it is because there is no institutional foundation from which a successful effort at mobilization can be launched. Political mobilization of those at the bottom of the social order is exceedingly difficult, because there are few patrons able or willing to risk the danger to their own political well-being that might arise from heavy political conflict over redistributive social programs. Elected officials, of course, are free to take the lead in promoting legislation designed to aid disadvantaged groups without prompting from any outside forces, but they know that once conflict begins over their proposals, there will be few organizations in place that can mobilize expressions of support, supply information and ideas, or raise the financial resources needed to combat the program's critics. The uneven pattern of political mobilization resulting from these forces is reflected in our bewildering array of narrowly focused social welfare programs, each dealing with some purpose upon which consensus among the political leadership has been achieved. The American system provides veterans of World War II with a wide range of services, including a comprehensive system of socialized medicine in government-owned hospitals with government-paid physicians, while providing little assistance at all for black teenagers, almost half of whom are unemployed (Steiner 1971).

This essay began by asking why certain groups were represented in Washington by political organizations while others were not, even though they seemed equally in need of representation. The explanation I have offered does not allow us to predict exactly which groups will be mobilized and which will not, but it does lead to the conclusion that only certain types of discontent are likely to gain expression. Political entrepreneurs are required to initiate the process of mobilization, but a successful set of political organizations representing a constituency will not come into being, no matter how clever or energetic the leaders of the movement may be, unless institutions can be identified that will serve as sponsors or patrons for their efforts. The behavior of potential patrons is largely determined by the degree of conflict or consensus revolving around the policies being proposed by the political movement. Some proposals and some groups are simply outside the prevailing consensus among elected representatives and the attentive public. It is doubtful that any political organizations could be maintained over a long period of time providing exclusive representation for such groups. The array of political advocates existing at any moment in our political system does not accurately mirror the pattern of discontents felt by the citizenry; it is a much better reflection of both the prevailing consensus over the legitimate scope of public policy existing among those active in politics, and the institutions in the society that are available as patrons of political action.

REFERENCES

Barringer, Felicity. 1983. "OMB Releases Proposed Restrictions on Lobbying by Contractors, Grantees." *Washington Post,* 3 November.
Brint, Steven. 1984. "'New Class' and Cumulative Trend Explanations of the Liberal Political Attitudes of Professionals." *American Journal of Sociology* 90:30–71.
Bruce-Briggs, William, ed. 1981. *The New Class?* New Brunswick, N.J.: Transaction Books.

Chubb, John E. 1983. *Interest Groups and the Bureaucracy.* Stanford: Stanford University Press.

Dahl, Robert. 1961. *Who Governs?* New Haven: Yale University Press.

———. 1983. *Dilemmas of Pluralist Democracy.* New Haven: Yale University Press.

———. 1985. *A Preface to Economic Democracy.* Berkeley: University of California Press.

Edelman, Murray. 1964. *The Symbolic Uses of Politics.* Urbana: University of Illinois Press.

Gaventa, John. 1980. *Power and Powerlessness.* Urbana: University of Illinois Press.

Hannan, Michael T., and John Freeman. 1978. "The Population Ecology of Organizations." *American Journal of Sociology* 82:924-64.

Hayes, Michael T. 1981. *Lobbyists and Legislators.* New Brunswick, N.J.: Rutgers University Press.

Heclo, Hugh. 1978. "Issue Networks and the Executive Establishment." In *The New American Political System,* ed. Anthony King. Washington, D.C.: American Enterprise Institute.

Jenkins, J. Craig. 1985. *The Politics of Insurgency.* New York: Columbia University Press.

Knoke, David, and Edward Laumann. 1982. "The Social Organization of National Policy Domains." In *Social Structure and Network Analysis,* ed. Peter V. Marsden and Nan Lin. Beverly Hills, Calif.: Sage Publications.

Laumann, Edward O., David Knoke, and Yong-hak Kim. 1985. "An Organizational Approach to State Policy Formation: A Comparative Study of Energy and Health Domains." *American Sociological Review* 50:1-19.

McAdam, Doug. 1982. *Political Process and the Development of Black Insurgency: 1930-1970.* Chicago: University of Chicago Press.

McFarland, Andrew S. 1984. *Common Cause.* Chatham, N.J.: Chatham House.

Moe, Terry M. 1980. *The Organization of Interests.* Chicago: University of Chicago Press.

Morris, Aldon D. 1984. *The Origins of the Civil Rights Movement.* New York: Free Press.

Mosher, Frederick C. 1980. "The Changing Responsibilities and Tactics of the Federal Government." *Public Administration Review* 40(6): 541-48.

Nelson, Barbara J. 1984. *Making an Issue of Child Abuse.* Chicago: University of Chicago Press.

Olson, Mancur, Jr. 1965. *The Logic of Collective Action.* Cambridge, Mass.: Harvard University Press.

Pratt, Henry. 1976. *The Gray Lobby.* Chicago: University of Chicago Press.

Salisbury, Robert H. 1984. "Interest Representation: The Dominance of Institutions." *American Political Science Review* 78:64-83.

Schattschneider, E. E. 1960. *The Semi-Sovereign People.* New York: Holt, Rinehart and Winston.

Schlozman, Kay Lehman, and Sidney Verba. 1979. *Injury to Insult.* Cambridge, Mass.: Harvard University Press.

—————. 1984. "What Accent the Heavenly Chorus? Political Equality and the American Pressure System." *Journal of Politics* 46:1006–32.

Steiner, Gilbert Y. 1971. *The State of Welfare.* Washington, D.C.: Brookings Institution.

Walker, Jack L. 1981. "The Diffusion of Knowledge, Policy Communities and Agenda Setting: The Relationship of Knowledge and Power." In *New Strategic Perspectives on Social Policy,* ed. John Tropman, Milan Dluhy, and Roger Lind. New York: Pergamon Press.

—————. 1983. "The Origins and Maintenance of Interest Groups in America." *American Political Science Review* 77:390–406.

Wilson, James Q. 1973. *Political Organizations.* New York: Basic Books.

Wines, Michael. 1984. "Ma Bell and Her Newly Independent Children Revamp Lobbying Networks." *National Journal,* January 28.

Zald, Mayer N., and Roberta Ash. 1966. "Social Movement Organizations: Growth, Decline, and Change." *Social Forces* 44:327–41.

Zald, Mayer N., and John D. McCarthy. 1980. "Social Movement Industries: Competition and Cooperation among Movement Organizations." *Research in Social Movements, Conflicts, and Change* 3:1–20.

CHAPTER 8

Formal Political Theory and the Design
and Evaluation of Institutions

John R. Chamberlin

Debates about institutional performance are commonplace in politics
and public policy, and the evaluation of alternative institutions presents a
major challenge to social scientists. Formal political theory is one productive vantage point from which to carry out this evaluation.[1] It pays
serious attention to the normative underpinnings of democratic institutions, and the mix of deductive, empirical, and experimental approaches
to institutions that one encounters in this literature helps us to understand institutional performance from a variety of perspectives.

Much of the early work in formal political theory was quite abstract
and focused on collective choices in institution-free settings. Although
such work is not directly concerned with specific institutions, it plays a
vital role in institutional evaluation by providing solid normative
grounding and by highlighting the difficulty of designing institutions that
meet desirable normative criteria. Until recently, much of the literature
focused on the evaluation of voting systems, but over the past decade a
great deal of attention has been paid to other institutions, with legislative
decision making being the most closely studied. This work has spurred
further developments in theoretical concepts and methodological
approaches. The increased attention that has been paid to strategic
behavior within institutions has given rise to new game-theoretic solution
concepts that yield insights into the performance of alternative institutional structures and rules. Laboratory experimentation has also been
shown to be an extremely productive method of studying both the new
solution concepts and the institutions themselves. These developments
have led to a wider recognition by other disciplines of the power of this

---

1. I use the term *formal political theory* to encompass a variety of literatures — social
choice theory, public choice theory, and some areas of public finance. I will restrict my
attention to the parts of these literatures that concern themselves with political institutions.

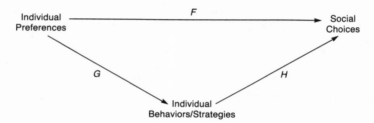

Fig. 1. The direct and indirect paths to social choices

approach to institutions, and the influence of formal political theory is very likely to increase in the future. In this essay I provide a brief overview of formal political theory, discuss some of the major findings from the literature, and present some of the principle challenges that face this approach to institutions.

In a recent article, March and Olsen (1987) discuss the important distinction between aggregative and integrative perspectives on institutions. The aggregative perspective, with its roots in neoclassical economics and its emphasis on rational decision making, takes individual preferences and endowments of resources as exogenous and is concerned with how institutions derive collective choices from individual preferences in accordance with various normative criteria. Formal political theory is firmly in this tradition.

The integrative perspective, which relies more heavily on political science and sociology for guidance, pays considerably more attention to the phenomena the aggregative perspective takes as exogenous. Thus the origin and evolution of preferences, the ways in which institutions shape the individuals they bring together or keep apart, and the ways in which collective outcomes can be more than "mere" aggregations of individual perspectives are questions that motivate work from the integrative perspective.

There is no doubt that a full theory of institutions must be informed by both perspectives, and much work remains to be done to bring together the insights of scholars who work in these two traditions. The insights of formal political theory are important ingredients for a general theory of institutions, since such a theory must place considerable emphasis on aggregative properties. In the final section I also call attention to some of the integrative questions that might profit from increased attention from formal theorists.

One way to view the landscape of formal political theory is with the aid of figure 1. The basic concern is with the aggregation of individual preferences (shown in the upper left) into social choices (shown in the upper right). The part of the literature usually referred to as social choice theory is concerned with the direct relationship between individual preferences and social choices that appears at the top of the figure. A social choice process from this perspective is a function F that specifies a social choice for every collection of individual preferences that might arise. We can specify conditions of various kinds that we want a social choice process to meet and then investigate the properties of processes (if any exist) that meet these conditions. Such analyses require that we provide rigorous definitions of the criteria to be met and they frequently result in a demonstration that we cannot simultaneously meet all the criteria that seem desirable. This literature has been particularly important in helping us to understand the nature of collective rationality and the ways in which our notions of rationality and other important normative criteria can conflict.

Another part of the literature, and the part that has most to offer in terms of institutional analysis, is concerned with the indirect path between individual preferences and social choices that is illustrated in the lower part of the figure, denoted by functions G and H. The indirect path from individual preferences to social choices gives separate consideration to institutions and to strategic behavior by individuals. Given a particular institution, individuals choose strategies that reflect both their preferences and their understanding of the institutions that generate social outcomes. On the basis of the behavior generated by these strategies, the institution arrives at a social choice. There are two separate, but not independent, processes at work here. In formal terms, an institution is a function H that specifies a social choice for every collection of strategies (behaviors) that might be encountered. One way in which this function may differ from that in the direct path of figure 1 is in terms of the information that an individual may convey in her actions. Some institutions offer a wide array of strategies; others, such as plurality voting, offer extremely restricted strategy sets. Another important way in which the indirect path differs from the direct path is that the indirect path considers the possibility that behavior does not always reveal individuals' true preferences. This possibility is dealt with by the other link in the indirect path, a function G that determines the strategies chosen by individuals with given preferences. It is here that the game-theoretic nature of collective choice enters the picture.

Along the indirect path, a social choice is seen as the output of function H operating on the output of function G. This portrayal of social choice is more complex than the simple function F of the direct path, and it is along the indirect path that we seek an understanding of the performance of institutions in practice. This formulation of the problem permits us to engage in the useful practice of comparative statics, holding one link in the path constant and varying the other. One of the performance criteria we might use in such analyses is the extent to which institutions lead strategic individuals to express their true preferences or, failing that, the robustness of an institution to varying degrees of strategic behavior by individuals.

The two paths from individual preferences to social choices thus both play vital roles in the evaluation of institutions. The direct path allows us to focus on the normative criteria we believe ought to govern social choices in a particular context and to identify outcomes that seem to be the "correct" outcomes in a given context. The indirect path allows us to study the performance of institutions under conditions that characterize individual behavior in actual institutions, including the important possibility of strategic behavior. The ability to vary both the features of institutions and the models of individual behavior provides a rich opportunity to investigate the extent to which it is possible to design institutions that yield appropriate outcomes.

Evaluation Criteria

Institutional evaluation requires that we have normative criteria with which to judge institutional performance. Formal political theory is centrally concerned with such criteria, and although it has not yet addressed the full range of criteria that might be thought relevant to institutional evaluation, the range of criteria that have been considered is broad. Among the important kinds of criteria are: (1) conditions of rationality, (2) moral and democratic principles as they relate to outcomes, (3) moral and political principles as they relate to "process" aspects of social choices, (4) the dynamic effects of institutions, and (5) the decision making or transactions costs associated with various social choice processes. Social choice theory has been concerned with investigating the compatibility of various norms that seem desirable for a social choice process to meet since its inception in the work of Duncan Black (1948, 1958) and Kenneth Arrow (1951). For the most part, the axioms in social choice theory are examples of the first two types of criteria listed above. A number of important criteria are noted below. The first several embody aspects of rationality; the rest reflect important moral and political considerations. These axioms, and the theorems that arise from them, frame the challenge that must be faced on the aggregative side of institutional design.

Social Choice Axioms

—**Transitivity:** *The social choice process should produce a social ordering of the alternatives that is complete and transitive.* Individuals are assumed to have transitive preference orders, so this condition makes a similar demand of the social preference ordering. This is a strong condition and may demand too much from a social choice process. Relaxations of it are discussed below.

—**Independence of Irrelevant Alternatives:** *The social ordering of a set of alternatives depends only on the individual orderings of these alternatives.* This axiom is by far the most controversial of Arrow's original set. It can entail the following: cardinal utilities are excluded, choices between alternatives x and y depend only on individual preferences between these two alternatives, and choices from a given set of alternatives depend only on preferences among alternatives in the given set.

—**Pareto Optimality:** *If all individuals strictly prefer alternative* x *to alternative* y, *then society strictly prefers* x *to* y. This axiom reflects the pursuit of efficiency that is assumed to be part of rational behavior; it is also a necessary condition for the maximization of welfare. To the extent that we care about the latter at all, which we must, this axiom seems difficult to fault.

—**Universal Domain:** *A social choice process should produce a social choice for all possible configurations of individual preferences. There are no restrictions on the preference orderings individuals may have.* This axiom speaks to the principle of autonomy and to our commitment to base social choices on the preferences of the individuals affected by the choices.

—**Nondictatorship:** *There is no individual such that the social ordering of the alternatives is always identical to her ordering, regardless of the orderings of the other individuals.* This is a very weak axiom that insures a very minimal relationship between social choices and the preferences of more than one individual. A democrat would demand much more.

—**Anonymity:** *The social choice should not depend on the labeling of the individuals.* This axiom implements the norms of impartiality and political equality. This axiom is usually violated by political institutions that assign special responsibilities or duties to particular roles. In institutional analysis it might be replaced by an equal opportunity axiom concerning access to these roles.

—**Neutrality:** *The social choice should not depend on the labeling of the alternatives.* This axiom demands impartiality with respect to alternatives. In particular, it does not permit the status quo to have a privileged position in the social choice process. Within institutions this axiom is frequently violated by rules that structure decision making.

— **Condorcet Criterion:** *If an alternative exists that defeats all others in pairwise majority comparisons, then it should be the social choice.* This axiom implements the democratic norm of majority rule. In social choice situations in which voting is considered the appropriate method of decision, this axiom is quite important, for a Condorcet winner has a strong claim to be regarded as the legitimate outcome of a voting process. In other settings, the selection of representatives, for instance, its relevance is open to question.

— **Positive Responsiveness:** *If society chooses x over y, and then some individual changes her preferences from x not preferred to y to x preferred to y, then society still chooses x over y. Also, if society was indifferent between x and y before the change, society must choose x over y after the change.* This axiom, and a variety of others with the same spirit, require that social choices be sensitive to preference changes among individuals in ways that accord with our sense of fairness. Thus, if *x* rises in the preference order of an individual, everything else equal, *x* should not fall in the social ranking of the alternatives. This axiom is often referred to as a monotonicity axiom. It seems like a reasonable requirement, and most voting systems meet it.

— **Liberalism:** *For each individual there is at least one pair of alternatives x and y such that she is decisive in the social choice between them in either order.* This axiom insures a domain of personal freedom, requiring that there be some things that individuals can determine on their own. Thus, if the only difference between social states *x* and *y* is that in the former I wear a beard, this axiom would be satisfied if the social choice between *x* and *y* were left up to me. This axiom is one way to build a concern for individual rights into the theory.

These are only some of the axioms that appear in the social choice literature. On its face, each has some appeal, and none seems an undesirable property of a method of social choice. But it turns out to be very difficult to satisfy many of these axioms at the same time, a fact that confronts us with hard choices among conflicting commitments. Social choice theory can make clear to us the logical constraints that apply to the project of aggregating individual preferences into social choices in ways that conform to moral and rational norms. It may require that we lower our expectations for such processes, but it does not mean that the pursuit of such goals must be abandoned.

Other Criteria

Because of its focus on the problem of aggregating known individual preferences into social choices, axiomatic work has paid less attention to criteria concerned with some very important aspects of real-world institutions. For instance, representative institutions have received little attention in social choice theory despite their central role in functioning democracies. The evolution of preferences and the ways in which institutions affect this process are also woefully understudied. In addition, social choice theory has also had little to say about the dynamic effects of institutions, although Nicholas Miller, in an article discussed below, has taken an important step in linking social choice theory with traditions in democratic theory that emphasize the dynamic stability of institutions. There have been only a few attempts to formulate axioms that capture important distributional criteria, a few of which I comment on below. Future work that addresses these issues will be particularly useful contributions to the development of a richer theory of institutions.

The Direct Path from Individual Preferences to Social Choices

Although quite abstract, the portions of social choice theory that examine the direct path from individual preferences to social choices play an extremely important role in a theory of institutions. In particular, this work allows us under some circumstances to identify outcomes that have the strongest claim to being the "right" social choice and to see the extent to which various combinations of norms may be logically consistent with one another. The major effect of results in this literature has been to make clear how difficult it is to find a set of social choice axioms that are both normatively attractive and logically consistent.

The Impossibility Theorems

The most famous result is Arrow's Impossibility Theorem (1951), which shows that the transitivity, universal domain, Pareto optimality, independence of irrelevant alternatives, and nondictatorship conditions are incompatible. Since at first glance the conditions seem to be rather minimal requirements for a social choice process, the theorem is an incredibly strong one. It is important to note that the theorem concerns all methods of making social choices, not just voting systems.

Over the years, there have been many attempts to weaken various conditions in the hope that some way out of the dilemma could be found, but no escape has been or is likely to be found. One might settle for an occasional failure to meet the Pareto criterion if that were the price for honoring a set of important conditions, but there is certainly nothing offensive about the condition itself.

We may consider limitations on individuals' preferences in the hope that a well-behaved social process will emerge, but the prospect of simply not honoring some kinds of individual preferences seems too offensive to individual autonomy to receive serious attention.[2] If the alternatives have certain properties that result in a natural structure to individuals' preferences, this would not be objectionable. The assumptions underlying the spatial model of voting and economists' assumptions about preferences over commodity spaces provide such a structure. Indeed, many of the most promising analyses of institutions proceed under such assumptions. This condition arises in social choice theory from economists' agnosticism concerning the origin of preferences; an integrative account of preferences that is consistent with the spirit of the principle of autonomy might provide the basis for an alternative reformulation of this criterion.

The transitivity condition can be weakened in reasonable ways. It is actually quite a strong condition. Disposing of it means giving up the notion of a "social preference" that corresponds to our accepted notion of an individual preference, but that seems a reasonable price to pay if it gets us anything, since the notion of social preference probably involves the fallacy of composition anyway. Unfortunately, we do not get much for our money on this. If we give up the transitivity of indifference and retain the transitivity of strict preference, we can avoid having a dictator, but we get an oligarchy instead.[3] In general, what we get if we weaken the transitivity condition are social choice processes that either retain some

---

2. Because it does not address the origin of preferences or how they might change, social choice theory has little to say about institutions that might give rise to collections of individual preferences that regularly possess a structure that is more limited than that permitted by this condition. Such institutions no doubt exist, and their existence can potentially take some of the sting out of the impossibility theorems, but my own judgment is that they cannot help us to avoid the sting entirely.

3. That is, there can exist conditions under which there is a set of individuals such that if they are unanimous in their preferences they can dictate the social choice; if they are not unanimous, then society is indifferent among the alternatives. This is hardly sufficient to satisfy democratic theorists.

flavor of dictatorship and/or are very indecisive (i.e., we may get social indifference over all or most of the set of alternatives).

Indecision is frequently encountered, for instance, if we abandon the search for a social ordering over the alternatives (and along with it the notion of a social preference relation) and simply demand that a social choice be made (that the "choice set" be nonempty). A full social ordering of alternatives is unnecessary, and there is a corresponding literature on the choice sets of individuals that we can draw on for inspiration. Sen (1970) demonstrated that it is possible to have a social choice process that has a nonempty choice set and meets the universal domain, nondictatorship, irrelevant alternatives, and Pareto conditions. The process is the Pareto-extension rule — it selects as the social choices the set of alternatives that are Pareto optimal. Such a process is obviously of little help in solving matters of social conflict, since it is so indecisive. That such a result is about the best we can get illustrates the extent to which a commitment to the spirit of Arrow's conditions constrains the nature of social choice processes.

Weakening the independence of irrelevant alternatives condition has been a tempting way of trying to exorcise Arrow's demon. Some do not like the fact that only ordinal individual preferences are permitted, and without the condition (and with suitable changes in other conditions) one might try to base social choices on cardinal preferences. Utilitarianism has been a dominant moral theory in philosophy for a long time, and its exclusion from social choice theory at the level of the axioms is unfortunate. That one important function of institutions might be to promote aggregate social welfare is difficult to reject, yet only a few studies of social choice processes have examined this aspect of performance in a way that goes beyond the fence of Pareto optimality beyond which economists are reluctant to tread. Fortunately, some axiomatic and empirical work that speaks to the utilitarians' concerns has begun to appear (for instance, see Maskin 1978).

The best reason for requiring some form of this condition is that if we do not, some unappealing things can happen in voting processes when the set of alternatives is itself a matter of choice among the participants. Winning alternatives can become losing alternatives if new alternatives are added or old (losing) alternatives are omitted. As Fishburn (1974) has demonstrated, drastic changes in the rankings assigned to alternatives by the Borda rule can result from changes in the set of alternatives. When social choice processes are viewed from a game-theoretic perspective, the failure to meet the independence condition can introduce large degrees of arbitrariness into the process, highlighting the importance of strategic considerations in institutions in which reasonably sophisticated individuals compete for the fruits of scarce resources.

The Indirect Path: Basic Institutions

By setting forth the normative criteria that guide institutional evaluation and making clear the difficulty of meeting many of these criteria simultaneously, investigations that focus on the direct path from individual preferences to social choices set the stage for studying institutions that can be used to actually make social choices. These analyses focus on the indirect path in figure 1, and the most frequently studied class of institutions in the literature is voting rules.

Voting rules are among the simplest forms of institutions. They take individual preferences and process them to arrive at a social choice. As institutions, they lack many of the attributes of full-blown institutions, such as hierarchy, formalized roles, and complex interactions among individuals within the institution. As the literature of formal political theory demonstrates, however, the choice of a voting system is an institutional choice with important implications. The different kinds of information that can be collected from individuals and the various ways in which "votes" can be counted give rise to a rich array of voting systems. In addition, there is ample empirical evidence that the choice of systems affects outcomes.

Majority Rule and the Instability Theorems

The most basic and most studied institution for making collective decisions is simple majority rule. It is about as simple as an institution can be, but majoritarian logic is so fundamental to democratic theory that attention to majority rule in its simplest form is a necessary prerequisite to considering more complex institutions of social choice. Since Condorcet, it has been known that majority rule can "cycle" among alternatives under certain configurations of preferences. The possibility of a majority voting cycle is the standard example in formal political theory of how problematic collective choice can be, and a great deal of attention has been devoted to understanding the conditions under which a cycle will not occur. In such a case, there will not be an alternative that cannot be defeated by any other alternative, and this lack of equilibrium calls into question the normative meaning of whatever outcome ultimately issues from a voting process.

By far the most influential results in this area come from analyses that have considered the process of majority rule over a set of alterna-

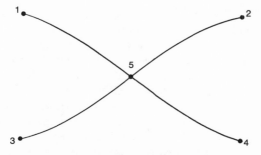

Fig. 2. Plott's conditions for majority-rule equilibrium

tives represented by a *n*-dimensional issue space. Individual preferences
for alternatives are assumed to be inversely related to the Euclidean
distance between the alternative and the individual's "ideal point" in the
issue space. The conditions under which a majority rule equilibrium
exists in such a model are too restrictive to give us any reason to believe
that they are ever met. One version of these conditions that is easy to
understand is due to Plott (1967), and is illustrated (for the two dimen-
sional case) in figure 2. The lines connecting the ideal points of persons 1
and 2 and persons 3 and 4 are the "contract curves" for these pairs — the
sets of alternatives for which it is impossible to make both persons better
off by a change. Plott's condition for an equilibrium is that it must be
possible to partition the individuals into pairs such that the intersection
of all the contract curves for the pairs intersect at one point. If there is an
odd number of individuals, then the remaining individual's (here number
5) ideal point must also lie at the point of intersection. Clearly, such
conditions will seldom, if ever, hold.

What does this mean for the stability of majority rule? It seems to
mean that something we can call *the* majority will does not exist. It is this
result that Riker (1982) considers to sound the death knell for what he
calls the "populist" interpretation of voting — no single, well-defined popular will exists, and therefore voting processes cannot hope to articulate
it. Some reacted to this result by accepting the fact that a majority rule
equilibrium will generally not exist, but reserved the hope that majority
rule would choose an alternative from a small set of "best" alternatives
that lie near the center of the set of the individuals' ideal points (i.e., near
the ideal point of individual 5 in fig. 2). This would surely be sufficient to
deliver on some of the spirit of Riker's populist interpretation of voting
and perhaps result in outcomes that would acceptably promote aggregate
utility (even if it did not maximize it). McKelvey (1976) and Schofield
(1978) dashed this hope. They showed that when no equilibrium exists, it

is possible to design a series of pairwise majority votes between alternatives that will lead from any point in the issue space to any other point in the issue space. Thus there is no reason to believe that a sequence of votes will lead to a "good" outcome, however that might be defined — majority rule will cycle around arbitrarily and at the whim of the agenda setter for voting until it is finally brought to a halt through some arbitrary means — parliamentary procedure, the fiat of some official, fatigue, etc. While any outcome may reflect the preferences of some majority of individuals relative to the previous status quo, there is no reason to believe that in the absence of more elaborate institutional structure the outcome so chosen has much normative standing.

Other Aggregation Rules

Despite the fundamental instability of majority rule, voting by citizens and within representative institutions must be carried out, and there are a number of voting systems whose characteristics recommend them to us.

In an important early paper, May (1952) showed that the method of pairwise majority comparison is characterized by four conditions: anonymity, neutrality, universal domain, and positive responsiveness. If the transitivity condition is added, an impossibility result is obtained, as the case of cyclical majorities illustrates. This instability is one justification for parliamentary procedures that restrict the comparisons that can be carried out.

Young (1974) provided an elegant axiomatization of the Borda rule, which most of us are familiar with as a method of compiling "Top 20" lists of athletic teams.[4] On the other side of the ledger, however, the Borda rule fails to meet two important criteria. First, it fails to meet the Condorcet criterion, which implements the fundamental norm of majority rule. Second, the Borda rule, as already noted, is susceptible to violating a variety of "subset rationality" conditions when the set of alternatives is varied. In practice, this is a particular problem when the set of alternatives is determined endogenously within an institution.

Another extensively-studied voting system is approval voting, which stands as the major innovation to date by social choice theorists. Developed by Brams and Fishburn (1978, 1983), approval voting permits voters to cast votes for as many candidates as they wish. The candidate

---

4. If there are n alternatives, each individual assigns n points to her first preference, $n-1$ to her second preference, and so on. The alternatives are then ranked by the number of points they receive. The social ranking of the alternatives that results corresponds to the ranking of the mean ranks given the alternatives by the individuals.

receiving the most votes wins. Approval voting combines an easily understood procedure with impressive axiomatic credentials. Because it is less than a decade old, the scholarly debate about the properties and performance of approval voting is far from complete. In the meantime, efforts by advocates of approval voting have met with some success in professional societies and political caucuses, and an empirical literature on approval voting is developing. Because of its simplicity and ability to produce desirable results in multicandidate elections, we may yet see it used in primary elections.

Axiomatic work has also been carried out on other rules of social choice that differ from the voting procedures just mentioned. In particular, the literature contains axiomatic investigations of utilitarianism and of Rawls's maximin principle. The utilitarian's quarrel with the standard social choice formulation of the problem is easily illustrated. Suppose one individual prefers x to y and another has the opposite preference. If the social process is to be impartial (neutral and anonymous), and if social choices are to depend only on the ordinal rankings of the two individuals, then society must be indifferent between x and y. But a utilitarian believes that we can coherently do more than compare ordinal preferences, and I think most of us agree that there are many instances in which this can be done without inordinate arbitrariness. Thus a utilitarian will want to reject the independence of irrelevant alternatives condition in the form in which it is usually used and substitute some other axiom about what information about individual preferences should be the raw material of social choices. The utilitarian will want to say, for instance, that based on the utilities involved, one person's preference for x over y has more moral weight than another's opposite preference. This does not violate the impartiality axiom, since it is not because of the labeling of the alternatives or of the individuals who make the judgment, but because of the nature of the preferences themselves.

Strasnick (1976) has proposed a modification of the independence of irrelevant alternatives condition that recognizes that in two person cases like that above, society may be able to assign a priority to one person's preference over another. If this is possible for all pairs of individuals, then an entire priority hierarchy can be constructed. If it is required that social choices be made consistent with such a hierarchy, then Strasnick shows that the resulting choice process will be similar to Rawls's maximin principle—a situation Strasnick refers to as that of a "justified dictator."[5]

---

5. For those unfamiliar with Rawls's work, the maximin principle requires that we seek to maximize the welfare of the least advantaged members of society.

Harsanyi (1977) has provided a defense of utilitarianism that has axiomatic roots. In particular, he shows that the axioms that underlie the case for maximizing expected utility in individual decisions under uncertainty can be restated in a form that supports the maximizing of aggregate utility as the proper choice when a collective choice must be made. The hole in this argument, at least in my eyes, concerns the "sure thing principle," which (in the collective formulation) requires that in a two-person society we must be indifferent between an alternative in which each of the two individuals receives one utile and another alternative that consists of an equiprobable lottery between two outcomes, one in which person 1 receives two utiles and person 2 receives none, and the other in which the distribution of utiles is reversed. Most conceptions of distributive justice or equality argue strongly for the first alternative as the appropriate social choice. This is another case in which importing an axiom that makes sense at the individual level into a discussion of collective decision making warrants deeper consideration.

Maskin (1978) has provided another axiomatic comparison of utilitarianism and the maximin principle. He shows that the former meets a continuity condition that the latter does not and that the maximin rule meets an equity condition that utilitarianism does not. The continuity condition is too complicated to pursue here, but the equity condition can be stated more easily. If $u(x,i)$ is the utility individual i gets from alternative x, then the equity condition says that if all but two individuals are indifferent between x and y and if $u(y,i) < u(x,i) < u(x,j) < u(y,j)$, then society chooses x. This axiom insures a preference for equality, other things equal, and will choose a more equal distribution over an unequal one with a greater aggregate utility.

The Liberal Paradox

Despite the general belief among those committed to democratic politics that majority rule is an appropriate method of solving political disputes, few believe that all questions are appropriately resolved in this manner. In particular, liberal democrats believe that there are some questions for which individuals ought to determine the choice (another kind of "justified dictator"). Ronald Dworkin's (1977) defense of rights is of this kind — there are some choices that ought not be determined on utilitarian (or other collective) grounds, but that properly lie with the individual. A number of interesting impossibility theorems show that there is an inconsistency between a commitment to the liberal principle of individual choice over some pairs of alternatives and the Pareto principle. Sen (1970) has shown that the universal domain, Pareto, and liberalism conditions are inconsistent. Gibbard (1974) has also done very interesting work on this problem. This work is of particular importance because it gives some indication of how formal political theory can cope with questions of individual rights as constraints on social choices.

The Other Challenge to Institutions:
The Manipulability Theorems

To this point, almost all of the discussion has focused on the problem of aggregating known individual preferences into a collective choice. A matter of great importance must now be considered. There may be a difference between an individual's true preferences and what she reveals about her preferences through her behavior in an actual social choice process. For strategic reasons, individuals may misrepresent their true preferences, a practice known in the voting literature as sophisticated (as opposed to sincere) voting. This possibility makes the task of institutional design represented by the indirect path between individual preferences and social choices in figure 1 even more difficult, for we have no guarantee that behavior is a true reflection of preferences (in Riker's terms, we observe the deed but not the thought). Another impossibility theorem drives home the force behind the possibility of strategic behavior: no interesting social choice process is invulnerable to manipulation through the misrepresentation of preferences (Gibbard 1973; Satterthwaite 1975). That is, for every decisive method of social choice there can exist conditions under which individuals can misrepresent their preferences and thereby bring about a social choice that they prefer to the choice that would have resulted from the expression of sincere preferences. This theorem is a stark reminder that we must consider the costs of strategic behavior when we evaluate alternative institutions, and makes susceptibility to manipulation an important criterion by which to judge institutions.[6]

Riker (1982) has seen this theorem as another telling blow to democratic theory. The instability theorems tell us that there is no such thing as "the majority will" and that left to itself majority rule will cycle around the entire issue space. Now we learn that however we bring a voting process to a stop, we have to face not only the fact that we have terminated it arbitrarily, but that the behavior that got us to where we are may not even reflect the true preferences of individuals. The instability

---

6. In economics, there has been a great deal of attention paid to "demand-revealing processes" that avoid incentives to misrepresent demand for public goods. See the special edition of *Public Choice* (1977) for an excellent discussion of work in this area.

and manipulability results lead Riker to the conclusion that only the "liberal" interpretation of voting can been sustained. On this interpretation, voting is a valuable institution because it offers us a chance to throw out tyrants, but it cannot be counted on to deliver outcomes with firm moral underpinnings—the whole process is simply too arbitrary to fulfill that function.

This is truly a depressing scene if we view it the way Riker does. Fortunately, I do not think we have to do so. Perhaps the best antidote to Riker's pessimism is found in an important paper by Nicholas Miller (1983). Miller returns to democratic theory as exemplified by thinkers like Madison and Schattschneider, and makes the argument that the very instability that Riker bemoans is the key to the long-run, peaceful operation of a democratic society. The knowledge that no majority will exists, and along with it the knowledge that there exists a way to oust an incumbent, whomever it may be, gives rise to the "wait 'til next year" spirit than gives losers good reasons to accept outcomes and devote their efforts to planning for the next election. Seen from Miller's vantage point, the instability theorems are not such bad news after all. His analysis also forces us to confront the important tension between static equilibrium and dynamic stability. Miller's analysis gives us reason to think seriously about the notion of meta-preferences for institutions, since it leads us to look not just at the one-shot performance of an institution but at the performance of an institution over time.

If the instability of majority rule is not as disturbing as Riker intimates, then we need not be so attentive to the problems of equilibria in the abstract, and we can attend instead to the study of the other effects that institutions have on outcomes of voting games. If democratic theory does not demand equilibria in the abstract, we can ask more of political institutions than Riker believes they are capable of and get on with the work of studying the performance of various institutions. Equilibria will still be a primary concern, but we will be freed from having them as our only concern. We can then turn our attention to the ways in which particular features of institutions bring about *structure-induced equilibria* when *preference-induced equilibria* would not exist in their absence. A good deal of work of this kind has been done, particularly in the last decade, and it is this line of work that warrants the interest of institutionalists of all kinds.

Designing and Evaluating Complex Institutions

Impossibility theorems, instability theorems, and manipulability theorems make clear the difficulty of designing voting systems that produce appropriate collective outcomes. Analyses that focus on more elaborate institutions allow us to confront this challenge in a productive way by separating institutions (function *H* in fig. 1) from individual strategic behavior (function *G*) and to investigate the ways in which they interact.

The Preference-Behavior Link

The manipulation theorems make it obvious that we cannot ignore the implications of strategic behavior, and this greatly complicates the analysis of institutional performance. Solution concepts from game theory become central to the analysis, and with this arises the question of just how we model the behavior of individuals who find themselves in very complicated strategic situations.

The performance of a given institution is likely to depend on what model of individual behavior we use, and there is a wide range of models to choose from. Some are noted for their elegance, while others may have a greater claim to capturing naturally occurring behavior. For instance, we can use the Nash equilibrium concept of noncooperative games, in which each individual (acts as if she) has knowledge of the entire game structure, including the preferences of all players, and solves for equilibrium strategies for all players. Or one can impose an even stronger standard, the notion of a strong equilibrium, which requires not only that no individual have a unilateral incentive to switch from her equilibrium strategy, but also that no coalition be able to coordinate changes in their strategies such that all coalition members are better off.

Such superrational behavior on the part of individuals runs counter to other insights into individual behavior, some of which come from the public choice literature itself. From the Downsian (1957) tradition of utility-maximizing political behavior we observe the tendencies for individuals to remain ignorant of much of what goes on around them. From the Olsonian (1965) tradition concerned with collective action we observe the tendency toward nonparticipation in collective action. Ignorance and passivity are difficult to reconcile with the demands of game-theoretic solution concepts, and some tough decisions have to be made when it comes to modeling this link in the process. Some studies have used game-theoretic solutions to model this link, while others have used various conceptions of bounded rationality to craft models of behavior. For instance, in my work on the manipulability of voting systems, I have usually restricted manipulation strategies to those that can be easily communicated and do not require complete information about voter preferences (1985).

This link in the indirect path is particularly important to those concerned with institutions that go beyond mere voting rules. For those interested in proving theorems, the game-theoretic models will do just fine, but those who must cope with the naturally occurring behavior of mass and elite actors embedded within complex institutions may not find such analyses sufficient for the task of evaluating these institutions. Game-theoretic models seem most appropriate for modeling elite behavior, so they may be appropriate for models of legislatures and bureaucracies. But students of these institutions have doubts about the ability of formal models to capture the richness and subtlety of political and bureaucratic behavior. Progress in developing more sophisticated models has been slow, but considerable activity in this area has occurred in the last decade. Ultimate success for formal theory in helping us with institutional questions depends on the continued development of work on this link.

The Implementation Problem

The manipulation theorems drive home with a vengeance the game-theoretic nature of social choice. Not only do we face obstacles in determining which outcome *ought* to occur given individual preferences, but we face the additional problem of designing institutions that can deliver the right outcome even if individuals behave strategically. This possibility means that it is along the indirect path from preferences to social choices that answers must be sought. The direct path can tell us what is possible and can tell us what the "right" social choice is once we decide what conditions we want to honor, but the real work comes in designing rules, incentive structures, or other processes that are capable of delivering the right outcome in the face of potentially strategic behavior by individuals. This is usually referred to as the "implementation" problem.

The implementation problem shares many characteristics with procedural justice as John Rawls discusses it. He refers to three levels of the problem — perfect procedural justice, imperfect procedural justice, and pure procedural justice. At the first level, we know what the right answer is and the task is to design a rule that can generate the desired answer. Rawls cites the "cake-cutting" problem as the prototype of pure procedural justice: the right answer is to cut the cake in half, and this can be accomplished if we let one person cut the cake into two pieces and let the other choose first. The pursuit of equilibria and economic efficiency are frequently studied in this way; existence proofs make up much of this literature.

The case of imperfect procedural justice is one step more complicated; there is a right answer, but we can never know whether in any actual instance we have achieved it. A jury trial is Rawls' example of imperfect procedural justice. In a world in which we will seldom possess the kind of information that is necessary to determine whether we have the right outcome, particularly in the face of strategic behavior, the task is one of designing institutions that will do as good a job as possible. One attribute of a good institution from this perspective is robustness in the face of different models of individual behavior, for that will make the evaluation of the institution itself less dependent on the choice we make concerning the preference-behavior link. We might expect individuals to have preferences for institutions based not just on the outcomes produced by the institutions, but on procedural properties of the institutions that generate the outcomes.

The most challenging of Rawls' categories is pure procedural justice, and it is at this level that Rawls pursues a theory of justice. Here the right answer requires a simultaneous and mutually reinforcing determination of principles and institutions. Formal political theory has had some impact here, particularly the impossibility theorems, but on the whole its contributions have been more on the side of demonstrating the difficulty of the problem than on the side of lending a hand in solving it.

The implementation problem thus faces us at several levels of complexity, and presents the basic challenge of institutional design: we must simultaneously develop and evaluate models of institutions and of strategic individual behavior within them.

Insights into Institutions

The formal theory literature helps us to understand the performance of a variety of more complex institutions, and such work has become more prominent in recent years. I focus here on political institutions and rules.

The Empirical Evaluation of Voting Systems

Evaluations of the performance of voting systems in practice make up an important part of the literature. Where the axiomatic work has clarified the logical properties of voting systems, the empirical literature has attempted to provide estimates of how often the various difficulties that *can* happen *will* happen. Most of this work has relied upon Monte Carlo methods to generate voter preferences, although there are a few studies of naturally occurring elections, my own work on elections of the American Psychological Association (Chamberlin, Cohen, and Coombs 1984) being an example. This literature has focused on several criteria in evaluating voting systems: the ability of a system to select a Condorcet winner when one exists, the frequency with which the system can be manipulated, and occasionally the ability of the system to select an alternative with a high aggregate utility. The literature indicates that the performance of a voting system usually depends on the character of preferences of voters and that the frequency of anomalies is greater in so-called impartial cultures (where all preference orders are assumed to be equally likely to occur) than is the case when preferences are generated by a spatial model of preferences.[7]

In addition to studies of particular voting systems, attention has focused on the frequency of occurrence of majority voting cycles. Early studies investigated this question for impartial cultures, and showed that the probability of a cycle increased with the number of voters and the number of alternatives. More recent work using spatial models has found a much lower frequency of cycles.[8]

The Spatial Model of Electoral Competition

This is probably the best known body of work within this tradition. It investigates the ability of electoral competition among political parties to generate political outcomes with certain desirable properties — usually an outcome that corresponds to a majority rule equilibrium. Downs (1957) showed that if individuals' preferences over candidates for election to an office could be arrayed on a single dimension so that each voter's preferences were "singlepeaked," then a two-party system of electoral competition would induce each candidate to announce a platform that corresponded to the ideal point of the median voter, a position that could defeat all others in pairwise majority comparisons. Over the years this model has been elaborated in a great variety of ways. The effects of voter indifference and alienation have been incorporated. The strong assumption that voters always vote for the candidate closest to them has been replaced with the concept of a "support function" that requires only that the likelihood of voting for a candidate is responsive (in appropriate ways) to the candidate's positions and the individual's ideal point. The recent book by Enelow and Hinich (1984) provides an excellent summary of developments in this area.

---

7. See Chamberlin and Cohen 1978, and particularly Merrill 1984 for further details on this point.

8. See Chamberlin and Cohen 1978; Merrill 1984, 1988.

The Structure of Legislative Decisions

The problem that has received the most attention in recent years concerns decision making in legislative bodies. This work usually focuses on decisions over alternatives situated in a spatial model and has arisen in response to both the instability and manipulation theorems. The force of the latter theorem has been illustrated by work on the effects of agendas on social choices. McKelvey's theorem says that an agenda can be constructed to get us from any status quo to anywhere we might want to go, and this formal result was followed by empirical demonstrations that those who control the agenda have a major impact on voting outcomes. Plott's work (1978) is particularly compelling on this question. The earliest work on agendas showed that experimenters could substantially control voting outcomes by dictating the agenda to be followed.

Recent work has recognized that in most legislatures the agenda is endogenous. This has required more sophisticated analyses, and new solution concepts have been put forward that enable us to see how stable legislative decisions will occur in situations in which the absence of any institutional constraints would have led to endless cycling around the issue space. This work represents an instance where interest in particular institutions has led to important new concepts at the theoretical level, illustrating the productive interaction between concern for institutional analysis and the development of theory that makes it possible.

Kenneth Shepsle (1979, 1981) has been the leader in this line of work, but an increasing number of scholars have turned their attention to this set of questions. We now understand that many of the kinds of rules that we observe in legislative bodies are capable of bringing about structure-induced equilibria.[9] Among the institutional features that have been analyzed are: bicameral legislatures, committee systems, closed rules governing floor votes, germaneness rules, line item vetoes, and parliamentary procedures. These analyses typically assume quite sophisticated behavior on the part of participants, but this may not be such an excessive assumption when professional legislators are under investigation. They also frequently show that sophisticated behavior, rather than making institutions work less well, actually leads to a greater stability of outcomes.

In addition to assuming prodigious reasoning powers on the part of participants, these analyses also assume that each participant possesses perfect knowledge of the preferences of the other participants. This

---

9. See Denzau and Mackay 1983; Ferejohn, Fiorina, and McKelvey 1987; Krehbiel n.d.; Shepsle and Weingast 1981.

assumption is more difficult to reconcile with the reality of legislative decision making, and work that relied on weaker assumptions about information would move this literature a considerable step closer to the concerns of congressional scholars and others who might benefit from the insights of this theoretical literature. Another major deficiency in this part of the formal political theory literature is that it has focused almost exclusively on questions of stability and Pareto optimality. Work that brings in other important criteria, particularly distributional criteria, is badly needed, and it is important that future efforts in this area have broader reach.

Representative Democracy

One of the reasons that studies of legislative decision making have difficulty in bringing in other evaluative criteria is that the links between these representative bodies and those who are represented have not been much studied by formal theorists. This is one of the areas that is ripe for future work. Paul Courant and I have done some formal work on representation (1983), as have Grofman and Feld (1986), and Sugden (1984). Representation raises new challenges; for example, the nature of preferences for representatives, the multiple purposes of representation, and the principal-agent relationship. It would be an important advance if one could tie together work on representation with the work discussed above on legislative decision making. One could then study the effects of different legislative structures and different methods of selecting representatives, and tie all of this back to the preferences of the electorate. This would permit evaluative criteria like welfare maximization, protection of minority interests, and other normative concerns besides efficiency and stability to be brought into institutional evaluation.

Experimental Work

Formal theorists have also made an important methodological contribution to the study of institutions by demonstrating the usefulness of laboratory experiments in helping us to understand the performance of institutions. Interestingly, rather than the field splitting into theorists and experimentalists as often happens, some of the major theorists have been at the forefront of experimental work. Laboratory experiments are particularly useful to the study of institutions because of the difficulty of making singular predictions about political outcomes. The work on structure-induced equilibria has managed to find a sense of stability in the chaos established by the instability theorems, but it has done so by identifying sets of outcomes that would be stable rather than by singling out specific outcomes. Such results are more difficult to check with empirical studies grounded in naturally occurring legislatures, and the laboratory provides a rich and flexible alternative for studying the new solution concepts that are being developed by theorists.

Experimental work has focused both on the evaluation of institutional rules and structures and on the validation of game-theoretic solution concepts. The experimental route provides the opportunity to build in contextual factors and to observe individual behavior in strategic situations. Experiments that involve continuing interactions among subjects also offer the opportunity of observing changes in behavior over time and may well provide some insights into the integrative aspects of institutions as well. To date, experiments have yielded important findings concerning the effects of agendas on outcomes of collective decisions, the ability of solution concepts to predict outcomes, and the kinds of decisions about social decision rules that subjects make when placed in a situation akin to Rawls's "original position" (Frolich, Oppenheimer, and Eavey 1987). Plott (1979) provides a general discussion of the use of laboratory experiments in this field, and the discussion that follows his paper raises some additional points concerning the strengths and weaknesses of this approach.

Important Remaining Challenges

Despite the considerable contributions that formal political theory makes to our understanding of institutions, there are some fundamental features of this approach that stand in the way of its providing fully satisfying results. Among these are the insufficient attention to distributional criteria and the narrowness of the assumptions about individual preferences. I close with a few comments on this latter issue.

The heavy debt that formal political theory owes to neoclassical economics entails both strengths and weaknesses. This is nowhere more evident than in the assumption that individual preferences are exogenous, fixed, and known by the individuals who possess them.[10] Indeed, individuals in this literature are little more than bundles of preferences coupled with reasoning abilities of specified kinds. Although these assumptions permit considerable insight into the behavior of individuals and the performance of institutions, they also raise major problems. It is axiomatic among sociologists and political theorists that there is no such

---

10. See March and Olsen 1987 and Wildavsky 1987 for two recent discussions of these issues.

thing as an exogenous preference; preferences are molded and constrained by experience and context. Nor is there reason to accept preferences as fixed. Our preferences develop and change, often as a result of
political and social interaction with others. These assumptions have
important implications for the evaluation of institutions. For instance, to
the extent that our preferences become more truly our own through the
process of political deliberation, analyses of institutions (like the market)
that try to decentralize decision making and reduce face-to-face contact
among citizens may overlook a fundamental function and purpose of
public institutions.

The notion that each individual has a single, well defined set of
preferences is open to serious question as well. It may be the case that
individuals have more than one set of preferences, or that what individuals prefer may depend on where and how the question is asked. For
instance, individuals may be able to distinguish between their narrow
egotistic preferences and their "social" preferences. There is considerable
empirical evidence in support of this structure of preferences, and a
number of contemporary theorists who have tried, do get some mileage
out of such a notion. If individuals do not have unique, well defined
preferences, then it seems likely that the ways in which preferences
invoke behavior will depend on the institutional context in which behavior takes place. If it is also true, as seems to be the case, that our
preferences change over time, then it is almost certain that whatever
feedback processes determine preference change are affected by the outcomes of previous decisions and the nature of the institutions through
which they were made.[11] Grofman and Uhlaner (1985) have raised the
possibility that individuals have "meta-preferences" for institutions that
can affect whether and how they assign legitimacy to social choices. Such
meta-preferences may be important in bringing some order out of the
chaos that so often characterizes social choices in the formal theory
literature.

Finally, the assumption that preferences are known by the individuals who possess them is often heroic. Determining one's preferences can
be a costly undertaking, and individuals may have good reasons to avoid
these costs. This is particularly true when decisions are made collectively,
where free rider behavior may frequently be coupled with lack of intro-
spection concerning preferences. The murky nature of preferences is
particularly important to the question of representative democracy, for it

---

11. Cohen and Axelrod (1986) illustrate one formal process by which preference
changes may arise; additional work on formal models of learning, persuasion, deliberation,
etc. is badly needed if progress is to be made on these issues within formal political theory.

matters a good deal whether a representative institution is merely to be a conduit for already formed preferences or an arena in which representatives deliberate not only about what issues should be on the public agenda but about the nature of their constituents' preferences (either their actual preferences or the preferences they would have if they had the inclination and/or the time to reflect on them).

This criticism of the methodological foundations of formal political theory are, of course, not new, and work continues on a variety of fronts to push forward our ability to model the evolution of preferences in rigorous ways. One must admit, however, that until formal approaches to these issues can deliver a more sophisticated understanding of preferences, institutional evaluation will require that we supplement the insights of formal political theory with large doses of "integrative" insights as well.

Conclusion

In this essay I have attempted to show how formal political theory as it has developed over the past forty years provides a particularly useful way to think about institutions. Normative considerations can be embedded in the axioms that provide the abstract underpinnings of the enterprise. Game-theoretic analyses can capture the complex interactions between actors who behave strategically in attempting to influence outcomes to their own advantages, and permit us to examine the performance of alternative institutional structures and rules under varying assumptions about individual behavior. Laboratory experiments offer the opportunity to observe behavior as a means of testing both models of individual behavior and models of alternative institutions. Taken together, the various parts of this literature thus offer a powerful perspective on the design and evaluation of political institutions. Despite the progress to date, I believe that there remains much important work to be done, work that will bring together the findings of formal political theory and other bodies of social science scholarship that are less dependent on economics for its foundations. Future work in this vein has the promise of placing in our hands a more general and more insightful theory of institutions.

R E F E R E N C E S

Arrow, Kenneth J. 1951. *Social Choice and Individual Values.* New York: Wiley.
Black, Duncan. 1948. "On the Rationale of Group Decision Making." *Journal of Political Economy* 56:23–34.

_____. 1958. *The Theory of Committees and Elections.* Cambridge: Cambridge University Press.

Brams, Steven J., and Peter Fishburn. 1978. "Approval Voting." *American Political Science Review* 72:831–47.

_____. 1983. *Approval Voting.* Boston: Birkhauser.

Chamberlin, John R. 1985. "An Investigation into the Relative Manipulability of Four Social Choice Functions." *Behavioral Science* 30:195–203.

Chamberlin, John R., and Michael D. Cohen. 1978. "Toward Applicable Social Choice Theory: A Comparison of Social Choice Functions under Spatial Model Assumptions." *American Political Science Review* 72:1341–56.

Chamberlin, John R., and Paul N. Courant. 1983. "Representative Deliberations and Representative Decisions: Proportional Representation and the Borda Rule." *American Political Science Review* 77:718–33.

Chamberlin, John R., Jerry L. Cohen, and Clyde H. Coombs. 1984. "Social Choice Observed: Five Presidential Elections of the American Psychological Association." *Journal of Politics* 46:479–502.

Cohen, Michael D., and Robert Axelrod. 1986. "Coping with Complexity: The Adaptive Value of Changing Utility." *American Economic Review* 74:30–42.

Cox, Gary W. 1984. "Strategic Electoral Choice in Multimember Districts: Approval Voting in Practice." *American Journal of Political Science* 28:722–38.

_____. 1985. "Electoral Equilibrium under Approval Voting." *American Journal of Political Science* 29:112–18.

d'Aspremont, C., and L. Gevers. 1977. "Equity and the Informational Basis of Collective Choice." *Review of Economic Studies* 44:199–210.

Denzau, Arthur T., and Robert J. Mackay. 1983. "Gatekeeping and Monopoly Power of Committees: An Analysis of Sincere and Sophisticated Behavior." *American Journal of Political Science* 27:740–61.

Downs, Anthony. 1957. *An Economic Theory of Democracy.* New York: Harper and Row.

Dworkin, Ronald. 1977. *Taking Rights Seriously.* Cambridge, Mass.: Harvard University Press.

Enelow, James M., and Melvin J. Hinich. 1984. *The Spatial Theory of Voting: An Introduction.* Cambridge: Cambridge University Press.

Ferejohn, John, Morris Fiorina, and Richard D. McKelvey. 1987. "Sophisticated Voting and Agenda Independence in the Distributive Politics Setting." *American Journal of Political Science* 31:168–93.

Fishburn, Peter C. 1974. "Paradoxes of Voting." *American Political Science Review* 68:537–46.

Frolich, Norman, Joe A. Oppenheimer, and Cheryl L. Eavey. 1987. "Choice of Principles of Distributive Justice in Experimental Groups." *American Journal of Political Science* 31:606–36.

Gibbard, Allan F. 1973. "Manipulation of Voting Schemes." *Econometrica* 41:587–601.

_____. 1974. "A Pareto-Consistent Libertarian Claim." *Journal of Economic Theory* 7:388–410.

Grofman, Bernard, and Scott Feld. 1986. "On the Possibility of Faithfully Representative Committees." *American Political Science Review* 80:863–79.

Grofman, Bernard and Carole Uhlaner. 1985. "Meta Preferences and the Reasons for Stability in Social Choice: Thoughts on Broadening and Clarifying the Debate." *Theory and Decision* 19:31–50.

Harsanyi, John. 1977. "Mortality and the Theory of Rational Behavior." *Social Research* 44:623–656.

Hotelling, Harold. 1929. "Stability in Competition." *Economic Journal* 39:41–57.

Krehbiel, Keith. N.d. "Sophisticated Committees and Structure-Induced Equilibria in Congress." In *Congress: Structure and Policy,* ed. Mathew McCubbins and Terry Sullivan. New York: Cambridge University Press. Forthcoming.

McKelvey, Richard D. 1976. "Intransitivities in Multidimensional Voting Models and Some Implications for Agenda Control." *Journal of Economic Theory* 47:1085–1112.

March, James G., and Johan P. Olsen. 1987. "Popular Sovereignty and the Search for Appropriate Institutions." *Journal of Public Policy* 6:341–70.

Maskin, Eric. 1978. "A Theorem on Utilitarianism." *Review of Economic Studies* 45:93–96.

May, Kenneth O. 1952. "A Set of Necessary and Sufficient Conditions for Simple Majority Decision." *Econometrica* 20:680–84.

Merrill, Samuel, III. 1984. "A Comparison of Efficiency of Multicandidate Electoral Systems." *American Journal of Political Science* 28:23–48.

_____. 1988. *Making Multicandidate Elections More Democratic.* Princeton, N.J.: Princeton University Press.

Miller, Nicholas R. 1980. "A New Solution Set for Tournaments and Majority Voting: Further Graph-Theoretic Approaches to the Theory of Voting." *American Journal of Political Science* 24:68–96.

_____. 1983. "Pluralism and Social Choice." *American Political Science Review* 77:734–47.

Niemi, Richard G. 1984. "The Problem of Strategic Behavior under Approval Voting." *American Political Science Review* 78:952–58.

Olson, Mancur. 1965. *The Logic of Collective Action.* Cambridge, Mass.: Harvard University Press.

Plott, Charles R. 1967. "A Notion of Equilibrium and Its Possibility under Majority Rule." *American Economic Review* 57:788–806.

_____. 1979. "The Application of Laboratory Experimental Methods to Public Choice." In *Collective Decision Making,* ed. Clifford R. Russell. Washington, D.C.: Resources for the Future.

Plott, Charles R., and Michael E. Levine. 1978. "A Model of Agenda Influence on Committee Decisions." *American Economic Review* 68:146–60.

Rawls, John. 1971. *A Theory of Justice.* Cambridge, Mass.: Harvard University Press.

Riker, William H. 1982. *Liberal against Populism*. New York: Freeman.

Satterthwaite, Mark A. 1975. "Strategy-proofness and Arrow's Conditions: Existence and Correspondence Theorems for Voting Procedures and Social Welfare Functions." *Journal of Economic Theory* 10:198–217.

Schofield, Norman. 1978. "Instability of Simple Dynamic Games." *Review of Economic Studies* 45:575–94.

Sen, Amartya K. 1970. *Collective Choice and Social Welfare*. San Francisco: Holden-Day.

Shepsle, Kenneth A. 1979. "Institutional Arrangements and Equilibrium in Multidimensional Voting Models." *American Journal of Political Science* 23:27–59.

Shepsle, Kenneth A., and Barry R. Weingast. 1981. "Structure-Induced Equilibrium and Legislative Choice." *Public Choice* 37:503–19.

_____. 1984. "Uncovered Sets and Sophisticated Voting Outcomes with Implications for Agenda Institutions." *American Journal of Political Science* 29:49–74.

Strasnick, Steven. 1976. "The Problem of Social Choice: Arrow to Rawls." *Philosophy and Public Affairs* 5:241–73.

Sugden, Robert. 1984. "Free Association and the Theory of Proportional Representation." *American Political Science Review* 78:31–43.

Tideman, T. Nicholas, ed. 1977. *Public Choice* 29, Special Supplement.

Wildavsky, Aaron. 1987. "Choosing Preferences by Constructing Institutions: A Cultural Theory of Preference Formation." *American Political Science Review* 81:3–22.

Young, P. 1974. "An Axiomatization of Borda's Rule." *Journal of Economic Theory* 9:43–52.

CHAPTER 9

Building the Impossible State: Toward an Institutional Analysis of Statebuilding in America, 1820 – 1930

Terrence J. McDonald

In his great work *The American Commonwealth*, published in London just about one hundred years ago, James Bryce aptly characterized the peculiar pervasiveness of the American state. For Bryce, the American citizen lived with a duality that few Europeans could understand: a national government that claimed his allegiance, but state and state chartered local governments that helped shape the parameters of his daily life.

> An American may, through a long life, never be reminded of the Federal Government, except when he votes at presidential and congressional elections . . . . His direct taxes are paid to officials acting under State laws. The State, or a local authority constituted by State statutes, registers his birth, appoints his guardian, pays for his schooling, gives him a share in the estate of his father deceased, licenses him when he enters a trade (if it be one needing a license), marries him, divorces him, entertains civil actions against him, declares him a bankrupt, hangs him for murder. The police that guard his house, the local boards which look after the poor, control highways, impose water rates, manage schools — all these derive their legal powers from his State alone. (Bryce 1888, 1:411–12)

Bryce might have gone on, for state and local governments were not only pervasive at the individual level in nineteenth-century America, but at the level of society and economy as well (Campbell 1980). In the broadest sense, in fact, the legislative and judicial branches of the state and local levels of the American federal system were fundamentally and continuously involved in the definition and redefinition of "public" and "private" in terms of property, interests, and realms of action. As economic historian Jonathan Hughes has pointed out, for example, nonmarket social controls of private activity — especially economic activity — were characteristic of the American political economy at the state and local levels from the beginning, legends of laissez-faire notwithstanding (Hughes 1977). Moreover, as legal historian Harry Scheiber has noted, state and local governments engineered a massive shift of resources from public to private uses through the distribution of public lands, the granting of legal privileges and immunities, direct capital investment in some projects — especially railroads — and the provision of a wide variety of police, education, and social welfare services. Conversely, through their fiscal policies, these governments shifted a sizable portion of private resources to public uses via regressive excise and property taxation and the approval of long-term bonded indebtedness (Scheiber 1975).

The sheer extent of these activities, however, is not as important as the recognition that in all of these ways state and local governments were continually constituting and reconstituting conflicting political actors; "winners" and "losers" in the process by which government conferred privileges and created or extracted resources. On one side of these actions might stand the railroad entrepreneur and his workers whose enterprise the state subsidized; on the other the artisan whose wages plummeted when the railroad brought more workers to town or the farmers whose heretofore "common" lands were enclosed by railroad fences. Yet at another time, say over the issue of taxation of real versus personal property, entrepreneurs, artisans, and farmers might stand together against the state or against banks, speculators, and others whose holdings were usually not taxed or not assessed "fairly." In the course of frequent local and state elections and constitutional conventions the agrarians and aristocrats, producers and drones, people and monopolists, machines and reformers fought over the appropriate role and size of the state. Moreover, these battles were frequently among forces constituted by the heavy hand of the government — e.g., taxpayers, bondholders, corporations, feeders at the public trough, and so on — rather than the hidden hand of the economy.

It is this sense of an active and controversial state in nineteenth-century America that has been lost in much recent work. Even in the midst of a widely noted campaign to "bring the state back in," historians, political scientists, and sociologists have had a hard time rediscovering the contours of an American state that were familiar to Bryce as well as to most nineteenth-century Americans. In 1982, for example, a leading political scientist could write that the "exceptional character of the early American state is neatly summarized in the paradox that it failed to evoke any sense of a state," while another would state flatly the next year that "there was no state" in America before 1860 (Skowronek 1982, 5;

Keohane 1983 cited in Keller 1987, 681). In a similar vein, a prominent historical sociologist studying the "late" development of the American welfare state would write in 1985 that late nineteenth-century American politics served "primarily symbolic-expressive and entertainment functions" and was not a matter of using politics to articulate demands for policies, but rather of "getting out the vote" within the "various ethnically and religiously based local residence communities" (Skocpol and Ikenberry 1983).

These writings and many others like them share a number of problems. First, they look for the American state at the national level where it is supposed to be rather than at the state and local level where the federal structure located it. Second, they reduce politics to a matter of symbolism and culture, rather than considering its role in political economy. Finally, they substitute relatively vague notions of "sensations" of the state for much clearer—if changing—ideologies about the proper role and size of the state in these years. These attempts to find the state keep coming back empty handed, therefore, in great part because they fail to think carefully about what they are looking for.

This essay considers the possible benefits of a more institutionally oriented approach to the history of the statebuilding process in America during the years when some fundamental patterns in both society and polity were constructed. It does not intend to put forward a new interpretation of that process, for that would take a good deal longer than the space of one essay. It does, however, attempt to show how a focus on structure, ideology, and the tasks of the state itself might help change what we find when we go looking for the state. To do this it will attempt to answer three questions: first, where was the state in America in these years located structurally; second, where was it located ideologically, and third, given these locations, how might a focus on the changing fiscal capacity of the state enrich our understanding of its interactive relationship with society.

Before turning to these more political historical questions, however, it is worth considering briefly some issues from intellectual history: why did social science move away from institutions in the first place?

The Rise and Fall of Institutional Analysis

Bryce noted that, relative to the attention lavished on the federal government, the state and local levels of the federal system had at that time received little attention. The study of these government activities, he wrote, was a "primeval forest, where the vegetation is rank, and through which scarcely a trail has yet been cut." Yet he had high hopes that what he called "the new historical school which is growing up at the leading American universities" would ultimately "grapple with this task" (Bryce 1888, 399–400).

Bryce's confidence in the rising institutional focus of American social science was not entirely misplaced, because for about the first three decades of the twentieth century institutionally focused historians, political scientists, and sociologists did produce detailed studies of these levels of government. As the century moved on, however, the focus on institutions as the constituent elements of society gave way to a focus on individuals in that role and the aggregations of their behavior as the components of institutions. Hand in hand with this change went a change in emphasis from the ways in which institutions shaped individual behavior to the ways in which they were shaped by it, and from the autonomous logic of institutional development (especially of political institutions) to institutional development as simply an epiphenomenon of stronger socioeconomic forces. By the middle of the century these new foci had almost totally subsumed the "state" to "society" rendering it neither pervasive nor controversial.

The story of the changing interest in institutions in general and the state in particular is a complicated one involving changes in liberal politics and social scientific theoretical and methodological agendas. For the reform-oriented institutionalists trained in the so-called progressive era, American institutions were important because they were problematic, potential obstacles to the cause of political reform. Moreover, historical and descriptive methods were the only ones available and institutions made a good focus for such work.

For the self-proclaimed "realist" generation that succeeded — and criticized — the progressive institutionalists, American institutions were less problematic and less interesting. Writing in the shadows of depression, fascism, war, and cold war, social scientists of the forties and fifties became convinced that American institutions were both more successful than their predecessors had thought and less important than the political culture that underlay them. Moreover, by means of powerful quantitative methods this generation had access to the components of that culture that their predecessors had lacked.

As Edward Purcell, among others, has written, the institutional tendency in the social sciences was led by men who believed in the ultimately rational nature of the universe and thought that science could lead to a full understanding of the social process and "an intelligent reordering of American institutions in a spirit of social harmony" (Purcell 1973, 24). By revealing the process of institutional change, authors like Bryce, Charles Beard, later even V. O. Key, hoped to discover the best ways for institutions to be changed so as to unleash the rationality and good will of the populace. Moreover, their interest in institutions was driven by their interest in reform: successful reform demonstrated that institutions could change; reform-oriented intellectuals argued that they should change and believed that social science would help (Purcell 1973).

Somewhat ironically, both the scientific work that they called for and the events of the 1930s and 1940s began to undermine these views, however. To begin with, the empirical studies that the leaders of the social sciences themselves advocated—e.g., those of political scientist Harold Lasswell in the thirties—began to discover irrational aspects of personality and behavior within individuals, leading to the possibility that the problem was not institutions at all. The nearly simultaneous rise of fascism and the onset of war in Europe seemed both to confirm these findings and to highlight the success of American political institutions—as embodied in the New Deal—in preventing similar developments. In Europe, democratic institutions had been swept away in a wave of popular irrationality; in America, the same institutions that had been lambasted by the progressive institutionalists had stood firm (Seidelman and Harpham 1985). Why?

One answer was offered in political scientist E. Pendleton Herring's enormously influential 1940 book *The Politics of Democracy*, which was essentially a paean to American political institutions and a call for more analysis of the democratic culture in America. For Herring the problem was not American institutions, but "the application of critical standards too high for human attainment" by reformers (Herring 1940, x). According to Herring, reformers failed to realize that men were not rational, but rather passionate and greedy. Because they were, political institutions were needed to stand in as a disciplining and moderating influence. In Herring's view, it was the reformers themselves who tended to produce a sense of frustration and cynicism about American political institutions because of their unrealistic standards (Ricci 1984; Herring 1940).

In addition to his attack on the reforming institutionalists, Herring's book contained two related arguments that contained the seeds of the predominant approaches to American institutions in the postwar period. The first was simply the revision of their problematic status; Herring argued that America's much maligned political institutions worked better than or in ways other than their critics thought. The second argument was that institutional mechanisms were less important for the preservation of American democracy than what he called a "democratic ideology," the set of primarily cultural attitudes that allowed democratic institutions to work.

In the postwar years, Herring's more "realistic" evaluation of both the performance and centrality of institutions in America triumphed over the alleged naivete, simplistic dualism, and rationalism of the early institutionalists. The view that American institutions were better than they seemed was coincidentally supported by the theory of "latent functions" popularized by structural-functional sociologist Robert Merton. The view that institutions were less important than "culture" was explicitly taken up in the work of pluralist political scientists, perhaps most prominently Robert Dahl.

Alternatives to Institutions: Culture and Functions

The methodological and substantive differences between an institutionalist like Bryce, on the one hand, and Dahl and Merton, on the other, are enormous and instructive. For Bryce there were three things that one needed to know about a commonwealth: "its framework and constitutional machinery, the methods by which it is worked, the forces which move it and direct its course (Bryce 1888, 1:5). For Dahl, writing in *A Preface to Democratic Theory*, published in 1956, these things were the "chaff" of democratic politics; institutions were less important guarantors of American democracy than the widespread "consensus" that underlay them. "Prior to politics, beneath it, enveloping it, restricting it, conditioning it, is the underlying consensus on policy that usually exists in the society among a predominant portion of the politically active members" (Dahl 1956, 132).

Substantively, their views of local politics—the critical locus of political activity for all three—were also worlds apart. For Bryce, as is well known, municipal government was the infamous "one conspicuous failure of the United States" because, as his intricate analysis of charters, parties, and so on revealed, city politics was dominated by the boss, who sat "like a spider, hidden in the midst of his web," with the power to dispense places, reward the loyal, and punish the mutinous because he was the best among the "knot" of political operators that "pulled wires for the whole city, and, thereby, riveted their yoke upon it (Bryce 1888, 2:75–76).

For Merton the focus on the corruption in local politics was simply misplaced moralism. Merton's famous distinction between "manifest" and "latent" functions, which first appeared in the 1949 edition of *Social Theory and Social Structure*, was part of his own polemic against the reforming zeal of earlier institutional sociologists, especially E. Stuart Chapin. Such a distinction, he said, clarified the analysis of seemingly irrational social patterns and directed attention to theoretically fruitful

fields of inquiry. It also precluded "the substitution of naive moral judgments for sociological analysis," and in this way presented the possibility
of a scientific analysis of even apparently repugnant social institutions
(Merton 1949, 71).

Merton exemplified this approach with his analysis of the functions
of the political machine. According to Merton, in spite of its apparently
manifest corruption, the machine satisfied basic latent functions, including the organization of power in an atmosphere in which political authority was legally fragmented, the humanizing and personalizing of assistance to what Merton called the "deprived classes," the provision of a
route of social mobility for those with limited opportunities elsewhere,
and the provision of political privileges to business which stabilized the
economic situation. Failure to recognize such functions led reformers
like Bryce and his generation to indulge in "social ritual rather than social
engineering" (Merton 1949, 80).

In his 1961 book, *Who Governs*, Dahl's conception of the functions
of local politics was strikingly similar to Merton's. For him, the famous
shift from "cumulative" to "dispersed" inequality in American society
was facilitated by the expansion of the state produced by a linkage
between political integration and social mobility. In New Haven, new
socioeconomic groups — especially ethnic groups — entered society at the
bottom and experienced an initial period when their proletarian status
prevented them from engaging in political activity. However, as members
of the group began to achieve lower middle-class economic status and
therefore had the leisure to work in politics, they began to experience
political mobility as well; as more members of the group became active
the public sector grew in response to their needs through a patronage-
based process similar to the "latent" functions described by Merton (Dahl
1961).

For Dahl, however, the most important "function" fulfilled by local
government was one not mentioned by Merton, namely the reproduction
of the "Democratic Creed." The argument in his famous "Book I. From
Oligarchy to Pluralism" of *Who Governs* was not about how local government institutions operated, but about how they reproduced the all-
important political consensus. At a high level of generality, Dahl argued
that in the eighteenth and early nineteenth centuries, New Haven — and
by invited extension, American communities everywhere — had been
ruled by interlocked socioeconomic, political, and at times religious
elites. However, the effects of large-scale social changes such as industrialization, immigration, and population growth were to destroy the socioeconomic basis of this elite by creating new sources of economic power,
generating greater social complexity, and permitting population growth.

All of these changes multiplied the bases of political power and thereby multiplied the number of political elites. As society became a mosaic of groups, the rational approach to politics was one rooted in political conflict among self-interest groups — or their leaders — whose goals were short-term, pragmatic, negotiable, and capable of being fulfilled within the existing framework of social and political institutions of American society. Agreement on these conditions formed a consensus on the rules of the game, and competition among the many groups maintained a rough political equilibrium. For Dahl, the transition from "patricians" to "ex-plebes" in control of the government, from "cumulative" to "dispersed" inequality as a social condition, and from the minimal to the responsive and expanding public sector were all part of the process by which the political consensus was maintained and reproduced (Dahl 1961).

For a generation of historians who were, as Richard Hofstadter wrote in 1955, "far more conscious of those things they would like to preserve than they are of those things they would like to change" (Hofstadter 1955, 14) these views provided useful ammunition for their own assault on the moralism of prewar reform as well as useful tools in the construction of a "usable" past for New Deal style liberalism. Therefore, the classic accounts of urban politics in Oscar Handlin's 1951 book *The Uprooted* and Richard Hofstadter's 1955 book *The Age of Reform* both trivialized the work of Bryce and his generation as status-anxious moralizing and imported these conceptions of urban politics — especially those of Merton — into history. For both historians, the focus of reformers on the alleged corruption and fiscal extravagance of the bosses was misplaced "moralism." More important was the fact that through the functions they fulfilled, the bosses placed human needs above inherited notions and inhibitions.

Although Merton himself had exemplified the way the machine "humanized and personalized" aid to the needy with a footnote referring to a story about Harry Hopkins's work under Roosevelt. The pro–New Deal view of the historians was even more explicit. Handlin argued that it was the machine that "opened to the immigrants the prospect that the state might be the means through which the beginnings of security could come," although it was not until the New Deal that immigrants were no longer "divided by the necessity of choosing between their own machines and reform," because by then reform had changed so that it could "swallow up their machines, bosses and all" (Handlin 1951, 226). Hofstadter's admiration of the boss's "pragmatic talents," and the machine's essential "humanity," was paralleled in his praise of FDR's opportunistic virtuosity and the ability of the New Deal to put human needs above "inherited notions." Like the machines, the New Deal avoided moralism and simply went about the business of dealing pragmatically with politics and society as it found them.

Whether undertaken to defend the liberal political economy of the New Deal, criticize the reform-oriented social science institutionalists, or shift the agenda of social science from political institutions to political culture, these works in combination rendered institutions in general and political institutions in particular uninteresting. For if American political institutions were either not problematic, but functional or less important than culture and individual values, then they were certainly not to be found at the top of anyone's intellectual agenda.

The problem with many recent works undertaken under the rubric of "bringing the state back in" has been their failure to understand the difference between this view of the role of the state in American life and the role of the state in American life itself. Works undertaken under the theoretical aegis of this view — which is to say most works of history and many of historically oriented political science and sociology written since — are predisposed to "discover" that the state was either functional or irrelevant. But that is a view that was constructed in the specific historical and intellectual conditions of the 1950s and 1960s. There was, as we have seen, a view that predated that one, and that view was obsessed with the state.

Structural and Ideological Tendencies in American Statebuilding

Indeed, one could do worse than turn to Bryce's formula for the analysis of a "commonwealth" for guidelines for an institutional attempt to "bring the state back in." Observation of the state's "framework and constitutional machinery, the methods by which it is worked, the forces which move it and direct its course" has the advantage of beginning with the state itself and working outward, rather than beginning with the needs of society, democracy, capitalism, and so on, and then deducing the functions of the state from those needs. It also correlates more closely with my questions about the location of the state structurally and ideologically.

There is abundant evidence that, as Morton Keller has recently written, regardless of whether there was a strong "state" in America there certainly were active "states" — and one might add local governments — in the nineteenth century. Fiscal data provide a crude measure of the relative magnitude of the activities of the various levels of the federal system. It is often forgotten that it was not until about 1940 that the major portion of government expenditure shifted to the federal government.

Instead, estimates suggest that on average between 1820 and 1930 federal expenditure accounted for only about 33 percent of all government expenditure, state 11 percent, and local almost 56 percent. (For purposes of comparison, in 1970 the federal share was 62.5 percent, the state share 19.4 percent, and the local share only 18.1 percent, when transfers are allocated to the donor level.) The larger expenditure at the local levels reflected the greater activity there. For example, municipal governments alone were responsible for 85 percent of the contribution of government to net capital formation between 1869 and 1929, and, until 1930, local nonschool employees numbered more than the employees of the federal government during all years except those of World War I (Keller 1987; Davis and Legler 1966; Anderson 1977).

Figures such as these have instilled a healthy respect for these levels of the federal system among some economic and political historians. For example, economic historians Lance Davis and John Legler argued in 1966 that "in the nineteenth century local units were without question the most important of the three levels of government" (Davis and Legler 1966, 523). Thomas Borcherding's analysis of government expenditure from 1870 to 1970 agreed that the nineteenth-century pattern was "growth at the periphery, not the center [i.e. the federal level]" (Borcherding 1977a, 24). Political historian Ballard Campbell has summarized some of this work in the argument that throughout the nineteenth century state and local governments were the government for Americans (Campbell 1980).

However, the fact that the most potent branches of the state were the closest to the electorate does not logically lead to the conclusion that the role of the state was not controversial. On the contrary, the appropriate role of the state was one of the burning political issues of the nineteenth century. In fact, the American state was located below the national level because of a pervasive ambivalence about the state that has been a characteristic of American politics from the time of the Revolution right up to the present.

For those interested in the development of American institutions, it is hardly necessary to review in detail the ideological underpinnings of American federalism, but a brief review will be useful. As Gordon Wood pointed out in his seminal work, *The Creation of the American Republic, 1776–1787*, at the heart of the "American science of politics" that emerged from the two decades of debate from the Revolution to the approval of the Constitution was a complete reversal of the classical theory of politics going back to Aristotle (Wood 1972). As Madison pointed out, the federal Constitution—and the state constitutions that imitated it—was not a charter of liberty granted by power, but a charter of power granted by liberty. The doctrines of popular sovereignty and representation developed by Americans located sovereignty—and thus power—in the people who, in turn, granted a charter of power to their representatives. This was not, however, an unlimited grant of power; on the contrary, as James Iredell wrote at the time, a constitution was a "declaration of particular powers by the people to their representatives, for particular purposes . . . under which no power can be exercised but what is expressly given" (Iredell quoted in Wood 1972, 600).

The crown on the head of the newly sovereign people did not, however, lie easy. On the one hand there were those who believed that popular sovereignty had to be reined in by a stronger executive and more powerful state that could prevent demagoguery and anarchy; on the other, many believed that the road to ruin was paved by a growing state and stronger executive that facilitated patronage and corruption. Layered on top of these abstract positions were also concrete interests in the protection of property—including slaves—and the maintenance of power in the hands of the elite (Keller 1987).

The structural outcome of this debate can be seen in both the federal Constitution and the state constitutions of the eighteenth and nineteenth centuries with their upper and lower house legislatures, relatively weak executive, and restricted grants of power which, in some states, required constitutional conventions almost as often as meetings of the state legislatures. These state constitutions were matched by similar city charters later.

These structural forms institutionalized and embodied the continuing ideological conflict that surrounded the state. By doing some damage to subtleties of their thought, one can range nineteenth-century state ideology on a continuum from Federalists, Whigs, and Mugwump Republicans on the one hand, to the Jeffersonian Republicans, and Jacksonian and Bourbon Democrats on the other (Heale 1977; Keller 1977). For the former, a growing state was a guarantor of stability, economic development, and, ultimately, social harmony. For the latter, a powerful state presaged corruption and the disruption of a natural social harmony as well as the domination of those favored by political-economic privileges over those without those privileges. Ironically, whatever other socioeconomic changes were to transpire in nineteenth-century America, these ideological poles in the debate over the role of the state would persist.

Furthermore, positions on the state and political democracy were linked unpredictably. Throughout the nineteenth century, those who professed to place their faith in "the people" objected to the expanding state, while those who tended toward political elitism lauded such expansion.

Whigs before the Civil War and Mugwumps afterward favored an expanding state but limited suffrage; pre-Civil War Jacksonian Democrats and post-Civil War Bourbon Democrats favored mass political mobilization and a small state. Those, therefore, whom one might have expected to expand the state purely for patronage reasons did not do so on ideological grounds, while those who favored expanding the state objected to political patronage beyond a certain level. Furthermore, those most dislocated by industrialization or the spread of the market were against the expansion of the state on principle and opposed it in practice (Thornton 1978; Watson 1985; Fink 1983).

The key to this opposition was the Jacksonian theory of the state, a theory that long outlived its presidential namesake. As John Ashworth has pointed out, in the ideology of Jacksonian Democrats nothing was more threatening to democracy than the state itself; therefore, nothing was less desirable than that the state be allowed to aggrandize itself at the expense of the citizen. It was not just political power that was zero-sum, but also economic power. According to the Jacksonians, because the state had nothing of its own, it could dispense with nothing of its own; resources or privileges given to one had to be taken from another. One of the great sources of inequality was, in fact, precisely what the Jacksonians called "partial" legislation that favored one group over another (Ashworth 1987).

Patterns of Growth and Constraint

Given these ideological and structural predispositions toward stasis, therefore, how did the state grow at all? Because it was decentralized, at one level the "state" was actually a large number of subunits in economic competition with one another. Harry Scheiber has noted that the public sector before the Civil War was characterized by decentralization and "rivalistic state mercantilism." Indeed, state and local jurisdictions perceived themselves as competitors with one another for economic development (Scheiber 1975). At the local level, as Eric Monkkonen has pointed out, local governments acted as "economic adventurers," using debt to underwrite and promote economic growth and attract outside investment, especially from railroads or manufacturing (Monkkonen 1984). State governments did the same, and they also felt the pressure from cities to do so, too. It is important to note, however, that these actions were viewed as special legislation at both the local and state levels. The politics of this fiscal capacity was by no means a pacific one. Far from granting the power to local or state governments to intervene in economic development generally, these decisions were made on an ad hoc basis, in the presence of sometimes strong opposition, and in the belief that they were temporary expedients or short-term investments. Caught between an ideological rock and an economic hard place, officials authorized such investments, but many of their hearts were not in it, and their actions granted no overall legitimacy to the expansion of the state.

Nonetheless, expand it did. For example, state debts — mostly for internal improvements — increased from almost nothing in 1800 to $191 million (about $10 per capita) by 1841 to about $257 million (about $8 per capita) by 1860. Municipal debt per capita was $23 in New York City, and $71 in Baltimore in 1860. Moreover, the need for regular revenue for interest and sinking funds, as well as for increases in fiscal oversight and elementary service provision produced an increased reliance on the property tax. Whereas in 1820 the property tax accounted for only 25 percent of the revenue collected in New York State, by 1860 it brought in 80 percent. In Maryland, the share of the property tax in 1830 was 0.006 percent; by 1848 it was 44 percent (Studenski and Kroos 1952).

On top of this, the Civil War set off even more expenditure and indebtedness leading to the highest decadal rate of change in expenditure in current dollars in American history to that time and the nineteenth-century peak in state and local expenditure in 1870. However, the unpopularity of the war in some states — and, especially the Reconstruction that followed it — led to calls for austerity throughout the land when it concluded. The burdens of this debt and expenditure set off a search for new sources of revenue that brought about an equalization of taxation and a restructuring and strengthening of the system of taxation of real property for the first time in American history. In this way, the actions of state and local governments in response to some groups created by the economy — e.g., entrepreneurs, railroads, and so on — created other groups whose existence was in the fiscal political realm — e.g., taxpayers, bondholders, and so on. As these groups became active, they put a powerful brake on the expansion of state activities.

Some of the most prominent examples of this postwar revolt against public sector expansion were seen in the public debt limitation campaigns conducted in state after state following the war. When the 1880 census surveyed these limitations on the state and local public sector for the first time, it found that fifteen of the thirty-eight states had added debt restriction provisions to their constitutions, while three others had authorized legislatures to do so. Twenty-four of the thirty-eight states had restricted the right of cities to invest in railways; twenty-five barred them from investing in private corporations. All but three of the constitutional debt ceilings were adopted before 1877, indicating that they were not just responses to the panic of the mid-1870s (Monkkonen 1986).

More important in the long run than the restriction of debt — but undoubtedly related to it — was the reorganization of the structure of taxation undertaken after the war, which resulted in a heavier and more strictly enforced reliance on the property tax for both state and local revenue. The most extreme example of this fiscal change was observed in the South, where before the war the public sector was run almost entirely on the basis of taxes on slaves and personal property, both of which fell mostly on the planter class. After the war, the abolition of slavery and impoverishment of the planters required the institution of a property tax for the first time and thus the mobilization of yeoman farmers as fiscal political actors for the first time (Thornton 1981, 1982).

A parallel transformation occurred in the North as state after state realized the hopelessness of personal property taxation and tightened up the assessment and taxation of real property. Beginning with the New York Tax Commission of 1871–72, the search for new revenue led to tightened assessment procedures, the most important of which was legal linkage of property transfer with property taxation by requiring county clerks to file records of real property sales with county treasurers for the purposes of taxation. Although personal property still escaped taxation, real property was now captured and its contribution to revenue soared (Yearley 1970; McDonald 1986).

Rather than increasing the legitimacy of government expansion, however, these actions caught more taxpayers in the fiscal net and, therefore, provided a growing material basis for the contest over that legitimacy. In the cities, for example, the level of homeownership — and thus eligibility for local property taxation — reached about 37 percent in 1890. Moreover, this homeownership spread remarkably deeply down the class structure, as it was not unusual for immigrants to own homes at a higher rate than the native born and for as much as 40 percent of skilled workers to own homes. Historical mobility studies have shown that those who accumulated property were those most likely not to migrate and that homeownership was age specific — those who aged in one place were very likely to own homes. Because the most important qualification for suffrage in the late nineteenth century was residence, those most likely to stay in one place — and thus count politically — were also likely to accumulate real property and thus pay property tax.

This new work suggests that groups that had been thought to be proponents of the expansion of local government may have had an interest in stopping that expansion since the only guaranteed result of such expansion was an increased tax bill. For example, throughout the nineteenth century the most highly mobilized ethnic group was the Irish, which was also the ethnic group with the highest rate of homeownership in many cities. However, as Stephan Thernstrom has pointed out, this property accumulation was achieved by means of what he calls "ruthless underconsumption," and the hold of immigrants on their property was tenuous at best. It is logically doubtful that these small property holders approved of sharp increases in their tax bills necessary to support patronage, and, in the only analysis of this question done on the case of San Francisco, municipal taxation and expenditure were driven to historic lows under administrations dominated by Irishmen (Thernstrom 1964; Zunz 1982; McDonald 1986).

This fiscal conservatism both played a role in and was reinforced by remarkably high levels of political participation and party mobilization in these years, which heightened the risk of unusual expansion of government capacities. Whereas from 1840 to 1872 political participation nationwide had averaged 68.5 percent of eligible voters in presidential elections and 57.2 percent in congressional elections, from 1876 through 1892 the same levels were 77.4 and 63.6, with even higher levels outside of the South. Historians like Paul Kleppner have attributed this rise in participation primarily to the prominence of so-called ethnocultural politics in the United States, which is to say political battles over issues like temperance, immigration, and sabbatarianism that were linked to religious values (Kleppner 1982). At the heart of this controversy, however, was a debate over the nature of the state: the question as to whether or not the state should enforce temperance and the observation of the sabbath was remarkably similar to the older debate involving the general question of state growth in terms of other activities. Moreover, the political alignments in these years were similar; Republicans favored state action on ethnocultural issues and in other areas; Democrats opposed the former and campaigned actively for retrenchment at both local and state levels.

In any case, one result of this mobilization was political stalemate, which undoubtedly helped stall the growth of the state. At the national level the margin of victory in presidential elections was less than 5 percent in every election from 1876 until 1900—less than 1 percent in 1880, 1884, and 1888. As Stephen Skowronek has pointed out, this produced minute majorities in Congress as well, with the result that innovation in national statebuilding was enormously risky politically in these years (Skowronek 1982). Although less is known about it, similar closeness was observed at state and local levels. In San Francisco, for example, no candidate for mayor won by a majority from 1882 through 1898 and divisions in the city's legislative branch were similarly close (McDonald 1986). The link among local, state, and federal political mobilization was, of course, the straight ticket voting procedure and the scheduling of all elections for the same date for most of the period from 1876 through about 1892.

Because of the original ideological ambiguity of the expansion of local and state government, its growth before the Civil War without overall political legitimacy, the necessity to extract resources primarily from lower- and middle-class small property holders, and the tiny mandates with which they took office, local and state leaders had to balance every specific demand for the fiscal expansion of the public sector with the more generalized and all-permeating demand for low individual tax liability, which could only be maintained by minimal local government activities, low expenditure, and thus a low tax rate and low assessed valuation. In this atmosphere, preelection promises of an expanded public sector were rare. In the case of the cities, Jon Teaford has argued that the "watchword of the age" in urban politics between 1870 and 1900 was "economy," not expenditure and in these years "pay as you go" was "one pillar of the general policy of fiscal conservatism," while low taxation was the other (Teaford 1984, 293).

It is not surprising, therefore, that as economic historian Alan Anderson has noted, the years from 1870 to 1910 witnessed increasing absolute amounts of municipal expenditure, but remarkable stability in outlays per capita (Anderson 1977). From 1880 through 1910, in particular, as Kenneth Fox has pointed out, while per capita national production of goods and services and federal expenditures rose, "city expenditures per capita declined between 10 and 20 percent . . . by 1912," although they rose again by 1927 (Fox 1977, 96). In 1902, average per capita, local expenditures amounted to 12 dollars (Anderson 1977). Even in the largest cities, heretofore thought to be the homes of the "big-spending" political bosses so crucial to the pluralist interpretation of political mobility, the trend in per capita expenditure was almost flat from 1890 to 1910 (Brown and Halaby 1984). State and municipal treasuries simply did not have the resources to create the "divisible incentives" that were alleged to have been the cement of politics in these years. In current dollars, 1870 levels of public expenditure were not seen regularly again until the twenties, although the decadal rates of growth began to increase after the turn of the century.

Motors of Change

From about 1910 onward, the trends in public sector activity moved dramatically upward. Between 1902 and 1932, for example, per capita state expenditures increased from $2.30 to $21.80, and local from $11.22

to $52.07 (these figures are not simply the result of the early years of the depression; by 1927 local per capita expenditure averaged $49.00). The standard explanations for this change have been variations on the theme of the response of government to social needs. Perhaps the most sophisticated of these has been the economic argument that the change resulted from the combination of rising per capita income and changing preferences for public services. Alan Anderson has argued, for example, that in the case of local government, as the externalities of urban development became more and more apparent and as additional income became available to do something about it, public sector activities increased (Anderson 1977).

While it would be foolish to ignore these changes, it is probably more true to say that they are necessary but insufficient to explain the change in the public sector. To begin with, the most recent estimates by economic historians Jeffrey Williamson and Peter Lindert are that the change in per capita income in these years was by no means as dramatic as the change in government activities; moreover, rising income was quite unevenly distributed (Williamson and Lindert 1980). An even more telling point about this argument has been made by James Buchanan. There is, he contends, no reason to believe that, other things being equal, goods and services supplied by government are those for which individual demands are highly responsive to income shifts (Buchanan 1977). The question is, then, what happened to make "other things" become less equal.

The institutional factors that have been the subject of this analysis may be the key to explaining the timing of a shift toward meeting needs that had been there all along. Most important are changes in ideology and political structure that again set in motion changes in the role of the state.

As Clifton Yearley has pointed out, beginning in the 1880s good government groups had consistently attacked what they perceived to be the mismanagement of state and local government. Their targets were two; first, the corrupt partisan management of government itself and, second, the conduct of elections. Regarding the first, the reformers shifted the Jacksonian argument from "government produces nothing" to "this government produces nothing," which was to say the government conducted by their partisan opponents. To make this argument, the reformers exaggerated the defects of the nonreformed system, issued local and state level investigations of the fiscal irresponsibility of the partisan operators of government, and in general extolled the virtues of an active government but at the same time undermined the capacity of partisan government to act. Yearley implies that there was, in fact, a fiscal crisis in the late nineteenth century. More careful studies of fiscal policy, however, have found that the crisis was more accurately political: abundant fiscal resources were available, what was lacking was the political will to tap them (Yearley 1970; Teaford 1984; McDonald 1986).

The opportunity to tap these resources was created by the campaign for the second goal of reform, electoral reform. This goal, then, was the purification of the electoral system by means of a set of changes aimed at reducing the influence of parties and shrinking the electorate at the same time. Studies by Kleppner and others have suggested that the introduction of the Australian ballot, which was used in 89 percent of the states with 92 percent of the voters by 1896, played an important role in reducing both participation and partisanship. Personal registration laws, lengthier residency requirements, literacy tests, and other qualifications for voting added in these years did the same. In his survey of who stopped voting, Kleppner argues that these changes had their greatest impact on blacks and poor whites in the South and immigrants and those of lower income in the North (Kleppner 1982). As noted above, it is likely that these changes in participation eliminated the obstacles to growth in the public sector — property holding whites in the South and immigrants in the North who had been the backbone of resistance to the public sector's expansion.

Having wounded the parties, reform politicians were forced toward a new basis for political mobilization. The public sector was, in both the theory and practice of the reformers, the only institution with the status and resources necessary for such a coalition. In the theory of progressive reformers, only the expanding public sector could overcome party and reintroduce a genuine political community. In practice, only the public sector had the resources that could provide the cement with which to hold their reform coalitions together. Furthermore, having denounced the "divisible" incentives allegedly provided on a broad scale by their partisan opponents, reformers were forced to offer indivisible incentives to the members of their coalition — e.g. services to middle-class neighborhoods, wage guarantees to workers, regulatory and protective legislation at the state level, "good government" to the middle class and professionals — including, most importantly, the reformers themselves (Wiebe 1967; Yearley 1970; Schiesl 1977; McDonald 1986).

Viewed in light of this political strategy, the rise of politically active functional interest groups at the local and state levels of government is as much the product of political mobilization as economic development. By inviting "interests" into the political arena, reformers both legitimated them and attached them to the state. Both the political demobilization that was well underway by 1900 and fully in place by the 1920s and the expansion of public sector activity at all levels in the same period are very likely part of the same development (McDonald 1988).

The (Re)Turn to Institutions

In recent essays on the "new institutionalism," James March and Johan Olsen, on the one hand, and Rogers Smith, on the other, have agreed that one important theme of this new movement is the point that political institutions appear to be more than simply "mirrors of social forces." I have tried to suggest that this is the case for the American state (March and Olsen 1984; Smith 1988).

It was the federal institutional structure that established the location at which social forces attempted to change the state and it was ideologies about the appropriate role and functions of the state that established the vocabulary within which such changes were discussed. Moreover, it was through the accomplishment of the state's own functions — in this case that of the extraction of resources — that a social or economic issue was translated into an issue of politics. For example, a request for a railroad subsidy became a request for a bond issue; a call for new streets became an issue of tax increase. In this way, political actors were created and mobilized who had little to do with the initial issue: bondholders, taxpayers, boodlers, etc. Finally it was the struggles of actors within the political institutions to change the electorate, or to expand or contract the state's fiscal capacity — that created or prevented the opportunity for the state to grow.

Given these abilities of the state to shape (or reshape) social and economic actors, it is not surprising that smooth functional fits between input and output or society and the state were rare in these years. This does not mean, however, that American institutions either failed (as the Progressives thought) or that they were actually fulfilling latent functions (as their critics believed). It simply means that the relationship between state and society was a good deal more contingent and historical and a good deal less determined than some have thought. In this respect, too, the relationship was — and is — a good deal more interesting.

As Bryce traveled through America one hundred years ago he claimed that "every chance acquaintance" asked: "What do you think of our institutions?" (Bryce 1888, 1:1.) This would seem like a rather queer question today. But perhaps there is hope that may change.

REFERENCES

Anderson, Alan D. 1977. *The Origin and Resolution of an Urban Crisis: Balti-more, 1890–1930.* Baltimore: Johns Hopkins University Press.

Ashworth, John. 1987. *Agrarians and Aristocrats: Party Political Ideology in the United States, 1837–1846.* New York: Cambridge University Press.

Borcherding, Thomas E. 1977a. "One Hundred Years of Public Spending, 1870–1970." In *Budgets and Bureaucrats: The Sources of Government Growth,* ed. Thomas E. Borcherding. Durham: Duke University Press.

———. 1977b. "The Sources of Growth of Public Expenditures in the United States, 1902–1970." In *Budgets and Bureaucrats: The Sources of Government Growth,* ed. Thomas E. Borcherding. Durham: Duke University Press.

Brown, M. Craig, and Charles N. Halaby. 1984. "Bosses, Reform, and the Socioeconomic Bases of Urban Expenditure, 1890–1940." In *The Politics of Urban Fiscal Policy,* ed. Terrence J. McDonald and Sally K. Ward. Beverly Hills, Calif.: Sage Publications.

Bryce, James. 1888. *The American Commonwealth.* London: Macmillan and Co.

Buchanan, James M. 1977. "Why Does Government Grow?" In *Budgets and Bureaucrats: The Sources of Government Growth,* ed. Thomas E. Borcherd-ing. Durham: Duke University Press.

Campbell, Ballard C. 1980. *Representative Democracy: Public Policy and Mid-western Legislatures in the Late Nineteenth Century.* Cambridge, Mass.: Harvard University Press.

Dahl, Robert A. 1956. *A Preface to Democratic Theory.* Chicago: University of Chicago Press.

———. 1961. *Who Governs? Democracy and Power in an American City.* New Haven: Yale University Press.

Davis, Lance, and John Legler. 1966. "The Government in the American Econ-omy, 1815–1902: A Quantitative Study." *Journal of Economic History* 26:514–52.

Fink, Leon. 1983. *Workingmen's Democracy: The Knights of Labor and Ameri-can Politics.* Urbana, Ill.: University of Illinois Press.

Fox, Kenneth. 1977. *Better City Government: Innovation in American Urban Politics, 1850–1937.* Philadelphia: Temple University Press.

Handlin, Oscar. 1951. *The Uprooted.* New York: Grosset and Dunlap.

Heale, M. J. 1977. *The Making of American Politics, 1750–1850.* London: Longmans.

Herring, E. Pendleton. 1940. *The Politics of Democracy: American Parties in Action.* New York: W. W. Norton and Co.

Hofstadter, Richard. 1955. *The Age of Reform: From Bryan to FDR.* New York: Vintage Press.

Hughes, Jonathan R. T. 1977. *The Governmental Habit: Economic Controls from Colonial Times to the Present.* New York: Basic Books.

Keller, Morton. 1977. *Affairs of State: Public Life in Nineteenth Century America.* Cambridge, Mass.: Harvard University Press.

————. 1987. "Powers and Rights: Two Centuries of American Constitutionalism." *Journal of American History* 74:675–717.

Keohane, Robert O. 1983. "Associative American Development, 1776–1860: Economic Growth and Political Disintegration." In *The Antinomies of Interdependence: National Welfare and the International Division of Labor,* ed. John Gerald Ruggie. New York: Columbia University Press.

Kleppner, Paul. 1982. *Who Voted? The Dynamics of Electoral Turnout, 1870–1980.* New York: Praeger Publications.

McCormick, Richard L. 1979. "The Party Period and Public Policy: An Exploratory Hypothesis." *Journal of American History* 66:279–98.

————. 1985. "Political Parties in the United States: Reinterpreting Their Natural History." *History Teacher* 19:15–32.

McDonald, Terrence J. 1985. "The Problem of the Political in Recent American Urban History: Liberal Pluralism and the Rise of Functionalism." *Social History* 10:323–46.

————. 1986. *The Parameters of Urban Fiscal Policy: Socioeconomic Change and Political Culture in San Francisco, 1860–1906.* Berkeley: University of California Press.

————. 1988. "The History of Urban Fiscal Politics in America, 1830–1930: What Was Thought to Be versus What Was and the Difference It Makes." *International Journal of Public Administration* 11:679–712.

McDonald, Terrence J., and Sally K. Ward, eds. 1984. *The Politics of Urban Fiscal Policy.* Beverly Hills, Calif.: Sage Publications.

March, James G., and Johan P. Olsen. 1984. "The New Institutionalism: Organizational Factors in Political Life." *American Political Science Review* 78:734–49.

Merton, Robert K. 1949. *Social Theory and Social Structure: Toward the Codification of Theory and Research.* Glencoe, Ill.: Free Press.

Monkkonen, Eric. 1984. "The Politics of Municipal Indebtedness and Default, 1850–1936." In *The Politics of Urban Fiscal Policy,* ed. Terrence J. McDonald and Sally K. Ward. Beverly Hills, Calif.: Sage Publications.

————. 1988. *America Becomes Urban: The Development of US Cities, 1780–1980.* Berkeley: University of California Press.

North, Douglass. 1979. "A Framework for Analyzing the State in Economic History." *Explorations in Economic History* 16:249–59.

Pells, Richard. 1985. *The Liberal Mind in a Conservative Age: American Intellectuals in the 1940s and 1950s.* New York: Harper and Row.

Purcell, Edward A. 1973. *The Crisis of Democratic Theory: Scientific Naturalism and the Problem of Value.* Lexington: University of Kentucky Press.

Ransom, Roger. 1982. "In Search of Security: The Growth of Government Spending in the United States, 1902–1970." In *Explorations in the New Economic History: Essays in Honors of Douglass C. North,* ed. Roger Ransom et al. New York: Academic Press.

Ricci, David M. 1984. *The Tragedy of Political Science: Politics, Scholarship, and Democracy.* New Haven: Yale University Press.

Scheiber, Harry. 1975. "Federalism and the American Economic Order, 1789–1910." *Law and Society Review* 10:57–118.

Schiesl, Martin. 1977. *The Politics of Efficiency: Municipal Administration and Reform in America: 1880–1920.* Berkeley: University of California Press.

Seidelman, Raymond, and Edward J. Harpham. 1985. *Disenchanted Realists: Political Science and the American Crisis, 1884–1984.* Albany: State University of New York Press.

Shefter, Martin. 1978. "Party, Bureaucracy, and Political Change in the United States." In *Political Parties: Development and Decay,* ed. Louis Maisel and Joseph Cooper. Beverly Hills, Calif.: Sage Publications.

Skocpol, Theda. 1985. "Bringing the State Back In: Strategies of Analysis in Current Research." In *Bringing the State Back In,* ed. Theda Skocpol et al. Cambridge: Cambridge University Press.

Skocpol, Theda, and John Ikenberry. 1983. "The Political Formation of the American Welfare State in Historical and Comparative Perspective." *Comparative Social Research* 6:87–148.

Skowronek, Stephen. 1982. *Building the New American State: The Expansion of National Administrative Capacities, 1877–1920.* Cambridge: Cambridge University Press.

Smith, Rogers M. 1988. "Political Jurisprudence, the 'New Institutionalism,' and the Future of Public Law." *American Political Science Review* 82:89–108.

Studenski, Paul, and Herman E. Kroos. 1952. *Financial History of the United States.* New York: McGraw-Hill.

Teaford, Jon. 1984. *The Unheralded Triumph: City Government in America, 1870–1900.* Baltimore: Johns Hopkins University Press.

Thornton, J. Mills. 1978. *Politics and Power in a Slave Society: Alabama, 1800–1860.* Baton Rouge: Louisiana State University Press.

————. 1981. "Fiscal Policy and the Pattern of Nineteenth Century Southern History." University of Michigan. Typescript.

————. 1982. "Fiscal Policy and the Failure of Reconstruction in the Lower South." In *Region, Race, and Reconstruction: Essays in Honors of C. Vann Woodward,* ed. J. Morgan Kousser and James M. McPherson. New York: Oxford University Press.

Watson, Harry. 1985. "Conflict and Collaboration: Yeomen, Slaveholders, and Politics in the Antebellum South." *Social History* 10:273–98.

Wiebe, Robert. 1967. *The Search for Order.* New York: Hill and Wang, Inc.

Williamson, Jeffrey G., and Peter H. Lindert. 1980. *American Inequality: A Macroeconomic History.* New York: Academic Press.

Wood, Gordon. 1972. *The Creation of the American Republic, 1776–1787.* New York: W. W. Norton and Co.

Yearley, C. K. 1970. *The Money Machines: The Breakdown and Reform of Governmental and Party Finance in the North, 1860–1920.* Albany: State University of New York Press.

Zunz, Olivier. 1982. *The Changing Face of Inequality: Urbanization, Industrial Development, and Immigrants in Detroit, 1880–1920.* Chicago: University of Chicago Press.

Contributors

Joel D. Aberbach is a professor of political science and the director of the Center for American Politics and Public Policy, University of California, Los Angeles.

John R. Chamberlin is a professor of political science and public policy, University of Michigan.

Mary E. Corcoran is a professor of political science and public policy, University of Michigan.

Paul N. Courant is a professor of economics and public policy, University of Michigan.

John E. Jackson is a professor of political science and director of the Taubman Program in American Institutions, University of Michigan.

Terrence J. McDonald is a professor of history, University of Michigan.

Malcolm B. Robinson is an assistant professor of economics, University of Cincinnati.

Frank P. Stafford is a professor of economics, University of Michigan.

Maris A. Vinovskis is a professor of history, University of Michigan.

Jack L. Walker is a professor of political science and public policy, University of Michigan.

Mayer N. Zald is a professor of sociology and social work, University of Michigan.